SPEECHES THAT CHANGED BRITAIN
ORATORY IN BIRMINGHAM

Andrew Reekes

Published by West Midlands History Limited
Minerva Mill Innovation Centre, Alcester, Warwickshire, UK.
© 2015 West Midlands History Limited.
© All images are copyright as credited.
Enoch Powell's 20 April 1968 speech reproduced by permission of The J Enoch Powell Literary Trust.

ISBN: 978-1-905036-23-3

Cover image: © Illustrated London News Limited/Mary Evans.
Caric Press Limited, Merthyr Tydfil, Wales.

To Terry Scammell Jackson and the Radley College History dons
1994 to 2012, inspiring and companionable colleagues all.

ACKNOWLEDGEMENTS

I am very grateful to Malcolm Dick for his invariably wise advice in the writing of this book, and to Mike Gibbs for his enthusiasm and his faith in the entire concept. I am indebted to my editor, Jenni Butterworth, for her scrupulous critical appraisal of the text and for her continuing encouragement. I am equally grateful for the challenge and stimulation, at every stage of the book, of Patrick Derham, and for the eagle-eyed scrutiny of Alison Goodfellow. Also to David Beattie for his rigorous proof-reading of the text and many valuable suggestions. I learnt much from talking to Roger Ward, Peter Marsh and Donna Taylor and from listening to the varied contributions of the speakers at the Conference: 'Joseph Chamberlain: Imperial Standard Bearer; National Leader; and Local Icon' organised by Ian Cawood at Newman University in July 2014. Thanks too to Matt Cole for his helpful observations on the chapter on Enoch Powell. Above all I am grateful to Lynne for her patience and her continuing support.

The courtesy, helpfulness and friendliness of the archivists at the Cadbury Research Archive: Special Collections, the University of Birmingham, have been invaluable, as has been the assistance of the staff of the Birmingham Archives and Heritage service at the Library of Birmingham, and that of the librarians of the University of Birmingham Library.

Contents

FOREWORD

This book combines three aspects of British history. Firstly, the role of speeches – oratory – since the early nineteenth century in advocating, defending or attacking political, social or economic ideas, policies or programmes; secondly, the importance of Birmingham in providing an environment which shaped their generation, presentation and reception; and thirdly, how concerns which were expressed locally, reflected and shaped national agendas.

Birmingham was the engine house of the 'workshop of the world' in the nineteenth century, and, according to one overseas commentator, 'the best-governed city in the world'. It remained economically and politically important for most of the twentieth century, but it declined both demographically and economically in the 1970s and 1980s and was reborn in the early twenty-first century as the youngest city in Europe with a diverse demography, a strengthening industrial base, a centre for higher education and research and a place of major cultural institutions, including the Museum and Art Gallery, Symphony Hall and, most recently, the new Library of Birmingham. These different histories, which, nonetheless, link the past to the present, cannot be understood without integrating local, national and global perspectives and revealing how the past and therefore the present are shaped by the interplay of rich and poor, men and women, natives and newcomers, and young and old. Much still remains to be researched, charted and analysed. Andrew Reekes' imaginative book offers a new way of seeing Birmingham by exploring how local speeches set new agendas and had an impact beyond the boundaries of the town and city.

These speeches expressed the aspirations, fears and obsessions of the individuals who delivered them. Reekes investigates the lives and words of individuals and their skills in presenting messages to provide an insight into the challenges which have faced British people for two centuries. The discourses of the speech maker were significant, but so were the contexts in which the speeches were made. The author combines an analysis of political, social and economic change with an understanding of how ideas, propaganda, organisation, symbolism and rhetoric interconnect, including, in one memorable phrase, the 'choreography of processions', which accompanied one of the speeches. The message and the medium were important, but so were the circumstances in which they were delivered.

The choice of individuals does not imply approval of what they said. The speeches are explored within their environment, by explaining why they were important and assessing their impact. The first chapters, which look at nineteenth-century speeches by Thomas Attwood (one of Birmingham's first two MPs), Chartist leaders, John Bright and Joseph Chamberlain in 1885, focus on political ideals: the attack on aristocratic privilege and the extension of the vote. George Dawson and R.W. Dale offered cultural and social messages: the importance of local libraries, the extension of education and a public urban culture dedicated to social improvement. Other speakers adopted different refrains, which revealed how local lives were affected by global issues: Joseph Chamberlain and tariff reform (1903), Oswald Mosley and unemployment (1925), Neville Chamberlain and the threat of Hitler (1939), Enoch Powell and immigration (1968), Malala Yousafzai and the education of girls (2013), and David Cameron and liberal values (2015).

Nineteenth- and twentieth-century speakers were conscious of how their speeches were received and transmitted in the media: newspapers in most cases, but also television for Powell and global electronic communication for Yousafzai and Cameron.

The closer the speeches are to the present, the more relevant they become to contemporary concerns. Reekes explores the distinctiveness and seemingly contradictory trajectory of Powell's opinions and the circumstances which led him to deliver the so-called 'Rivers of Blood' speech of 1968, one of the most controversial speeches of modern times. Powell expressed what many British people believed: that Black and Asian immigrants were alien and brought unwanted personal standards and cultural practices into the country. His electric language struck fear into the hearts of immigrants and was excoriated by much of the press, his own party leadership and advocates of liberalism and toleration, but his popularity amongst white working- and middle-class men and women was reflected in letters to newspapers, demonstrations in his support and opinion poll evidence. Powell's dire forecasts have not come to pass, but the fears his speech aroused and the hostility he expressed have persisted. Britain's demographic profile is more ethnically diverse than it was in 1968, but its people remain sharply divided over the value and contributions of immigrants to social and economic life.

This leads to the final speeches: Malala Yousafzai's at the Library of Birmingham in 2013 and David Cameron's at Ninestiles Academy in 2015. Yousafzai was a teenager at school, a Pakistani Muslim and an advocate of girls' education in her native country, a commitment which led to her being shot in the head by gunmen opposed to her beliefs. Medical treatment at the Queen Elizabeth Hospital saved her life and she resumed her schooling in Birmingham. Like George Dawson at the opening of Birmingham's Library in 1866, Malala stressed the moral value of education, books and libraries for individual and social enlightenment – a cause for which she nearly died. Cameron's focus was on the assertion of 'fundamental liberal values' against 'Islamist extremism', which, in its most fanatical form – Islamic State – became 'a cultish attachment to death'. Cameron might have had Malala in mind when he praised the 'huge number of Muslims in our country who have a proper claim to represent liberal values in local communities'.

One quotation from Malala Yousafzai's speech provides a reason why this book was written. For Malala, 'a city without a library is like a graveyard'. The archives, books and electronic resources contained in libraries preserve, shape and disseminate history, culture and identity. Andrew Reekes has used manuscript, printed and electronic resources to create an insight into Birmingham's people and their motives. The book is beautifully written, immediately accessible and based on the latest research; it adds to our knowledge of both local and national history and the concerns which animated people from the 1800s to the present. At a time when libraries – and the Enlightenment project which led to their creation – are being threatened, it is pertinent for those of us who believe in education to remember that the pursuit of knowledge has not always been accessible to all. In many places, as Yousafzai has shown, it remains a matter of life and death.

Dr Malcolm Dick, Director of the Centre for West Midlands History, University of Birmingham and Editor-in-Chief, *History West Midlands.*

INTRODUCTION

It is striking how many nationally significant political speeches have been made in Birmingham over the past two hundred years. The provincial voice which has been heard most consistently since 1815 has been that of Birmingham, a counter to London which is, of course, overwhelmingly preponderant in this country's political history, with Parliament and government operating in the capital city. This book looks at ten episodes when a speech made in Birmingham delivered an important message to the rest of the country, in all cases either advocating or effecting radical change.

What is more remarkable is that throughout the nineteenth century, while it articulated an insistent and influential Radical voice, Birmingham was not even the country's second city; only in 1911 did its population overhaul that of Liverpool, up to that point Britain's second most populous city. Through the early years of Queen Victoria's reign, arguably, Manchester predominated in terms of political influence. It established a special place for itself in radical mythology as a result of the massacre of supporters of parliamentary reform in 1819 at St Peter's Field, known as Peterloo. The successful crusade of Manchester's textile manufacturers (the Anti-Corn Law League) in the 1840s confirmed the northern city as the veritable bastion of what would become a national faith, belief in the unassailable superiority of Free Trade. Birmingham vied with it to be the mouthpiece of radical reform during these years (Chapters 1 and 2). Yet Manchester's very success in converting every Victorian government to the benefits of Free Trade ensured that it became a city content to defend the status quo; indeed right at the beginning of the twentieth century, when a Birmingham politician, Joseph Chamberlain, challenged Free Trade orthodoxy by advocating Tariff Reform (Chapter 6), Manchester bestirred itself, burnished its liberal economic credentials and led a Free Trade counterattack to preserve the existing dispensation. Chamberlain's campaign neatly exemplifies Birmingham's contrasting character, for as this book shows, far from defending the status quo it was a consistently sympathetic platform for those who would champion radical change.

Thomas Attwood (Chapter 1) articulated the case for the reform of Parliament and he, and his Birmingham organisation (the Birmingham Political Union), was more influential than any in persuading Westminster to concede the Great Reform Act, a momentous first step in the process of democratisation. It did not immediately bring about the anticipated new world order; as a result disappointed working men demanded a vote for every man, to emancipate all from government oppression. That Chartist campaign was devised in Birmingham (Chapter 2). Parliament's continuing stubborn refusal to enfranchise the ordinary responsible householders prompted a great Northern figure, John

Bright, to migrate to Birmingham, where he knew he would find an audience receptive to a new campaign for parliamentary reform (Chapter 3). Indeed that doyen of historians of Victorian cities, Asa Briggs, identifies this as the pivotal moment when provincial leadership in Britain passed from Manchester to Birmingham.[1] The electors of Manchester rejected the Radical hero John Bright, a leader of the Anti-Corn Law League, in the election of 1857 because of his outspoken criticism of Britain's Crimean policy; the electors of Birmingham promptly returned him as an MP. Manchester's loss of John Bright was very much Birmingham's gain, as the latter consolidated its reputation as a Radical city (Chapter 3), in which new ideas of civic responsibility and of a higher purpose for city government would be propagated, becoming a template for provincial cities everywhere (Chapter 4).

Chapter 5 on Joseph Chamberlain's speech in 1886 is partly, it is true, about the battle to defeat a projected reform, that of Home Rule for Ireland, advocated by Chamberlain's own party leader, William Gladstone. On another reading, however, it is just as much about promoting the alternative of radical social and economic change, a prospectus of educational, tax and land reform propounded by Chamberlain in his Unauthorised Programme a year earlier; to the latter's chagrin, it was ignored by a Prime Minister more interested in great moral missions such as solving the Irish Question.

Many in Birmingham were converted in the last decades of the nineteenth century to an economic heresy, Fair Trade, a policy of tariffs designed to protect the town's metal manufacturers from cheap imports dumped by German and American firms. Chapter 6 focuses on Joseph Chamberlain's famous speech calling for the creation of an imperial free trade area; later he extended this to urge protection from foreign manufactured imports. Again Birmingham was the platform for a clamorous voice challenging received wisdom. Its protectionist reputation, and partly the fact that it was an industrial giant in the twentieth century, also goes some way to explaining why Oswald Mosley used the city as a base for a new, Keynesian economic approach to unemployment articulated in his 1925 Birmingham Proposals (Chapter 7).

Even Chapter 8, Neville Chamberlain's abandonment of Appeasement in a Birmingham speech of March 1939, is a call – however late and however authentically felt – for a radically different government policy towards Hitler's Germany in light of its aggression towards Czechoslovakia. The extent to which Smethwick and Birmingham shaped Enoch Powell's prescription for immigration policy in Britain is debated in Chapter 9, but there is no doubting that his controversial speech articulated a strikingly different approach to race in Britain from that of official, politically correct, orthodoxy. The final chapter reflects on two twenty-first century speeches. Firstly that of Malala Yousafzai who issued a rallying cry for the education of children, especially of girls, all the world over when she opened the new Library of Birmingham in 2013. Secondly it considers the important speech made by the Prime Minister David Cameron on the need to confront Muslim extremism and the means by which it might be tackled.

It was no accident that Birmingham attracted campaigning politicians. Its people were renowned for an active interest and engagement in politics by the turn of the nineteenth century, an involvement which could spill over into violence. An imported troop of the Metropolitan Police learnt this in the Chartist riots of 1839; Lord Randolph Churchill found this at a Conservative rally at Aston Manor in 1884, as David Lloyd George did in 1901 when nearly lynched in the Town Hall pro-Boer War riots, and as Oswald Mosley witnessed when his New Party came calling on Birmingham in 1931.[2] Part of the explanation for their political involvement was a sense of exclusion from power and influence; until 1832 the only representation for Birmingham's 300,000 people was that of Warwickshire's county MPs. Birmingham was an *arriviste* manufacturing town, while national seat distribution at Westminster reflected centuries of influence and special pleading.

Only in 1885 with the Third Reform Act did its representation come broadly to do justice to Birmingham's size and its stature. Being distant from London, the seat of government, might have exacerbated the occasional feeling of impotence and accentuated difference; certainly Enoch Powell (Chapter 9) felt strongly that Westminster politicians were so divorced from reality that they had no idea what his ordinary Midlands constituents were experiencing, as immigration into Birmingham, Coventry and the Black Country brought particular strains on housing and health services. Yet, paradoxically, that distance could be an advantage. Early Chartists thought so in 1839, when they fled London to meet and plan direct action against the state in their Birmingham Convention, a hundred miles distant from an oppressive Parliament (Chapter 2).

That sense of exclusion was sharpened by nonconformity; the rapidly expanding Victorian city was imperfectly and incompletely ministered to by an Anglican church operating on historic parish boundaries. Nonconformist churches, most especially Baptists, Congregationalists and Unitarians, took advantage and settled themselves in the town. Unquestionably, as Chapter 4 shows, they brought a vigour and a reforming zeal to the town and a very real challenge to entrenched, establishment attitudes and practices.[3]

A distinctive characteristic of Birmingham was that for years its politics tended to be dominated by one party. Radical control in the mid-nineteenth century, then a Liberal monopoly, changed after 1886 to Liberal Unionist domination, the era of Chamberlainite hegemony. After the First World War Unionist, or rather Conservative, domination briefly gave place to Oswald Mosley's Labour Party campaign in 1929, but was then reasserted. Only in 1945 was the Conservative spell broken. This is important in two contradictory ways. Bright's loyal Liberal base and Chamberlain's solid, impregnable fastness (the Duchy) provided each with sympathetic, supportive audiences for decades. Yet that domination also invited a challenge. Randolph Churchill came to Birmingham in the 1880s to break that stranglehold. Oswald Mosley chose to contest Ladywood, then Smethwick, in the 1920s because he craved a spectacular victory over the Chamberlain dynasty in its last and latest guise, Neville.

This book reflects the importance of oratory in making a political, usually reformative, argument. Certainly until late into the twentieth century the set-piece speech was the means by which a politician connected with and sought to win over potential supporters. Crowds of around 200,000 heard Thomas Attwood plead for peaceful reform of Parliament at Newhall Hill (Chapter 1). Many of the speeches featured here are long and closely argued, and those delivered at the great outdoor meetings made extra demands on the speaker in an age before amplification. With the occasional exception – for example, a withering assessment of the behaviour of working-class men and women at an early Chartist meeting in *The Times* (discussed in Chapter 2) – in general it is the involvement, enthusiasm and capacity to listen attentively for hours which is striking. Great open rallies became the exception, for reasons of law and order. From John Bright onwards in this book, the occasions for the speeches featured were nearly all substantial gatherings of the local party faithful or of people known to be sympathetic, at places like Birmingham Town Hall or Bingley Hall.

While the speeches were made to convert, excite or enthuse the immediate assemblage, most were intended for instant publication to a wider national audience. Right at the start of this book, Thomas Attwood can be seen dispatching his speeches, made to the Birmingham Political Union, to London for publication in full. Chartist speeches, especially those of Feargus O'Connor, the acknowledged leader, were dutifully printed in his newspaper *The Northern Star*. The great Birmingham speech made by John Bright, his first in his newly adopted home, was such an event that *The Times* chartered a special train to hasten its journalists back to London to ensure the next edition carried the five full columns of dense text which comprised his efforts that night. The stamina and concentration of the nineteenth-century reader was every bit as impressive as that of those attending the event. This pattern of publication was continued into the Chamberlain era. Favourable local newspapers like the *Birmingham Daily Post* as well as the nationals, especially *The Times*, carried the full text as well as an exegesis. Even on the eve of the Second World War, his Prime Minister son's speeches (Chapter 8) were printed in their entirety, unsurprising in view of the gravity of the international situation on which the country's leader was commenting. Enoch Powell was as acutely aware of the importance of managing the media as were the Chamberlains; in the case of the notorious 'Rivers of Blood' speech he alerted *ATV, Midland Television* as well as local and national newspapers. However, perhaps in other ways Powell was by contrast the last of a dying breed of politicians who dared to argue a case closely and at length in rigorous and compelling oratory.

Reflecting a common perception that political discourse has become trivialised and debased, Mary Beard, Professor of Classics at Cambridge, has recently written that party machines are 'too risk-averse to countenance real speech', and so political leaders have abandoned the art of rhetoric, which is 'reasoned argument to persuade', relapsing instead into 'a series of endlessly repeated slogans from a teleprompt', sound bites for the day's headlines.[4]

All these speeches here, including those of Malala Yousafzai and David Cameron, fulfil Beard's requirement of rhetoric that they comprise a reasoned argument to persuade. Many of our speakers were among the most famous orators of their time – Attwood, O'Connor, Bright, Dawson and Dale, Joseph Chamberlain, Mosley and Powell all had a national reputation and attracted large audiences drawn by the prospect of both enlightenment and entertainment. Yet even if these Birmingham speeches are not their most memorable in terms of oratorical flourish (Powell's excepted), each and every one conveys strength of conviction, passion, intellectual rigour and a vision, which made them extremely important in their context. For many of these speeches distilled the essence of an argument and initiated a process of national change and reform.

Attwood's speeches unquestionably convinced many of the need to concede reform, and Chartist oratory underlined for Prime Minister Peel the importance of economic and social reform to ameliorate the condition of the working classes. John Bright's Birmingham speech anticipated over twenty years of parliamentary reform. Chamberlain's 1886 speech derailed Home Rule for a generation, and the Tariff Reform he outlined in Birmingham in 1903 profoundly affected party politics until he First World War. Oswald Mosley's Birmingham Proposals were Keynsian and visionary. Neville Chamberlain's Birmingham speech in March 1939 signalled a massive about-turn in his own approach to Hitler, and represented as significant a loss of face. Powell's Birmingham speech of 1968 remains the most dramatic and controversial contribution to the debate on immigration and race relations, and possibly the most divisive speech on any issue by a British politician since the Second World War. Malala Yousafzai's speech is less controversial, though her public espousal of the cause of children's education the world over in light of her own experience was to be every bit as influential. David Cameron's speech signalled a new determination in government to address the causes of Muslim extremism in Britain.

The overwhelming preponderance of men making important speeches in this book demands some explanation. Women did not achieve prominence in national politics until the twentieth century, a trail blazed by Emmeline Pankhurst and then by Barbara Castle, Shirley Williams and Margaret Thatcher among others; only in 2013 with Malala Yousafzai was Birmingham host to a notable female political contribution. Yet women were important in the history of political movements throughout the period covered by this book. They joined their husbands in the huge pro-Reform crowds listening to Thomas Attwood. Birmingham was at the forefront of radicalising women in the late 1830s, and the Birmingham Female Political Union founded by Thomas Salt had *c.* 3000 members.[5] Women attended Chartist rallies, canvassed, petitioned and spoke at meetings elsewhere nationally.

If they didn't get the vote until 1918 they were prominent in the Conservative Party's Primrose League from the mid-1880s, a formidable, one million strong volunteer organisation which raised funds, canvassed and electioneered with branches in the Unionist-dominated West Midlands. Joseph Chamberlain's Women's Unionist Tariff Association effectively involved women and, as the *Birmingham Mail* reported in 1906, 'the lady worker has contributed no mean part to the sweeping successes of the Unionist candidates. Up to 300 ladies, morning after morning have been setting out in fair and foul weather to canvass the constituencies.'[6] We find women enthusiastically attending the great public meetings addressed by Chamberlain and by John Bright. Cynthia Mosley sometimes joined her husband on the platform at electoral rallies of men and women. If women did not have the opportunity to take a national lead politically in the first century covered here, that did not connote a lack of interest or enthusiasm for political issues.

What follows here is an extended exploration of the context and the national significance of a dozen important speeches delivered in Birmingham by politicians and others for whom the Second city was a welcoming and supportive platform for their radical prescription.

CHAPTER ONE

Thomas Attwood by Unknown artist. Stipple engraving, 1832 or after.

__Thomas Attwood__ was born in Halesowen, Shropshire in May 1783 into a banking family. He succeeded to the family firm, and became convinced that only currency reform would bring Britain prosperity in the post-Napoleonic War years; failure to convert government to his cause led him to espouse reform of Parliament. He helped found the Birmingham Political Union in 1829 and led the campaign for the Great Reform Bill in 1831-32. The speech featured here was made in May 1832 at the culmination of the successful battle to carry the Bill.

THOMAS ATTWOOD AND THE BIRMINGHAM POLITICAL UNION

It was Thomas Attwood and his creation, the Birmingham Political Union, who first established Birmingham's voice and influence on the national stage. The occasion was the prolonged battle for the Great Reform Bill from 1830 to 1832, a campaign of lasting significance for democracy in Britain. However disillusioned Attwood, an articulate advocate of this Bill, might have later become, the fact was that – to employ Sir Robert Peel's homely analogy – a door had been opened which there was no prospect of being able to close, and the next century was marked by a series of parliamentary reform acts which by 1918 had so extended democracy as to enfranchise all men over 21 and about 6 million mature, propertied women.

Contemporaries were in little doubt of Thomas Attwood's importance in that first stage: fellow reformer Francis Place called him 'the most influential man in England', William Cobbett dubbed him 'King Tom', the Prime Minister – Lord Grey – consulted with him over tactics, and so implacable a foe of the aristocratic anti-Reform Tories was he that he became the Duke of Wellington's number one, most excoriated, enemy.[7] Those contemporaries were equally clear about the contribution of the Birmingham Political Union (BPU). Bronterre O'Brien, the Radical, wrote in his newspaper, *The Destructive*, in March 1833, 'to this body, more than any other, is confessedly due the triumph of the Reform Bill. Its well ordered proceedings, extended organisation and immense assemblages of people at critical periods of its progress, rendered the measure irresistible.' Daniel O'Connell, the Irish leader whose methods Attwood had imitated, praised the BPU – 'it was not Grey or Althorp (*the Whig leaders*) who carried the Bill but the brave and determined men of Birmingham' – and Lord Durham, a member of the Whig cabinet, thought that 'the country owed Reform to Birmingham and its salvation from revolution'.[8]

Although it would be unhistorical to attribute all its success to Thomas Attwood – others, like George Edmonds, were central to the organisation of the country's leading political union – there is no doubt that he was its most influential figure, its founder and national embodiment, and 'between 1830 and 1832 his ideas were dominant and his organisation supreme'.[9] It was he who articulated the philosophy of the BPU, and his speeches served to inspire, channel and discipline the disparate multitude of his supporters as well as to convey to London politicians the relentless determination of the industrious classes to win their reform. One of his most notable speeches made near the culmination of the campaign will be used later to illustrate his message and his methods.

Thomas Attwood did not emerge in 1830 as an instant, fully-fledged reformer. For a banker, scion of a successful iron, steel and copper business based in

Halesowen, to ally himself with Radicals demanding fundamental political change, a long and painful journey of disappointment and disillusionment had to be undergone. His political education started during the Napoleonic Wars. As Birmingham's high bailiff, the most powerful figure in the unincorporated town (recognition both of the importance of the Attwood and Spooner bank, and of his ability), he represented the interests of its manufacturers in asking the government to rescind the Orders in Council which embargoed trade with America and much of Europe. Birmingham trade was suffering and 1811 had seen an unprecedentedly deep depression. In this, and in his later advocacy of an end to the East India Company's monopoly on trade to the Orient (an area eyed opportunistically by Midlands industrialists), Attwood had some success and refined his skills – and reputation – as counsel and apologist. He also learnt about the inertia and conservatism of London's ruling classes, a characteristic amply illustrated by the battle on which he now engaged, one he fought for the rest of his life – currency reform.[10]

After the Napoleonic Wars had ended in 1815 the country sank into a prolonged recession. Demand, especially government demand, for Birmingham's metal-working products shrank alarmingly. In 1816 Attwood wrote a powerful polemic, *The Remedy: or Thoughts on the Present Distress*. Government policy was to blame – instead of expanding currency and ensuring full employment, influenced by the landed classes on the Commons backbenches, it had conspired to reduce taxation, reduce government expenditure and deflate. Furthermore it planned through Robert Peel's Committee of Enquiry in 1819 to return to gold as the basis of currency to ensure stability and to demonstrate economic strength.[11]

This would inevitably lead to a sharp reduction in the paper currency secured on gold reserves. Where the banker, Thomas Attwood, saw the value of the notes circulated by his bank in oiling the wheels of commerce and stimulating business, and understood that bills of exchange, transfers, and book debts quite as much as bank notes, gold and silver, constituted the means of exchange, the government – he believed – was hell-bent on a contraction of currency, with inevitably desperate consequences for Birmingham's economy. Businesses with high fixed costs, facing the fall in prices which would follow a severe deflation, would either go bankrupt or at the least shed jobs and cut wages.[12] For Thomas Attwood, a reversal of this policy – government adoption of paper money whose circulation could be expanded or contracted, always with full employment as its guide – was to be his holy grail. For him there was a crucial point – currency reform would benefit all classes in Birmingham, for both masters and men were suffering from the recession. 'If the masters flourish, the men are certain to flourish with them', he told a Town Meeting in 1830.[13]

That belief in the coincidence of class interests, in a town of small workshops where masters and men worked closely together, was to find expression in the BPU.[14] He might have been prompted to rethink by his failure to persuade Peel, and Prime Minister Liverpool, and his successor George Canning, of the benefits of currency reform, despite the encircling economic gloom at the end of the 1820s. The realisation dawned on him that he must tackle the lack of parliamentary representation for the middle and lower classes. Yet, even though he would then spend years engaged in the campaign to reform Parliament, for him currency reform and its corollary, prosperity for all, would always be the end, and political reform the means to achieving it.

Agitation for reform of the House of Commons had existed in Britain since the 1770s, but reformers had different motivations and different goals. Some saw the purpose of reform as being to diminish royal influence, which was founded on building phalanxes of support in the Commons by nominating friendly candidates to boroughs with few voters, controlled by the Treasury. Others, from Major Cartwright in the 1770s to Tom Paine during the French Revolution, saw a vote for every man (universal manhood suffrage) as an inalienable right. Some were driven by outrage at the anachronistic distribution of seats, where ancient boroughs with few inhabitants, such as Dunwich and Old Sarum, returned two Members of Parliament, and yet burgeoning new towns like Birmingham had no representation; others thought the system overwhelmingly weighted towards the landed interest, whose aristocrats controlled many Commons seats, to the exclusion of the newly enriched productive and industrious classes.[15]

In time some of these arguments would come to resonate with Thomas Attwood. Birmingham, like many other Northern and Midlands towns, had a Hampden Club to discuss and agitate for political change after the Napoleonic Wars, but he took no part in its Hampden Club campaign to elect a people's parliament in July 1819 at Newhall Hill, when Sir Charles Wolseley was solemnly chosen as 'legislatorial attorney and representative'. A number of reformers were arrested for conspiring to elect Sir Charles without lawful authority, and among them was George Edmonds, later Attwood's right-hand man in the BPU; but at least – as in 1830 – Birmingham had been seen to take the lead. Attwood's first involvement with parliamentary reform was in the unsuccessful campaign to get his partner Richard Spooner elected to one of the Warwickshire county seats in October 1820; many Birmingham businessmen keenly felt the need for one of their own to sit in the House and represent the issues of the manufacturing classes.[16]

His conversion to reform in the 1820s was largely a frustrated reaction to his failure to make any impression on government with his currency theories. For him, fears for the future of his own business elided with a wider concern for suffering fellow countrymen. He was contemptuous of ministers who remained inert in the face of a growing distress which threatened the solvency of his own bank in 1826. The rejection of two Birmingham petitions to Parliament, calling for action to alleviate the recession in 1827 and 1829, and the stalling of plans to transfer East Retford's corrupt seats to Birmingham, completed his disillusionment and fuelled his anger. If Parliament was unwilling to act, then it must be changed, a more empathetic body replacing it, to better reflect industrial Britain. As acknowledged leader and spokesman for Birmingham interests he, and a small like-minded group, resolved to act in late December 1829 by launching an organisation to agitate for Reform. It would be predicated on Attwood's principles and beliefs and underpinning it was a fear that, if working men were allowed to suffer they would turn violent and Jacobin mobs would wreak the kind of havoc France had suffered in his childhood and he had himself witnessed in Birmingham in the notorious 'Church and King', anti-French Revolution riots of 1791. He was ever aware that Birmingham manufactured small arms – more than anywhere else in Britain, an armed riot could quickly turn bloody.[17]

So it was that the Birmingham Political Union, established in December 1829 at a meeting at the Royal Hotel, had as its slogan, 'Peace, Law and Order', for Attwood was bent on keeping tight discipline, and ensuring peaceful legality, at every turn. He had been profoundly impressed by the example of Daniel O'Connell and his Catholic Association, which had won Emancipation in 1829 through impressive monster meetings of Irish peasants, whose eerie self-control and orderliness had been positively unsettling for the government. One way Attwood achieved this discipline was by running the Union through a large Council, which did his will. But as important was the word 'Union' in the BPU's title; he had an almost mystical faith in the alliance of the classes. By employing peaceful means, and espousing a relatively limited propertied franchise, he could draw on middle-class support, frustrated at Birmingham's exclusion from the Commons; by emphasising that reform of Parliament ('the origin of the evil' he said) would usher in economic reform and policies bringing employment and prosperity to all, he attracted Birmingham working men, with whose representatives he had developed good relations through the 1820s by his chairmanship of the Mechanics Institute in the town.

He could even appeal to artisan Radicals like James Bibb, who advocated universal suffrage and annual parliaments, yet was prepared to subordinate himself to the aims of the BPU.[18] At a meeting of 15,000 to 20,000 'of the Inhabitants of Birmingham' on Monday 25 January, at Beardsworth's Carriage Horse and Carriage Repository in the market quarter, Attwood rehearsed these themes.[19] He 'attributed the general distress to the gross mismanagement of public affairs, and that distress could only be effectually remedied by a Reform of Parliament'. He darkly alluded to what might happen and wanted to help avert 'the awful consequences which he anticipated'. He rejected violent means himself in the pursuit of the Union's aims, which were 'to meet, to consult, to resolve and to petition' for Parliamentary Reform – 'although they should not use the bow or the spear, they would wield the weapons of truth, reason and justice'. 'As far as law will justify me, I will go with you.' These avowals were met with tremendous cheering. He had established himself at the outset as a formidable public speaker.

More than this, the next two and a half years were to reveal skills of organisation and control which were to make the BPU preeminent among contemporary pro-Reform organisations.

That control was needed throughout 1830 when talk of reform made the atmosphere febrile; only at the end of the year, with the collapse of a Wellington government dangerously out of touch with public opinion, was it possible to make progress. A new Whig government under Lord Grey, and a surprisingly radical and far-reaching Reform Bill in March 1831, which proposed the cull of more than 160 borough seats and their redistribution, transformed the situation. Now the BPU committed itself to petition in support of Grey and the Bill, whatever its imperfections.

Attwood's mastery of his supporters, with Edmonds' command of the workers, was never more important than in October 1831 when – ignoring the pro-Reform feelings manifested in a monster meeting of perhaps 150,000 people at Newhall Hill on 3 October – the second Reform Bill was rejected by the House of Lords.[20] Where Bristol, Nottingham and Derby subsequently witnessed notorious acts of violence and were temporarily ungovernable, Attwood and his Council issued an address calling for 'Patience! Patience! – Be Patient and Be Peaceable'. Apart from a few broken windows, Birmingham stayed notably calm despite widespread unemployment. The BPU drew up plans to organise the Union on military lines so that members could quickly respond to any riot locally; but their sinister hints about Britons' right to arm seem to have been made to act as a spur to government to to keep faith with Reform rather than as a serious option and, at a hint from the Prime Minister, Attwood dropped the plans.

What the whole incident did show was firstly how seriously the Duke of Wellington took Attwood and the BPU: 'If we do not put down these Unions with a firm hand, they will destroy the country', he fulminated to Whig ministers – to him Birmingham and Attwood were the dark heart of national unrest. On this at least he was right – Birmingham's Union was now being widely imitated, from Leeds to Stow in the Wold, and these imitations based themselves on the constitution of the BPU, an organisation committed to petitioning, to mass membership of working and middle classes, to awe-inspiring meetings, and to peaceful agitation. Some 130 were established although many foundered through a lack of cohesion and leadership, and a single Reform movement between them was impossible in an age of localism, before the coming of the railways created the possibility of a truly national operation.[21] The incident secondly demonstrated how important the government considered Attwood. Lord John Russell famously confided to the Council of the BPU in late 1831 that 'it was impossible that the whisper of faction (*the Lords*) should prevail against the voice of the nation', Lord Grey counselled Attwood on the government's thinking regarding a proclamation against proposed military organisations in November 1831. The BPU's mass meetings were most valuable evidence for the government of the popularity of its Bill – and its potent membership an equally useful threat of what might happen if reform were to be obstructed.[22]

Fortified with the King's promises that, if needs be, the Bill would be carried through an intransigent House of Lords by the stratagem of a mass creation of peers, Grey returned to the fray and reintroduced a Reform Bill at the end of 1831. It passed safely through the Commons and by the beginning of May 1832 was being debated in the Lords. It was clear that many Lords were determined to eviscerate the Bill in committee and call the King's bluff. During these months the BPU had been largely quiescent; it was as a response to critics who thought it had sold out and lost enthusiasm for reform that Attwood and his committee organised another great monster meeting at Newhall Hill for 7 May 1832 as a way of proving the BPU's credentials as reformers, and as a warning to the Lords not to derail the Bill. Before looking at Attwood's speech to a crowd of 200,000 people, something should be said about Attwood's skills as an organiser and as a manager of these meetings.

The BPU reflected Thomas Attwood's need for domination and oversight of all aspects of the organisation. It involved itself in every parish matter in Birmingham, from proposals for Burials to appointments to Church Wardenships, posts of Constable and Governorships of the Free Grammar School. It controlled its own publicity, printing reports of meetings for wide circulation and in 1832 acquiring (through the Radicals, Francis Place and William Scholefield) *The Birmingham Journal*. That eye for detail is seen in the planning of these huge Reform meetings at Newhall Hill, chosen because it was a natural amphitheatre accessible by foot via the turnpike road, at a point where numerous roads fed into that turnpike.[23] To elevate them in importance they were dubbed – not meetings of the BPU but – 'Great Meetings of all the inhabitants'. Stewards (on horseback and wearing a sash of office embroidered with a Union Jack) were appointed to bring in delegations in an ordered way from all over the Midlands, starting – in the case of the 7 May 1832 meeting - over 24 hours before it commenced. Those different bodies arrived in Birmingham preceded by bands, and carrying banners and flags bearing patriotic devices and the names of their localities. On 7 May the Grand Northern Division, for example, which included Wolverhampton, Bilston, Sedgeley and Wednesbury, was represented in a four-mile procession of over 100,000 people, carrying about 150 banners and accompanied by 11 bands of music.

Shortly before noon 'the programme being all arranged, the immense multitude headed by Thomas Attwood, the Chairman and the Founder in company with the Council carrying white wands and followed by an immense procession, preceded by the Birmingham Union Band in their superb uniform, proceeded to the place of the meeting'.[24] Thomas Attwood and his advisors such as George Edmonds understood the theatrical power of pageantry, the thrill of being part of a huge, colourful gathering, all engaged in what one historian has called the 'politics of sight'; like 'Orator' Hunt with his famous white hat, Attwood employed a habilimentary device, that is distinctive clothing – the fox fur collared coat – as a recognisable trade mark.[25]

The choreography of these processions, designed to impress the establishment with the sheer numbers as well as with the discipline of the body, in some ways aped that of traditional election contests but, for Attwood, what was vital was that the crowds were well behaved. BPU medals had been cast and were worn by many, as were blue pro-Reform ribbons, sometimes tied round trees, all reinforcing a sense of belonging to this great Birmingham movement. The banners expressed the political message and sometimes the cult of Attwood; so 'Unity is Strength' was matched by the nationally popular slogan 'Attwood and the People'. And when all was ready on 7 May Attwood prepared to speak. His 'theatrical whisper', his poise, his clear voice and his quickness of mind made him something of a star turn and after over two years of campaigning for Reform, he had earned the right to be listened to with respect and even reverence. The speech was recorded and published as the 'Report of the Proceedings of the Great Meeting of the Inhabitants of the Midlands Districts held at Birmingham, 7 May 1832, convened by the Council of the Political Union for the purpose of Petitioning the House of Lords to pass the Reform Bill'.

Thomas Attwood (the Chairman) rose amidst loud cheering and addressed the meeting:

Men of Warwickshire, Staffordshire and Worcestershire – My dear friends and fellow countrymen, I thank you most sincerely for the immense, glorious and magnificent assemblage which you now present in the hour of your country's need... The enemies of the liberties of our country have spoken of re-action and indifference in the public mind towards the great cause of reform – how are they answered by the people of the Midland counties? We have had but to stamp on the earth as it were and from beneath the ground a hundred thousand brave men, besides the thousands of beautiful women I see before me, determined to see their country righted, present themselves at our call. (Great cheering)

(The assembly now, under the leadership of Mr. Edmonds, proceeded to sing the Union Hymn:

Lo! We answer, see we come,
Quick at Freedom's holy call,
We come! We come! We come! We come!
To do the greatest work of all –
And hark! We raise from sea to sea
The sacred watchword - Liberty!

God is our guide! From field, from wave,
From plough, from anvil, and from loom,
We come our country's rights to save,
And speak a tyrant faction's doom;
And hark! We raise from sea to sea,
The sacred watchword, Liberty!

God is our guide! No sword we draw,
We kindle not war's battle fires;
By Union, Justice, Reason, Law,
We claim the birthright of our sires –
We raise the watchword – Liberty,
We will, we will, we will be free!

After this spirit-stirring composition had been thundered forth by many thousand voices, silence was obtained by the sound of a trumpet; and the mighty murmurs of the multitude being immediately stilled, Mr. Attwood continued):

We have not hesitated to call this meeting for the purpose of petitioning their Lordships as soon as ever we saw the misrepresentations of the enemies of the People as to the state of public feeling and opinion. The enemies of the People have told their Lordships that the country is indifferent in this great cause. If we hold no meetings they say that we are indifferent – if we hold small meetings they say we are insignificant, and if we hold large meetings that we are rebellious and wish to intimidate them. (Laughter). *Now God forbid I wish to intimidate them – I only wish to speak the plain and simple truth – I would rather die than see the great Bill of Reform rejected or mutilated in any of its great parts or provisions.* (Immense cheering which lasted a considerable time.) *I would rather hide my head under the earth than live to witness the degradation and slavery of my country. Answer me then, had you not rather die than live like slaves of Boroughmongers?* (All, all.)
I have some means of understanding what public feeling is and I say that the people of England stand at this moment "like greyhounds in the slips", and that if

our Beloved King gave the word, or if the Council should give the word in his name, and under his authority, the grandest scene would be instantly exhibited.

The House of Lords are excessively ignorant of the state of this unfortunate country... there are not ten individuals in that Right Honourable House who knew that the country was in a state of distress. A noble Lord assured a friend of mine that the demand for Reform arose from the riches and prosperity of the middle classes who had become jealous of the Aristocracy. Never upon this earth was there a greater error. Here then is the proof of the absolute necessity of Parliamentary Reform. Give us a House of Commons, which is identified with the Commons, and with the feelings and interest of the Commons, and everything will be right with England.

Now my friends I must beg leave to explain the absolute necessity of the peace, order and the strict legality, which you have always exhibited. But for these great qualities our cause would have been lost. Within the law the People are as strong as a giant – beyond the law they are as weak as an infant. See now the prodigious strength which this meeting has peacefully and legally accumulated and compare it with the failures which, for want of due attention to these principles, have been exhibited in other quarters... In the town of Manchester lately, a considerable meeting was held; but a few individuals having made use of violent, inflammatory and illegal observations, the whole meeting was rendered illegal. If such meetings had strictly obeyed the law, no power on earth could have injured a hair on their heads. Under the wise and discreet management of that distinguished Member of our Union, Daniel O'Connell, the Irish people refused to break the law and yet they moved in a sullen, patriotic and determined course until they accomplished their object.

See now the prodigious power, which this Association has obtained. Under the sanction of the law we have here produced probably 200,000 human beings in one great assembly. Suppose we should erect the standard of the Birmingham Union in London. I can tell you that if we should so act, nine-tenths of the population of that immense city would instantly rally round the sacred emblem of the country's freedom. (Cheers.) *The same would be the case in Newcastle, Manchester, Glasgow, Dublin. The whole of the British people would answer to the call wherever the standard of the Birmingham Union was unfurled.*

When I met you here in October I asserted that every honest workman in England had as good a right for reasonable maintenance in exchange for his labour as the King had to the Crown on his head... I insist upon it, that of all the rights in civilised life, the oldest, and the strongest, and the most righteous, is the right of living by honest labour. (Cheers.) If the great Reform which we are now about to obtain does not have the effect of establishing this right, and confirming it for ever, it will never satisfy me.

Friends, I will trouble you no more. Your destinies are at this moment in the hands of the House of Lords. If that august body should neglect to discharge its duty towards us, and our country, upon their heads alone will rest the awful responsibility of the tremendous consequences which may ensue... I will tell the boroughmongers that they will find it as easy to turn the sun from its course as to make the English people now be content with less than the Bill of Reform.

We have not called this meeting from any distrust of Lord Grey, but in order to contradict the falsehoods of the enemies of Reform, and to place a weapon in the hands of his Lordship. When the enemies of Reform speak of indifference in the public mind, Lord Grey will answer, "Look at Birmingham", and no answer will be necessary. Remember my friends, our weapons are PEACE, LAW, ORDER, LOYALTY and UNION. Let us hold fast to those weapons, and I tell you that the day is not distant when the liberty and prosperity of our country will be restored. (Long and enthusiastic cheering.)

His mastery of a huge crowd can be seen by the way he commanded their attention – they listened in silence because he was worth listening to. One can see in the second paragraph of this, "his masterpiece" – in the judgement of his biographer David Moss – both Attwood's wit as well as his passion, especially in the oratorical flourishes such as 'I would rather die than see the great Bill of Reform rejected' and 'the slaves of the Boroughmongers'. The speech rehearsed familiar tropes. Firstly, he highlighted the paramount importance – repeated and underlined – of remaining within the law, of projecting a moral force founded on huge, well-disciplined numbers. Secondly, he hinted at a more revolutionary outcome if the will of the People is consistently thwarted – 'upon their heads alone will rest the awful responsibility of the tremendous consequences that may ensue' (if the Lords neglect to pass the Bill). Thirdly, there was that mantra of the economic underpinnings of Attwood's reform campaign, for ultimately Parliamentary Reform was all about ensuring, through economic reform, that every workman has 'the right of living by honest labour', that is, the right to work for a decent wage – if the Reform Bill failed to establish this, Attwood would be deeply dissatisfied.

Permeating this speech is a contempt for the ignorance, insensitivity and wilful incomprehension of many of the aristocrats, the boroughmongers who controlled small rotten and pocket boroughs and failed to sense the anger of the industrious classes at this anachronism. For Attwood, Grey was an honourable exception, and some of his admiration for the Prime Minister's patience and stamina comes through here. Finally, the speech reflects a profound pride in Birmingham and the BPU: its standard would be the totem around which the British people rallied, and its monster meeting would be all the proof Lord Grey needed 'to contradict the falsehoods of the enemies of Reform' who 'speak of indifference in the public mind'. One further observation concerns the Union hymn, quoted here, in which Edmonds led the singing; the process of singing developed audience participation, reinforced Union through unison singing, 'but also instructed the people on ideology, their rights, and the necessity for Parliamentary Reform to protect and defend those rights'. These hymns were then sung outside rallies, in pubs for instance, and so reinforced and reminded members of the message and bonded people in a shared identity.[26]

Yet the immediate impact of the speech was disappointing; reports did not arrive in London in time to influence the Lords, who proceeded effectively to wreck the Reform Bill in committee, precipitating Grey's resignation and bringing about a week of confusion (known as the Days of May) as Wellington tried to assemble a government. Still, the meeting had been an impressive show of strength and within days of the news of the Whigs' resignation reaching Birmingham, five hundred much publicised new members were recruited to the Birmingham Political Union, many of them respectable businessmen and professionals who had been wary of its populism but now – in frustration – threw in their lot with it. That Newhall Hill meeting had also consolidated Birmingham's preeminent position among pro-Reform campaign groups, and other unions like those in London, Leeds and Manchester held meetings (albeit with smaller numbers and less rigorous control) and followed Birmingham in petitioning Parliament. These were dangerous days; there were rumours of a warrant to arrest Attwood, there was wild talk of civil war, and in the judgement of an authority on the Great Reform Act, 'this was the most intense burst of agitation which anyone observing it had ever known', as petitions rained in on the House.[27]

The BPU took the lead – within days of that great meeting described above there was a second. Attwood presided over a funereal assemblage in which references to a King who had disappointed were eradicated, in which banners and flags were draped in black, and in which a tone not of earlier optimism and confidence, but of pessimism and shadowy defiance now prevailed. Rumours of infantrymen and Scots Greys, issued with ammunition, sharpening swords and prepared to act, heightened the sense of drama. Amidst treasonable anti-monarchical mutterings, and talk of violence elsewhere, Attwood was sober and measured. The aim of the meeting was to petition the Commons not to submit to a Wellington/Tory government foisted on it from the Lords. Once again, he urged patience – 'the new government might kidnap him... but thousands he doubted not, would follow him to imprisonment'. He asked simply that the crowd trust in him.

He remained in Birmingham while BPU allies such as Scholefield and Parkes took the petition to London; Attwood's command of his followers was vital in such a volatile situation. Across these Days of May, Radicals such as Francis Place in London advocated a run on the banks to bring the economy to its knees, while over 200 meetings of the political unions took place to demonstrate the strength of feeling against the Tories. Attwood capitalised on that by drafting a 'Solemn Declaration against the Duke of Wellington', an itemised indictment of the Duke's incompetence to be signed by every reformer in the land, which was then to be presented to the King.[28] Whether it was the palpable strength of pro-Reform feeling embodied by the unions and especially by the BPU, or the lack of support for the Duke at Westminster, where Peel's refusal to join Wellington was a mortal blow, a week after he started to try to pull together a ministry with the Speaker, Manners Sutton, Wellington conceded defeat. With Grey's return, an unadulterated Whig Reform Bill was assured; the King would make the necessary creation of peers.

Birmingham did not doubt its contribution. *The Report of the Proceedings of the Public Meeting of the Inhabitants of Birmingham held at Newhall Hill on May 16th 1832 to present an Address to Earl Grey on his Reinstatement to Office* faithfully records the spontaneous surge of the crowds early on the morning that the good news arrived of Grey's reinstatement as Prime Minister, choking the roads out to Attwood's residence in the village of Harborne, four miles distant from Birmingham's centre. Eventually bands led the procession back to Newhall Hill where Attwood regaled them. 'I cannot but express the great delight I feel in Birmingham having been mainly instrumental in this glorious consummation. I congratulate you on the courage, the strictly legal courage, which you have at all times exhibited. Surrounded by temptations of a hundred kinds, the powers of hell have not been able to prevail or succeed in diverting you from the strict path of justice or the law.' (Loud cheers)... 'The glorious cause of liberty has proved triumphantly victorious'... 'I have little doubt but a short period of time will elapse before the country will enjoy a greater degree of prosperity than ever recollected by the oldest man living among us.' (Cheers).[29]

Events now moved rapidly: the Bill became law. Attwood was fêted at a Public Entry to Birmingham on 28 May which saw an immense cavalcade traverse the towns of Coventry and Meriden, gathering beribboned, flag-carrying supporters all the while as it passed through Birmingham's outskirts. Ringing bells, shouting and singing crowds, a tricoloured balloon, banners and bunting all melded into one vast spectacle as the crowds pressed into the town centre where Attwood addressed them once more. The themes were familiar as Attwood – 'the Friend of the People', as numerous banners proclaimed – sought to distil the significance of what had happened. 'The Duke's hopes of despotism had forever been crushed.' Reform would 'relieve the distress and produce the amelioration and happiness of the people'. For a while his union of people from all classes believed it, but within a few years they were to be greatly disabused. Attwood, one of the newly enfranchised town's two MPs, was profoundly disappointed, for the 1830s did not see prosperity, there was none of his beloved currency reform, the Corn Laws remained in place and the hated New Poor Law was enacted. The BPU ceased to be active.

Yet Attwood remained a Birmingham hero, at least through the 1830s, for all that, and the wider importance of what he achieved cannot be gainsaid. He masterminded mass demonstrations in support of reform, which served to strengthen the resolve of advocates at Westminster at key moments in that epic saga; and he ensured that at every stage, and despite every provocation, these immense meetings were tightly choreographed and entirely peaceful. His fear of a Terror in England prompted him to retain an iron grip on the BPU. He might allude enigmatically to ulterior measures but he did not want to use arms and merely wished to nudge Parliament into conceding the Reform Bill. In truth he played a major part in ensuring that in Britain institutional reform would be carried out incrementally and peacefully. Furthermore, the central role in which he cast Birmingham for this constitutional drama would not be readily relinquished. Its opinions would now be treated with a healthy respect.

CHAPTER TWO

© National Portrait Gallery, London

Feargus Edward O'Connor after Unknown artist. Stipple engraving, mid-19th century.

Thomas Attwood *returned briefly to the fray demanding Parliamentary Reform in 1838 after bitter disappointment at the results of the Great Reform Act.* **Feargus O'Connor**, *born in Ireland in 1794, became a great Radical leader, inspired by Daniel O'Connell. He was a democrat, demanding universal manhood suffrage. A great orator, he also founded* The Northern Star, *the Chartist newspaper. His incendiary speeches landed him in jail in 1840. On release he founded the National Charter Association and the National Land Company, a scheme to return industrial workers to a healthy life on the land. His leadership of the Chartists failed in 1848 when the government effectively repressed the last despairing efforts at securing the Charter by a mass petition.* **Edward Brown** *was one of a new breed of Birmingham working-men who in 1838 rejected the middle-class leadership of Attwood, and instead followed O'Connor. He believed in physical force, specialised in violent speeches, and became a member of the Chartist Convention before his incitement to arms in a public meeting in the Bull Ring in 1839 led to arrest and, despite O'Connor's efforts, to a long stint in jail. That incarceration permanently sobered and moderated him.*

BIRMINGHAM AND THE EARLY CHARTISTS

Chartism was the first great working-class movement in English history, recruiting millions, spanning the country, enduring for a decade from 1838 to 1848, and for much of the time terrifying the propertied establishment. There were three peaks, periods of intense activity which to many seemed revolutionary, and for the first – and arguably the most significant of these, from 1838 to the end of 1839 – Birmingham was the acknowledged heartland. Every national Chartist figure travelled there to speak, including Feargus O'Connor, Henry Vincent, George Julian Harney, and Bronterre O'Brien, and three speeches made there during the movement's convulsive first year will be used to illustrate the aims and the methods of – and the tensions within – the Chartists.

Ever since its inception Chartism has, by its very scale and social and cultural importance, drawn journalists, writers and historians to it, from Thomas Carlyle, Elizabeth Gaskell and George Eliot onwards. There has been no debate about the fact of the Charter, the simple founding document of Chartism, demanding six points, the most important of which was universal manhood suffrage, but much else has been contested. For long, social and economic explanations for this national outburst of activity held sway, relating Chartist activity to unemployment, food prices and trade cycles. However, since the 1970s historians have experienced what has been called a 'political turn' in which they have reverted to an analysis framed in 1854 by Chartism's first historian, R.G. Gammage, according to whom the masses concluded 'that their exclusion from political power is the cause of our social anomalies'. [30] That explains why they supported a political movement for the vote, rather than resorting to the traditional manifestations of economic distress, food riots, arson and begging. [31]

The word 'exclusion' is the key; the working classes in the 1830s felt a keen sense of vulnerability – they had no protection from a tyrannical government, and taxation was inequitable. They inherited a folk tradition, a radical reading of English history in which the labouring classes had lost their land, their property and their rights: it stretched from the time of the Norman yoke (the oppression of the Norman Conquest and its denial of Anglo-Saxon liberties), on through the dissolution of the monasteries, to the enclosure movement and the Pitt government's repression of the French Revolutionary War years. Their anger was fuelled by an acute feeling of disappointment at the barrenness of the yield from the Great Reform Act.

It seemed to many that most of the middle class had joined the ranks of their oppressors in the 1830s, for the reformed Parliament heaped tyrannical ignominy on those already suffering from economic distress, imposing the Irish Coercion Act of 1833 and the hated New Poor Law of 1834, maltreating the Tolpuddle

Martyrs, and ignoring the plight of the handloom weavers. A young Benjamin Disraeli (the future Prime Minister) said as much in the Commons debate on the Chartist petition, under the shadow of the 1839 Bull Ring riots which form the subject of this chapter: 'The real cause of this ... was an apprehension on the part of the people that their civil rights were invaded.' [32] The answer was to focus on the source of the evil, Parliament; with the vote, working men would secure just taxation, good laws and fair government. The means to that paradisiacal end were various. One method involved voluminous petitions, well exceeding a million signatures. Another was of equally monster rallies – often torch-lit, highly colourful and theatrical – which awed spectators and challenged authorities. A further was by demagogic itinerant speakers and by a nation-wide press (especially *The Northern Star* with a circulation of 40,000 and a readership of up to a million a week). Finally they tried aping Parliament through an assembly, or Convention of the people, to debate strategy, and manage the practicalities of persuading Parliament to concede universal suffrage.

Birmingham was not the sole progenitor of Chartism: the London Working Men's Association (LWMA) drafted the charter, the Great Northern Union harnessed the hatred felt by the industrial classes of Lancashire and Yorkshire for the New Poor Law, and Feargus O'Connor's *Northern Star*, published in Leeds, educated, cajoled, and invigorated Chartists, and gave them a sense of belonging. Yet Birmingham pioneered many of the early Chartist strategies for expanding the movement, generating support and spreading ideas. Once again, it was the Birmingham Political Union, revived in 1837, which spawned these.

From its Council came the idea of a National Petition; after all, Birmingham Radicals had petitioned Parliament in the 1820s about distress and currency reform and had experience of the organisation required.[33] The BPU was the first Chartist body to use its members as missionaries, and John Collins had great success in rousing Glasgow, and Thomas Salt more modified success in Lancashire. It was Birmingham which, building on Collins' work, sent a deputation to Scotland to address a huge crowd at Glasgow Green in 1838 on the urgent need to reform. Birmingham initiated the recruitment and involvement of women in the Chartist movement with Thomas Salt's Female Political Union, founded in 1838, which was designed to support the push for men's suffrage, not to campaign for a vote for women; soon it would be 3000 strong, a model for many others to follow. The BPU first popularised among Chartists the idea of a Convention, a people's parliament in London, and adopted William Benbow's strategy of a sacred month, a general strike to halt national production and force Parliament to concede political reform.[34] It was Thomas Attwood and the BPU committee who first saw the potential in a National Rent to finance the Convention. It was to Birmingham that the Convention repaired for protection in May 1839 and Birmingham which became a by-word for violence in the summer of that same year with its riots, before the altogether bloodier events at Newport in November overshadowed it.

Finally, as its name 'Union' suggests, it was Birmingham's Political Union which most prominently represented that early Chartist ideal of an alliance of all the excluded and supplicatory, of working men and still dissatisfied middle classes. There was history, after all, for this had been a winning formula in the battle for Reform in 1830. If the working classes were disillusioned with the establishment, so was Thomas Attwood, who as early as 1834 had concluded of the Great Reform Act: 'It has given us a House of Commons but little better, I am sorry to acknowledge, than the old concern... the House is not what it ought to be; one half consists of Lawyers, Jews of Change Alley and monks of Oxford – the other consists of country gentlemen.'[35] He thought the government wilfully ignorant – and in denial – of the true state of poverty in the country, and wanted to revive an alliance of the productive classes in Britain against the idlers and *rentiers* currently in occupation at Westminster.

Nevertheless, the seeds for the dissolution of a united front between the classes were evidently present from the start. When the BPU was revived in 1837 it had as its goal household suffrage, and only progressed to universal suffrage, the vote for every man, on the prompting of members of Birmingham's Working Men's Memorial Committee (formed to campaign on the distress of the industrious classes) that autumn. For the next two years the worm of suspicion lingered that this was a pragmatic move. Clive Behagg believes that the BPU's leadership really wanted a sort of 'virtual representation' whereby the educated middle class would speak and act for the rest of the productive classes.[36]

At Glasgow the BPU had argued for only three of the Charter's six points (universal suffrage, the secret ballot and annual parliaments). Later it added in the LWMA's other demands, those of equal electoral districts (to which Attwood objected strongly because of its impact on Ireland's representation), payment for MPs, and removal of the property qualification for MPs. These latter two certainly promised much for working men; their earlier omission adds to an impression that the BPU wanted reform on its middle-class terms and did not want to extend political power too much.[37] At the great 6 August meeting at Holloway Head, the venue for the first speech we will later examine, Attwood also put on a brave face when he conceded that his hitherto middle-class Council should be broadened out to include some working-class representatives. By spring 1839 Chartists with long memories were building a case against their putative middle-class allies, who fuelled suspicion by the lukewarm nature of their support for the way the movement was evolving.

One last claim must be made for Birmingham in the history of early Chartism – that monster meeting of 6 August 1838 at Holloway Head, to choose delegates to the newly announced Convention, was designated by Mark Hovell, Chartism's first modern historian, 'the official beginning of the Chartist movement'.[38] It was significant in that from 100,000 to 200,000 people attended (though 300,000 met at Kersal Moor outside Bradford the previous year); all these numbers were estimates and must be very provisional. Nevertheless, they formed huge crowds, drawn from all round the Midlands, processing according to their trades to the natural amphitheatre, but it was the more significant because it was the moment when the movement's 'tactics were extended beyond petitioning'.[39] The speeches of the two leading speakers were widely reprinted. As the local hero, and founding light of the BPU, Thomas Attwood spoke first:

Lafayette said 'for the nation to be free it is sufficient that she wills it.' (Loud cheers); *but how is the will to be known? We must have twenty such meetings; they have had one at Glasgow like this, and another at Newcastle. When we have others we will have a little gentle compulsion upon the boroughmonger. We will do nothing violent. We will gently but firmly screw them out of the seats they have usurped and we will plant the people of England there. (Loud cheers). Now my friends, petition, petition, petition. When I have 100,000 about me as I have today, when I produce two million as I shall by Christmas Day, banded together (Great cheering), you shall see that the voice of the masses will make itself heard and respected.*

We shall have no blood – no blood. Far from me is the guilty ambition of wishing to be a Robespierre... I will take care that the millions of men shall act as one man, and shall act peaceably and never break the law... Let us agree to send delegates to London; we shall propose to you to nominate six to eight from this great meeting. These men will supervise the National Petition. Forty nine delegates of the people, acting according to the law, will knock at the gates of government and tell them that two millions of Englishmen demand justice and liberty. The question is, what are the best means we can attain our holy objects? You have heard of the sacred week (Loud cheers). You all know what a strike is. The time is coming when we should all have a strike against the House of Commons. Suppose we establish a sacred rest for one week, when no plough, or shuttle shall move and no anvil shall sound... and every man should forego his labour.' [40]

This *Birmingham Journal* account was inevitably partial, its editor being BPU Council member and author of the National Petition, R. Douglas, and it is important to recognise a more general partiality in the reporting of Chartism. One of the most comprehensive sources for Chartist gatherings is *The Northern Star*, but the historian has to be conscious of the influence Feargus O'Connor had over its opinions. Regarding 6 August, *The Times*, as a contrast to the accounts of passionate, enthusiastic crowds, dubbed the meeting 'a miserable failure', reported that the people 'were cheerfully employed in regaling themselves with Brummagem ale and pipes of tobacco', and that the speeches 'fell dead upon the ears of the auditors'. 'The charm of Radicalism appeared to be completely broken.' [41] In light of the meeting's instant fame and later significance to Chartists, this seems a jaundiced narrative from a newspaper consistently opposed to this Chartist movement, but it is a reminder of the caution with which one should read contemporary journalism. On the content – what Attwood said – there is unanimity, and what the passages above show are his enduring desire for a non-violent campaign, his continuing belief in the impact of sheer weight of numbers, his importance in popularising the Convention (and desire to stay within the law by limiting the membership to under 50) and the sacred month, and – it must be said – a certain blindness to its consequences. A strike on the scale he envisaged would lead to violence, without doubt, as employers and ministers sought to get men back to work, and suggests that Attwood's rejection of violence was in part wishful thinking.

Feargus O'Connor, an Irish gentleman Radical consciously modelled on the iconic 'Orator'

Hunt, was the self-styled national chief of the fledgling Chartist movement and unquestionably the most charismatic and popular of its leaders, celebrated by millions of devoted followers as 'the Lion of Freedom'. His presence at Holloway Head testified to the importance both of the meeting and of the BPU, but his message differed in tone from Attwood's. O'Connor declared that:

'He was here representing the wishes and feelings of three millions of determined minds. There was not a man among them who was not satisfied to trust the moral power of the nation, even to fawning pliability. They were ready to do this rather than rush into maddening conflict... But he was not to be understood to imply that he was content to live as a slave. No!

> *Come he slow, or come he fast*
> *It is but death that comes at last!* (Tremendous cheering)

But when the moral strength was expended, and the mind drawn out at last, then cursed be that virtuous man who refused to repel force by force. His moral creed was to do unto others as they would do to him. They sought to prevent the rich from applying the national resources to the purposes of corruption, violence and injustice... He had travelled over 2000 miles within the last six months. He had seen the soldiers intrude upon the people and, as if prepared for better days, everyman stood unawed. (Cheers). *He told the soldiers that if they were going to start the work of carnage, to give him time to muster his battalions and if two millions were not sufficient, then five millions would stand up to them to do justice. He would not be led rashly to take up arms. The purpose of universal suffrage was worth living, and worth dying, for.*

This was a glorious meeting; it would be a signal to the rest of the country. He looked for 50 such meetings. If they were refused redress, he would refer them to the 4th chapter of Lamentations – 'it is better to be slain by the sword than perish by famine'. Let there be a strong pull, a long pull, and a pull together, until they had pulled down the citadel of corruption and entered the temple of the constitution. [42]

O'Connor's tone was altogether more threatening than Attwood's. It is the language of physical force, a vocabulary of swords, arms, carnage and dying for causes, rather than that of Attwood's moral force, and the differences between advocates of the two schools would grow across the next year to shatter the unity of the movement. In truth O'Connor was like Attwood in that he hoped the mere prospect of violence would persuade the government to yield, so rendering its employment unnecessary; subsequent history shows O'Connor full of braggadocio until the time came to commit to real violence. So, he cancelled the sacred month in August 1839, was mysteriously absent when the Newport uprising occurred in November 1839, was unwilling to commit to a general strike of Northern factories in the febrile summer months of 1842, and bowed to government pressure at Kennington Common, London in 1848. All that was in the future; back in 1838 his threat of force seemed to Birmingham's reformers, by turns, thrilling and deeply unsettling.

In the months before the Convention met in London in March 1839, Birmingham and its BPU Council meetings was as close to an organisational centre as Chartism had. Yet through the autumn and winter of 1838/9 the fault lines in Birmingham widened between BPU middle-class Council members and O'Connorites, overwhelmingly local working men. It seems that O'Connor attracted many with talk of 'trying their right arms to get their rights', and of setting a deadline for Parliament to accept the Charter. This prompted a long-running dispute between O'Connor and Thomas Salt, over the latter's trenchant criticism of a strategy which seemed sure to end in bloodshed, and it was patched up only in December.

In the meantime there was growing evidence of working-class unhappiness with middle-class leadership in Birmingham – criticism of the very essence of the BPU, inter-class cooperation. The Working Men's Committee of the BPU met separately through the autumn; their leaders such as Edward Brown then formed a Managing Committee for the collection of the National Rent whose affiliations were transparent – it supported O'Connor in advocating physical force, and endorsed the controversial Methodist minister J.R.Stephens, who had sanctioned the utility 'of an ounce of lead and the cold steel'. It was the BPU Council's failure in the spring of 1839 to disband this recalcitrant group which led to open hostilities. The Rent Committee held fast and its leaders, including John Fussell, harangued the BPU's middle-class delegates to the Convention for a failure to do their duty to expedite the long-awaited presentation of the Petition to Parliament. Those middle-class members (Wade, Douglas, Salt and Hadley) promptly resigned to be replaced by working-class radicals like Fussell. The BPU quietly quit the scene, meeting for the last time on 9 April 1839. Although Attwood would loyally introduce the Petition to the House in July, he had lost his enthusiasm, his attendance at BPU meetings having tailed off through the previous year. [43]

Now Birmingham's working men were on their own. Brown and Fussell set up a Birmingham Observational Committee to look after the interests of the workers, and increasingly they took the argument to the streets; according to the Borough of Birmingham Report into the causes of the summer riots, a physical force group (O'Connorites) 'had acquired a kind of independent existence by holding nightly meetings in the Bull Ring'.[44] The language, the message of many of the orators, reflected the anger of a hungry, desperate workforce, as well as Chartist frustration at news of fellow Radicals attacked and beaten that spring at Devizes. Edward Brown is relatively unknown – but he had his moment in the sun as soap-box orator, Rent Committee member, and as prisoner defended unavailingly by none other than Feargus O'Connor himself. His March 1839 Bull Ring speech to a large, boisterous crowd, as related in court, will stand for scores of others in that perfervid atmosphere of spring/early summer 1839:

'I call upon you all to do as I shall do – arm yourselves and be ready and then you

will be prepared to meet your enemies whether they come from France, or Germany or Russia, or your own domestic tyrants. I don't know how long you mean to bear the tyranny of the rich aristocrats but I can tell you I mean to bear it very little longer. The man that does consent to do it is a rank coward. Arm yourselves, and be ready to resist your oppressors. Depend upon nothing but the Almighty God and your own right arms.

Gentlemen, you know that the aristocrats have left you scarcely enough to support nature, while they are wallowing in wealth and luxury on their sofas, and rolling through the streets in their carriages, and if a poor beggar looks up to them and asks for a trifle, they throw themselves back in their carriages and treat him with disdain and contempt. Damned scoundrels, they rely on the soldiers for putting us down, but they won't. They are taken from among our ranks but if we are united what can they do? We have only to walk arm in arm and we could trample them under our feet... We will demand our rights and if our aristocratic tyrants do not grant them then we must seize them by force of arms. They are violating the Constitution every day – they are the enemies of the country and we must arm to resist them. They may hang me up at the rope's end if they like – I am ready to shed my blood for the sake of posterity. Prepare yourselves with pikes and muskets and bayonets and swords and be ready to fight for your lives and liberties... Let the aristocracy make their laws; we, the working classes will make ours – we will do no work for them, and we will take care they shall have nothing to do with our rights... My opinion of physical force I have often told you. It is this. I believe we shall never get our rights without it.' [45]

Of course there are caveats to be made; this is a witness's deposition, made the morning after the speech and related under cross-questioning by Feargus O'Connor. Nevertheless, one can hear the authentic voice of the Chartist physical force working man that summer. To the authorities it was further, worrying evidence of a desperate mood seemingly prepared to have recourse to arms. Throughout the winter and spring that year reports of Chartist leaders prompting men to arms were coming in: Peter Bussey was urging the purchase of firearms, George Harney believing 1839 would be as memorable as 1793 in Bourbon France, and John Markham the Primitive Methodist preacher encouraging men to 'ornament their mantelpieces with ARMS'. Cutlasses and pikes were openly traded in Lancashire, nocturnal groups paraded with pikes, and arms were being produced in ironworks on Tyneside. Although the aim was to persuade a government, with intelligence of this, peaceably to concede the Charter, it was still a matter of real concern. Would those arms be used? [46] The authorities sought to avoid confrontation – instead, through the summer, men like Brown were arrested, held for long periods in custody to allow time for popular support to cool, and sentenced, in ones and twos across the country, so beheading Chartism.

Those nightly meetings in the Bull Ring continued despite the magistrates banning them; they culminated in violence on 4 July when the Convention, having relocated to Birmingham in May (where they could be 'under the shelter of the guns made by the people there', as O'Brien put it), had first prorogued, then reassembled. Mayor Scholefield, concerned about law and order and concluding that its existing enforcement officers of constables, 'specials' and Chelsea pensioners were not up to the task, negotiated with the Home Secretary, Lord John Russell, in London for 60 Metropolitan Police to augment them. Their arrival that evening provoked a riot, as men armed with shutters and railings resisted police furnished with truncheons, determined to break up an unlawful meeting as the Mayor had instructed them to do; the police were routed and the armed forces had to restore order.

At one level this episode appears a straightforward expression of physical force from Chartist sympathisers radicalised by talk of violence by the Edward Browns and the John Fussells in their leadership. But even at the time, observers discerned another more deep-seated motivation. Brown in his defence in court argued that the 'responsibility for the meetings lay with the gentlemen who drew us into it, and then left us'.[47] O'Connor in March 1839 published an open letter in *The Northern Star* to the 'Working Men and Women of Birmingham', and wrote 'you have been invariably used ...for the benefit of men who, at this moment, are sounding a retreat. They have got their share.' [48] Thomas Powell, a friend and ally of Brown, was more specific, denouncing the leaders of the moribund BPU for using the people to win the Charter of Incorporation in 1839, enabling Birmingham to elect its own local government to run its own affairs; then 'only to desert the artisans of Birmingham, after they themselves had been put in possession of the rest'.[49] Most publicly of all, William Lovett, the founder of the LWMA and secretary of the Convention, published three Resolutions on 5 July, so outraged was he by the violence of the previous day. The first blamed an unconstitutional force from London acting 'under the authority of men who, when out of office, sanctioned and took part in meetings of the people, and now when they share in public plunder, seek to keep the people in their social and political degradation'. For this he was arrested and later jailed in Warwick along with the printer, that working-class BPU member, John Collins.

The common theme was betrayal. The middle-class members of the BPU had been involved in gross deception, a ploy to convince Parliament of the unity of Birmingham's classes while the application for Incorporation was being made which, once successful, could be abandoned.[50] Working men observed the shift in priorities of former BPU members – of 34 BPU Councillors, 14 were to be elected to the first Town Council. Three ex-BPU Council members were part of the bench which declared the Bull Ring meetings illegal, and one of them, P. Muntz, sat in judgement on those arrested for obstruction after the riots. Mayor Scholefield, who summoned the hated agents of tyranny, the Metropolitan Police, was a prominent BPU leader.[51]

A narrative favoured by the Chartist crowds developed around the theme of falsity and exclusion. Recent analysis of the Chartist 'groan', a rather terrifying, choreographed, collective roar, shows the crowd, on the day when the Convention first arrived in Birmingham in May, performing this sign of mass disapprobation outside certain selected targets: Douglas's

Birmingham Journal offices, Salt's factory, the Public Office and the barracks. When the second riot of 15 July commenced on news of the humiliating rejection of the Petition by the Commons, and on rumours of police heavy-handedness, the crowd destroyed the property of members of the shopocracy who had shown their true colours by demanding police protection; some of them were transparent supporters of the Town Council. All these targets represented 'the other', the establishment side.[52]

The extent to which the excluded were expressing pure class animosity has been the subject of debate. According to John Belchem: 'The language of exclusion acquired an uncompromising, democratic tone and, abandoned by the middle class, the working class acquired a sense of class pride.'[53] For Donna Taylor, the turbulence of the summer reflected 'a single division society' in which organisations and people were either 'in' or 'out' of the Chartist community, 'with us or against us', irrespective of class.[54] Still, for a while at least, Birmingham's cross-class unity, on which Attwood and others had so prided themselves, was broken, shattered by the self-interest of those business and shopocrat citizens who saw Incorporation as giving them what they wanted. That involved democratic authority at a local level, the power to re-shape the town, by-pass medieval structures like the vestry and the Street Commissioners, and govern on behalf of the ratepayers.[55] What need now did they have of further parliamentary reform? The immediate issue was one of law and order, to ensure they held on to what they had.

The Chartists 'saw an inescapable correlation between the success of middle-class Radicals at the municipal elections of 1838 and their gradual withdrawal from the Chartist movement'.[56] Unsurprisingly, this betrayal hurt; the strong language manifested by Chartist speakers that year simply reflected that 'they were goaded to it by their rulers', as Edward Brown put it.[57] There was a later attempt to rebuild the old alliance – by Joseph Sturge, corn factor, Quaker, prominent anti-slaver, founder of the Birmingham branch of the Anti-Corn Law League and then of the National Complete Suffrage Union in 1842. This movement for universal suffrage briefly promised much in the autumn of 1842. That members of Birmingham's working class were prepared to collaborate at all shows that they recognised an important truth; without middle-class advocacy within the establishment, especially at Westminster, parliamentary reform would remain a chimera. In this case, the alliance foundered on Sturge's refusal to adopt the label 'Chartism'. Mutual suspicion had won out.[58]

The Chartist meetings of 1838/1839 were 'rituals of assembly which created and affirmed Chartist identity. Audience participation was vocal.'[59] The rhetoric, the flags, the banners, the coloured Chartist favours and the groans created a theatrical performance. For a while during the winter of 1838/1839 torchlit processions added to that sense of theatre. As we have seen, the latent threat of large numbers could, as at Birmingham in July 1839, turn to real violence when the crowd was provoked. Many in the authorities feared a Revolution transplanted from across the Channel. It did not help that England's magistracy was amateur, propertied and often out of its depth. Little had changed since Peterloo in this regard. The diarist Charles Greville noted gloomily at the start of the year that '... there is no military force in the country at all adequate to meet these menacing demonstrations; the Yeomanry have been reduced, and the Magistracy are worse than useless, without consideration, resolution or judgment'.[60]

Stealth, cunning, and growing experience combined to allow those authorities to get on top of Chartism. In Birmingham, the arrests of Brown, Fussell, Powell, Lovett, Collins and Harney, and the continued use of police and soldiers to control meetings in public places, ensured there was no Chartist revolution in the town. Birmingham did pioneer one more device for discomforting the authorities. Malcolm Chase claims that 'Birmingham Chartists were the first to use the tactic' (of mass attendance at church services in August 1839).[61] The strategy evaded the ban on meetings and it challenged the social elitism of the Anglican Church with its private pews and Tory clergymen. It was ineffective in winning the six points but it was a welcome way of irritating the establishment.

Nationally, the rejection of the Chartist Petition of 1839 saw many wondering 'what next'? The failure of the movement to agree on a sacred month in August left it without an agreed alternative strategy. The year ended with a bloody but abortive uprising in Newport – perhaps part of a planned conspiracy which nevertheless came to nought outside Wales. Energies were now poured into ensuring the pardon of the three men condemned to hang for their part in the uprising. That and the jailing of O'Connor in York Castle for eighteen months quietened Chartism. By the time of the next real surge in 1842 there was a new central organisation, the National Charter Association, and Birmingham was peripheral to the dramatic events in the industrial North.

If Chartism was essentially a political movement then its defeat would be by political initiatives applying to Birmingham as much as to the whole country. It was partly that the state showed it could effectively bring force to bear: in August 1842 Sir Robert Peel dispatched the guards by train to deal with industrial workers striking for the Charter; in 1848, Prime Minister Russell recruited 80,000 special constables to overpower Chartists in London bent on marching on Westminster. It was also that Peel called into question their entire *raison d'être*. Radicals like Attwood and O'Connor had argued that only by having political power could good laws be enacted; the vote was a necessity to improve the People's lot. Peel's government showed that wasn't necessary – it imposed income tax on its own supporters, it reduced indirect taxes, it abolished the Corn Laws which kept bread prices high, it introduced a Bank Charter Act which was aimed at rash bankers, and it enacted factory legislation.[62] An essential argument for Chartist universal suffrage was undermined. It therefore took many years for the Chartists' central demands to be realised. As for our three speakers: long before then, Attwood had succumbed to disillusion and disappointment, O'Connor to financial impropriety and incipient madness, and Edward Brown – cowed by a prison sentence – to moderacy and religion, as a member of the Christian Chartists who flourished in Birmingham after 1841.[63]

CHAPTER THREE

John Bright by Walter William Ouless. Oil on canvas, 1879.

John Bright *was born in Rochdale in 1811 into a Quaker family. He became Britain's leading Radical, successfully campaigning with his friend Richard Cobden for the Repeal of the Corn Laws, symbol of aristocratic dominance, in 1846. He went on to struggle unavailingly against Britain's decision to go to war with Russia over the Crimea in 1854; he would abandon the North and Manchester and take his crusade for greater democracy to Birmingham in 1858 when he made the speech featured in this chapter. By the time of his death in 1889 he could reflect with real satisfaction on the great strides made in the reform of Parliament since his move to Birmingham thirty years earlier.*

BRIGHT AND BIRMINGHAM

John Bright was the outstanding orator of his age and, along with Richard Cobden and Joseph Chamberlain, was one of 'the most famous and influential reform agitators of the Victorian era'.[64] They, with Thomas Attwood, established the right of the big city to participate in the political process of Victorian Britain and helped put Birmingham and Manchester on the political map.[65] Bright influenced both cities profoundly. He made his name in Manchester, but when that town rejected him, or rather his trenchant views on Britain's involvement in the Crimean War, Birmingham offered him a lifeline, an opportunity to re-launch his stalled career. His first big speech as a Birmingham MP in 1858 is explored later on in this chapter; a political event of the first magnitude, it articulated afresh his mission, that of reforming Parliament, one which was to dominate the next fifteen years of his career.

The members of the Birmingham Liberal Association who approached Bright in 1857 to fill a vacancy for one of the town's Parliamentary representatives wanted what he offered: 'a national celebrity... who would project the reforming vigour of its (*Birmingham's*) local politics onto national politics'.[66] Because Birmingham politics was, in truth, dominated not by Whigs or Tories but throughout the nineteenth century by Radicals, there seemed logic in securing the country's leading Radical. The Radical agenda of winning democracy, securing civil and religious liberties, and establishing economic justice was one shared by both Bright and his sponsors in Birmingham. The town's Radicalism was expressed in its popular tradition whereby 'the people of Birmingham were invited to see themselves as heroic subjects, chief actors in their own democratic project'.[67] This they did through the monster meetings we have seen in earlier chapters. Contemporaries were struck by their attachment to liberty; the evidence of their passionate involvement in the agitation for both the Great Reform Act and then for the Charter accords with this perception.

John Bright's views on Parliamentary Reform in 1857 were in a long tradition of vigorous criticism of undue royal and aristocratic influence over the Commons, and of the often flagrant corruption accompanying it. As a corollary, he was a champion of cheap government, low taxation, and measures to ensure that the establishment's penchant for waste and extravagance was contained. He and Birmingham could agree on this programme; it helped that his fellow Quakers in Birmingham such as Joseph Sturge were not of the conservative bent that characterised Quaker communities in much of the country, but had a distinctly Radical tinge.[68] John Bright was no conventional Radical either, as will be seen, and he sometimes took a line diametrically opposed to Radical allies over the use of force, over temperance and later, notoriously, over Ireland and Home Rule. [69] The truth was that he was more of an Independent than a Radical; following his conscience, responding to his Inner Light, made him occasionally impatient with party labels and discipline. What he brought his new constituency was the ability to elevate and articulate the cause of reform on which they both agreed. 'How is it', he asked at a dinner for the great American anti-slave campaigner William Lloyd Garrison, 'that any great thing is accomplished? By love of justice, by constant devotion to a great cause, and by an unfaltering faith that what is right will succeed in the end.' [70] He would be constantly devoted to that 'great cause' while representing Birmingham, and would achieve signal success.

Yet he never truly became a Brummagem native, remaining a Rochdale man to the end. His outlook was determined by his upbringing, son of a Northern Quaker mill-owner. In some ways he himself was not a traditional Quaker, for he sought to break down Quaker seclusion and open up the Society to greater participation in the world. He believed, for example, that in getting rid of tyranny there might be necessary violence, which was anathema to many pacific Quakers. Yet in other ways he was profoundly influenced by his faith. He saw radical activism, like fighting for Corn Law Repeal, as a 'calling': 'I felt in my conscience that there was work which somebody must do and therefore I accepted,' he said – referring to Cobden's invitation to become involved in the Anti-Corn Law League's campaign. [71] His career can be seen in terms of the Quaker imperative to 'bear witness'.

Indeed his family's religion first led him into political campaigning. He was outraged by the persecution his father suffered for non-payment of Church Rates, that invidious tax which forced all, Anglican or not, to contribute to the upkeep of the parish, and he led a –locally successful – campaign for their remission. For Bright, the issue was of a piece with a larger injustice, of a tyrannical establishment exploiting the common people, with whom Bright aligned himself. The Quaker 'belief in the equality of all men before earthly governments, naturally leads to a strong sympathy with the great body of the people,' he wrote. [72] His Radicalism was determined by his reading of history, in which the persecution of the Society of Friends elided with the oppression of unpolished, unlettered Northern working people, for all of whom Bright saw himself as a mouthpiece. A significant moment was his first experience of this class, as a young and impressionable man campaigning shoulder to shoulder with working men, at the Preston by-election in 1830, where 'Orator' Hunt, their champion, exhilaratingly triumphed over a scion of the aristocratic Derbys.

For such aristocrats, Bright had a deep, life-long animosity. He couched the great victory for Corn Law Repeal in the 1840s in terms of being one for humanity, and as a termination of aristocratic, landed power – after all, the landowners had kept bread prices high to line their own pockets at the expense of the people. He said in 1849 that Corn Law Repeal meant 'that the power of the landed aristocracy has reached its height and henceforth it would find a rival to which it would be subjected'. He meant the middle classes, and perhaps that shows that whilst he may have been the people's tribune, he was also a gentleman and a mouthpiece for the class from which he emerged.

During the Anti-Corn Law campaign he had experienced the corruption and abuse of that landed class first-hand, when he contested the Durham by-election in 1843, initially losing to Lord Dungannon, before it was established that the erstwhile victor had used bribery and treats to secure the poll, and Bright was declared the winner. A year later he commenced a ferocious, though ultimately vain, assault on the Game Laws, which allowed landowners to preserve game for hunting at the expense of tenants' crops.[73] His stance over the American Civil War was coloured by a belief that the North represented democracy and the working man, against the aristocratic slavers of the South. Back at home, the rejection by the Lords of Gladstone's Paper Duties Repeal in 1860, which would have ended the 'tax on knowledge', merely confirmed in Bright's mind their anti-democratic persuasion. We will see later on his hostility towards the Peers restated in his great Birmingham speech.

The issue of Corn Law Repeal was not simply about reducing the power of the aristocracy; it was part of a bigger campaign to abolish all tariffs, which kept prices higher than they need be, and introduce Free Trade, that would oil the wheels of international trade. Industry, businessmen and employees, would benefit from reciprocal reduction of tariffs. In all this, Bright was Cobden's assistant – 'I can in no degree take your place but as a second I can fight', he wrote to him in 1845.[74] He was distinguished by the force of his oratory, and by his occasional impetuosity, as in his seeming encouragement in the bleak recessional summer of 1842 to League members to close their factories, so driving already desperate men to turn to violence, to bring to a head the fight for reform.[75]

Once Peel had carried Repeal in 1846, the relative importance of Cobden and Bright changed. It was Bright who made the running on Parliamentary Reform, seeing Repeal 'as the commencement, rather than the conclusion, of an era of reform'.[76] It was Bright who took the fight to the successive governments of Aberdeen and Palmerston (the latter of whom he cordially disliked) over Britain's involvement in the Crimean War, lasting from 1853 to 1856. His youthful Grand Tour round the Near East had convinced him of the plague-ridden and despotic character of Turkey; would it be such a crime if Russia occupied Constantinople and civilised it? Why was Britain fighting another Christian power? Wasn't the 'balance of power vicious and mad'? Most disagreed, fearing the emergence of a newly powerful Russia. For his pains he was excoriated by many, in Manchester where he was burnt in effigy, and nationally, where he was labelled a coward, a traitor and a Russian agent. He was aware that 'the country is drunk just now, and will hear nothing against its passion'.[77] His Quaker faith gave him courage and self-assurance, as seen in a famous Commons speech of December 1854: 'Even if I am alone (*in my condemnation of war*), I should have the consolation I have tonight – that no word of mine has tended to promote the squandering of my country's treasure or the spilling of one single drop of my country's blood.'[78]

He was by turns depressed and confounded by the public's callousness, a public in which he normally had such faith. Early in 1856 he broke down from the strain of fighting his corner and facing an unremitting barrage of criticism. It was not altogether surprising that he and Cobden, another critic of the war, should be defeated in the subsequent General Election of 1857, when the war was won. It was still deeply satisfying that in the same year, on the death of their MP George Muntz, leading Birmingham Liberals should have invited Bright to stand in the town, overlooking the recent past, for after all the war was now over, and elected him. Cobden was exuberant at the turn of events: how gratifying, he wrote, that the voters of Birmingham 'should have in so handsome a way kicked the posteriors of those political snobs and fops in Manchester'.[79]

A year elapsed from the date of his return to Parliament to his meeting his constituents and unquestionably there was a growing pressure on him; after all, anticipation was keen in Birmingham and in the country. Was he still up to it, after his recent depressive breakdown? Would there be a new mission? The cause was not, in the event, difficult to determine. He had since the late 1840s 'seemed anxious to keep domestic politics in movement while others wished to keep it in repose', wrote Asa Briggs, and that had meant articulating the case for another, substantial tranche of parliamentary reform.[80] He was not alone; 'a reform party was in continuous existence at Westminster' in the 1840s and 1850s but its main interest, one shared by Bright, was in the redistribution of seats to the new industrial conurbations and from the small boroughs controlled by the landed interest. Reform bills were proposed – by Russell, even by the Conservatives – but, for Bright, they were characterised by their modesty, by the naked pursuit of party interest and by a depressing lack of real commitment among the sponsors of reform.[81] In 1859 another bill was to be laid before the House, this time by Benjamin Disraeli. It was Bright who exposed its inadequacies, shoddiness and partiality and in doing so he precipitated the Conservatives' fall from office.

If the subject clarified itself, there remained the question of whether he had lost his touch. For Bright had a towering oratorical reputation. He knew he possessed a gift and felt a religious duty to use it – 'I cannot discern that there is anything wrong in exercising a talent for the furtherance of a great and good object', he wrote. That talent had been honed and practised, at his Quaker school, Ackworth, which was known for its teaching of Diction, and then at the Rochdale Literary and Philosophical Society, and the local Temperance Society, where Bright performed orations.[82] So skilled did he eventually become that his speeches were published by *Everyman* until 1907 as models of oratory. It was partly that he had a gift for the memorable turn of phrase: he dubbed Liberal Party rebels 'the Cave of Adullam' (the Old Testament refuge for the discontented) in 1866 and that has stuck; he dismissed the complicated and exotic votes for the propertied planned by Disraeli as 'fancy franchises'; he coined the term 'residuum' for the undeserving poor at the bottom of the social ladder; and he mocked Disraeli's party in 1867 as it struggled to keep up with his tortuous reform plans – 'the whole Tory party has been dragged from its anchorage', he said.[83] Most famously he found a poetic image to encapsulate the case against the bloodshed of the Crimean War:

> 'The angel of death has been abroad throughout the land. You may almost hear the beating of its wings. There is no one as when the firstborn were slain of old, to sprinkle with blood the lintels and the sideposts of our doors, that he may spare and pass on; he takes his victims from the castle of the noble, the mansion of the wealthy and the cottage of the poor and lowly.'[84]

There was more here than technique. This Biblical allusion illustrates a central truth about Bright, that his power came from the ability to convey his inner conviction simply, in what

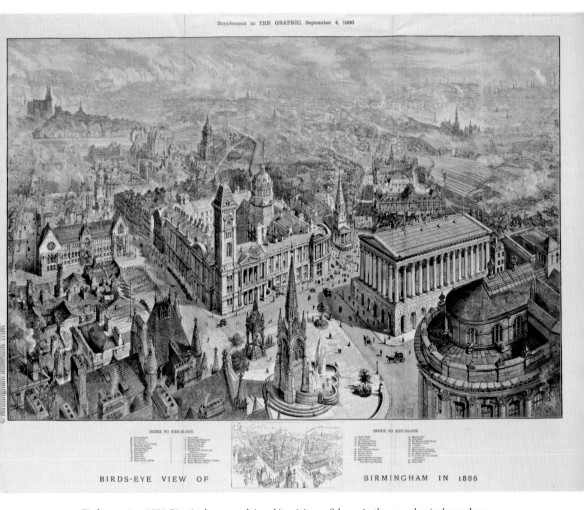

INDEX TO KEY-BLOCK

INDEX TO KEY-BLOCK

BIRDS-EYE VIEW OF   BIRMINGHAM IN 1886

Birds-eye view 1886. Birmingham proclaimed its civic confidence in the neo-classical grandeur
of its municipal buildings, grouped around the newly laid-out Chamberlain Square in the foreground.
Beyond lies the source of its wealth – the industrial districts, hazy with smoke.

In 1832 Thomas Attwood addressed about 200,000 people at a Parliamentary Reform rally on Newhall Hill, Birmingham, which saw some of the largest political assemblies the country had ever witnessed.

A commemorative medal struck to celebrate the Reform Bill of 1832, showing Thomas Attwood. This was a fitting tribute to a man whose oratory had achieved so much for Parliamentary and currency reform.

In 1839 the Chartist campaign for Parliamentary reform became violent. In Birmingham the July
'Bull Ring' riots saw serious clashes between protestors and officials. Here firemen come under attack.

Joseph Chamberlain (front left) talks with his Party Leader Gladstone (centre) in the lobby of the House of Commons. Another of Birmingham's Radical champions, John Bright, stands in the background (third from left).

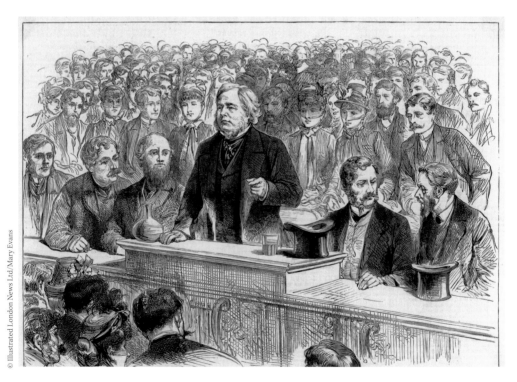

John Bright was already a Radical hero and popular speaker when he became a Birmingham MP in 1858. Here he addresses a packed assembly of his new constituents at the Town Hall.

OPENING OF THE BIRMINGHAM CENTRAL FREE LIBRARY.

The opening of Birmingham's first Reference Library in 1866, 'a great diary of the human race', by George Dawson, part of the establishment of a Civic Gospel to provide a framework for the government of Birmingham.

In this political postcard, Joseph Chamberlain's Tariff Reform policy of 1903 is shown as a runaway car. Chamberlain's passenger is Prime Minister Arthur Balfour, whose government was fatally weakened by the divisive policy.

The role played by Birmingham politicians at Westminster over the vexed question of Irish Home Rule. Joseph Chamberlain (bottom right) broke irrevocably with Prime Minister Gladstone over the issue in 1886.

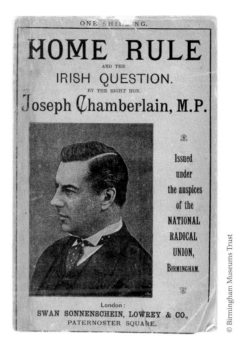

Chamberlain fought a desperate battle to retain the loyalty
of Birmingham Liberals in 1886, the source of his power, over his opposition to Home Rule.

Home Rule bitterly divided the Liberal Party, with Joseph Chamberlain at the centre of the controversy.

The Rt. Hon. Joseph Chamberlain
addressing his constituents in the Town Hall, Birmingham.

Cox C9 L^{TD}

Always a powerful and persuasive orator, Joseph Chamberlain argues the case for abandoning
Free Trade in 1903 at Birmingham Town Hall.

Trevelyan calls a 'homely' way.

'He was singular among orators for his want of gesture; there he stood, foursquare, and sometimes raised an arm; his oncoming was as the surge of the full swollen tide, not of the sea in storm; he awed his listeners by the calm of his passion, a terrible steed restrained by a still stronger hand.'[85]

Even more than Gladstone, 'Bright tapped into the religious feeling in which the age was suffused'.[86] He was, in the words of a contemporary, John Morley, 'the prophet of democracy.'[87] So it is not altogether surprising that his maiden speech in his Birmingham constituency should be one of the political events of the year. For Bright the occasion, on 27 October 1857, the first big speech since his illness, was 'an ordeal'. The Town Hall was stripped of its seating to accommodate a great crowd of over 5000 people. Bright archly wrote in his diary: 'Attended meeting and dinner at Birmingham. Speeches. Reporters were more numerous than at any meeting ever held before in the country. Telegraph and special trains – as if some very important person here to utter words of great import.'[88] *The Times*, not always kind to Bright, was one to have arranged its own special train to speed news of this event back to London in advance of the morning editions. And in a hall in which – it reported – not an inch of ground was unoccupied, Bright stood to speak:

It is now nearly three years since I was able to stand upon any public platform to address any public meeting of my countrymen. From apparent health I have been brought down to a condition of weakness exceeding that of a little child, in which I could neither read nor write. And from that condition I have been restored to comparative health. In remembrance of all this, is it wrong in me to acknowledge here, in the presence of you all, with reverent and thankful heart, the signal favour which has been extended to me by the great Supreme? ...

I never imagined for a moment that you – who conferred on me the honour of returning me as one of your representatives to the House of Commons – were prepared to endorse all my opinions or to mention every political act with which I was connected; but I accepted your resolution in choosing me as meaning this – that you have watched my political career; that you believed it an honest one (Cheers)*; that you are satisfied I have not swerved knowingly to the right hand or to the left* (Cheers)*; that the attractions of power had not turned me aside* (Cheers)*; that I have not changed my course for any fleeting popularity* (Cheers)*; and further, that you were of this opinion – which I religiously hold – that the man whose political career is on a line with his conscientious convictions can never be unfaithful to his constituents or his country* (Prolonged cheering) *...*

They (the party leaders) *all pretend now to be very fond of the question of reform but they remind me of that American cable, 'that the currents were visible but the signal wholly indistinct.'* (Loud laughter). *But having admitted that Parliamentary reform is necessary, they therefore admit that the present House of Commons does not satisfactorily represent the nation. Now, I do not believe that the Parliament as at present constituted does fairly represent the nation. Let us come to figures...*

There is this great significant fact that wherever you go in Great Britain and Ireland five out of six men you meet have no vote. And the law has selected 1,000,000 to be the electors of members of Parliament but having got that they have contrived, very much by intention so that the political power of the majority of this 1,000,000 is frittered away and fraudulently disposed and destroyed by the manner in which members are distributed among the voters. We want to substitute a real honest representation of the people for that fraudulent thing which we call a representation now. And when you are about to reform the House of Commons, are your eyes to be turned to the House of Peers or to the great body of the nation? The House of Peers as you know does not travel very fast – even what is called a Parliamentary train is too fast for its nerves; in fact it never travels at all unless somebody shoves it (Laughs). *But the question between the peers and the people is one which cannot be evaded. It is the great difficulty in the way of our friends at headquarters who are for reform but don't know how to do it.*

With regard to the question of the suffrage, I have no doubt that there are persons who on reading my speech will say, 'Subversive doctrine, violent language this.' But I do not want to propose any new principle which it may be found difficult to adopt. There are many men probably among those I see before me who are of opinion that every man should have the vote. (Loud cheers). *They are for what is called 'universal' or 'manhood suffrage.' I should not act on that principle. There are scores of thousands who imagine that they could not sleep safely in their beds if every man had the vote; and there are rich people in this country who believe that if every man had the vote it would actually give him a weapon wherewith to attack their property. It is, then, clearly the duty of government to frame a measure which shall fairly represent the reform opinion of the whole country. For generations, for ages past, there has been an extensive franchise in all our parishes. We have a franchise in our Poor Law unions. We have a corporation franchise. I will ask any man here whether he believe that in all the parishes, unions and corporations men have not conducted themselves with great propriety and managed their affairs satisfactorily. And I should like to ask them whether they would object to having the same franchise conferred on them for the election of members to the House of Commons. It would admit the working people to electoral power just as fully as it would admit the middle, or the higher, classes...*

Every elector is of the same importance in front of the law; why then should not every elector vote for the same portion of the whole Parliament? What a miserable delusion it is that this great capital of midland industry, with its 250,000 or 300,000 inhabitants, sends only two members to the House of Commons (Cheers). *Whenever a Reform Bill is brought into the House of Commons, be as watchful and exacting as you like on the franchise but never, I beg, take your eye for one moment from the question of the distribution of members.*

There is one other point to which I must refer and it is one on which I presume I shall have the cordial assent of this meeting. Any Reform Bill, which pretends to be generally satisfactory to Reformers, must concede the shelter and protection of the ballot. Those who are for the ballot are for it because they wish free elections. Those who are opposed to it are so chiefly because they believe it would liberate the great body of constituencies from the control and influence of the rich. (Cheers). *I say that it is especially wise and just that the humble elector in every county and borough should have from the law, if the law can give it, an equal protection in the exercise of his franchise.*

This question of Parliamentary Reform then is a great and serious question. I want to give a word of warning to those who are engaged in constructing a Reform Bill. Let them not bring in a delusive and sham measure. It will disappoint everybody; it will exasperate reformers; it will render a feeling that is not now bitter, bitter and malignant and within twelve months after such a bill has passed and the cheat is discovered we shall be entered in all probability upon another agitation of a very different character from any we have yet seen. Now I have a suggestion to make; the Reformers now are more numerous than ever they were before. Why should they not have their own bill, and have it introduced into Parliament and supported by this great national party? Why should we not, with all the unanimity of which we are capable – by public meetings, by petitions, by presenting ourselves at the polling-booths – do everything in our power to carry that bill into law? I say that we are great in numbers; that united we are great in strength; that we are invincible in the solidity of our arguments; that we are altogether unassailable in the justice of our cause. Am I not in the town of Birmingham – England's central capital; and do not these eyes look upon the sons of those who, not thirty years ago, shook the fabric of privilege to its base? (Cheers). *Not a few of the strong men of that time are now white with age. They approach the confines of their mortal day. Its evening is cheered with the remembrance of that contest and they rejoice in the freedom they have won. Shall their sons be less noble than they?* (Cries of No! No! and cheers). *I speak with a diminished fire, I act with a lessened force; but as I am, my countrymen and my constituents, I will if you will let me be found in your ranks in the impending struggle.* (The honourable gentleman sat down amid great cheering which was renewed again and again).[89]

G.M. Trevelyan, an early biographer, memorably described how the 'great audience swayed, like a cornfield beneath the wind… and the magic that swayed them was not some hard appeal to the lower part of their nature but drew its compelling virtue from the simplest invocation of moral principles'. Robert Dale, a noted orator himself, as well as a leading Birmingham minister, wrote later of 'the hush which had fallen on the vast and excited assembly deepen(ing) into awe… We suddenly found ourselves in the presence of the Eternal, and some of us, perhaps, rebuked ourselves in the words of the Patriarch, "Surely the Lord is in this place and I knew it not".[90] Dale is referring to that confessional passage about illness and recovery; to modern eyes the language seems sententious, and Professor Burn described it as 'nauseating', but the enthusiasm with which this, and the image which conjured up the old Birmingham reformers 'white with age,' was received suggests a different sensibility in the mid-nineteenth century from ours.[91]

The full speech – for the above is a necessarily abridged version – was an epic performance filling five closely printed columns of *The Times*. It represents impressive stamina; he was clearly restored. Bright was back. What he said was partly about self-justification, portraying himself as the sea-green incorruptible holding fast to principle whatever the worldly inducement to abandon it – he defies his Crimean war critics. He is fulsome about his new constituency, grateful for the opportunity for a second chance, honouring its unique pedigree in agitating for reform and recognising Birmingham's special claims for greater representation. That constant, his hatred of the peerage and the landowning classes who monopolise power, is once again rehearsed. Above all he sets out a clear reform agenda, sensible and achievable, one designed to allow the propertied classes to sleep easy in their beds at night. So, he proposes household (not manhood) suffrage, highlighting the precedents for this in historic parish and Poor Law elections. He then demands root and branch redistribution of seats fairly to reflect the population growth in industrial centres. He also advocates a secret ballot to allow men freely to vote without the coercion of employer or landowner. He is quite prepared to lead a vigorous campaign and contribute his own poor, weakened constitution to the fight. He even countenances an 'agitation of a very different character from any we have yet seen' – a euphemism for violence – in the event that a reform bill be a 'sham.'

This speech is significant in a number of ways. His enthusiastic reception re-invigorated Bright, and emboldened him; crusading against the landowning classes through the medium of great meetings in Edinburgh, Glasgow and Bradford led him eventually back to Manchester in December 1858, an altogether more rewarding experience than his recent electoral defeat there. The sum of attendances 'had exceeded in numbers and influence almost every meeting that was held by the Anti-Corn Law League', he boasted in the Commons in 1859.[92] The Birmingham speech was the first of many which articulated nationally a coherent reform case, so different from the tactical manoeuvrings of the two main parties' leaderships. However, it was not to be translated into a successful reform bill just yet. Russell's Bill in 1860, which did little for redistribution (for Bright at the time a real priority), foundered on the lack of enthusiasm in both the House and in its aristocratic sponsor, but most of all, from the obstruction of the Prime Minister, Palmerston. In any case, as Bright averred, 'there is no howling wind, and no imminent convulsion' in the shape of a popular outcry for reform. By 1866 it was different, and within months Parliament was to take a giant step towards realising the democratic vision John Bright had conjured up in that Birmingham speech.

Palmerston's death in 1865 removed a roadblock on the road to reform. The Chancellor of the Exchequer, William Gladstone, the Liberal Party's coming man, had indicated in 1864 a new sympathy for enfranchising respectable working men. The visit of Garibaldi to England, a revolutionary nationalist but also a liberal hero, rejuvenated popular working-class enthusiasm for greater democracy, expressed in a new Reform League and Reform Union. The victory of the democratic North in the American Civil War in 1865 seemed both propitious and a precedent. So, a Reform Bill drafted by Russell and by Gladstone was presented in the Commons in 1866. Despite great demonstrations of popular support at meetings across the country – and Birmingham was to host one with an estimated 200,000 attending – the Bill was defeated in the House when a group of Liberal MPs led by Robert Lowe (Bright's Adullamites) helped vote it down. The autumn of 1866 saw 'the anger of the provincial towns blazing fiercely as working men were thoroughly aroused and flocked to the banner of John Bright'.[93] At these meetings, Bright's arguments were simple and logical: the House of Commons was a travesty elected by a small proportion of adult males; seats were inequitably distributed; great landowners dominated the House and pursued their narrow, selfish interests rather than those of the nation; whereas the working classes had the vote in other countries, in the home of the mother of Parliaments they did not.[94]

It was a paradox that reform should eventually come not from the Liberal Party but from Derby, Disraeli and the minority Conservative government. The great Reform meetings across the winter of 1866/7 convinced Disraeli of the need to produce some measure of reform to satisfy popular demands. Initially timid proposals in March 1867 soon gave place to household suffrage, at first hedged around with limitations. Over the next few months Disraeli accepted amendments, which radically altered the bill, widening the suffrage to include most tenants. For him and for his party 'it was like a moonlight steeplechase. In negotiating the fences few of them saw where they were going, nor much cared, as long as they got there first.'[95] It was the excitement of doing down the Liberals, holding the initiative and discomfiting the Tories' particular *bête noir*, Gladstone, and it resulted in a more far-reaching bill than Bright could have hoped for. He had got his household suffrage, just as he had set out in that 1858 Birmingham speech. Complete redistribution would have to wait (until 1885), as would the ballot (achieved in 1872), but Birmingham got its extra seat. Vince wrote that 'the passing of the Second Reform Act was the crowning triumph of Bright's career'. Bright was quietly satisfied

– 'the invective and vituperation that have been poured on me have now been proved entirely a mistake'.[96] By the end of his life, in 1889, the programme of reform he had envisaged in Birmingham had been achieved.[97]

His popularity there had been established as early as 1858 when, by articulating the case for more reform, he had 'revived the traditions of the Birmingham Political Union'. The Second Reform Act set the seal on his prestige in Birmingham. Much later, local liberals would laud that reforming achievement: 'Owing largely to your exertions in the cause of freedom, the constituency has been multiplied tenfold by household suffrage.'[98]

In many ways his career faded after this crowning achievement of reform. The twenty years after the Act were punctuated by illness; he did achieve cabinet rank in Gladstone's first two ministries, and he influenced Gladstone in the adoption of the secret ballot, a Radical totem for forty years, and in the extension of the vote to rural householders, in practice the agricultural labourers, another long-standing Radical goal. As the acknowledged grand old man of the Liberal Party his views on Irish Home Rule were eagerly sought in 1886, by both Gladstone and his proto-unionist opponents. Bright was deeply concerned about a Dublin Parliament, and about 'the views and feelings of the Protestant and loyal portion of the people'.[99] A letter to Chamberlain, expressing grave reservations about Gladstone's Home Rule initiative, was unscrupulously leaked, against its author's wishes. It did considerable damage to Gladstone's hopes for a Liberal united front, and boosted Chamberlain's emerging Liberal Unionist position. Above all, it showed the weight John Bright still carried – his reputation remained formidable, and his opinion continued to matter.

Recent scholarship on John Bright has reassessed his career and his legacy. It is clear that the mostly uncritical, hagiographical, portraits of the man do insufficient justice to the chiaroscuro, light and shade, in his career. For example, not everyone welcomed him to Birmingham in 1857, for he was not a local man and his stance on the Crimean War was controversial. Even back then it was his reputation rather than the reality, which local Liberals wanted. He was frequently absent from the constituency, either ill, or at home in Rochdale. He seemed, to some, increasingly to be trapped in the past, with a political vision shaped in the 1830s and 1840s; he was, for example, unsurprisingly out of sympathy with the growing Fair Trade (that is, pro-tariff) movement in Birmingham in the 1880s. He remained to the end suspicious of a vote for every man, of Votes for Women, and of working men becoming MPs. He proved to be a relatively ineffectual Cabinet member; he was happier on the platform than round a conference table, but even there his oratorical powers were fading in the 1880s. None of this diminishes his stature or importance, but it brings a necessary complexity to any portrait of John Bright.[100]

He was an immensely popular figure to the end and Birmingham's week-long celebrations in 1883 – when an estimated 500,000 attended the commemoration of his birthday and the silver jubilee of his parliamentary representation of Birmingham – attest to this. It was, according to *The Birmingham Post*, 'one of the most remarkable tributes of popular approval ever bestowed on a public man'.[101] Processions, speeches, a banquet, the unveiling of a statue – all spoke of great public affection. Yet for Patrick Joyce this was all about stage-management, the careful cultivation of an appearance of Liberal strength in the industrial heartlands, and the moulding of an ideal of Bright – a man of simplicity, honesty, true nobility of the soul, the tribune of the People. This, too, would serve the party. Bright was being commodified – the engravings, the souvenir books, cheap editions of his Life, kitchen crockery and medals with his likeness, all reinforced a carefully manufactured image, and were an extension of the impeccably choreographed programme of public events which comprised these celebrations.[102] By now it mattered little whether critics griped about his absences or his lower profile in the Commons; and for Joseph Chamberlain, such misgivings would be heretical. In his speech that week he articulated the party orthodoxy (and meant it), giving thanks for the way John Bright had 'illustrated the dignity of the political voice of our town. He has been our leader and our teacher, he has been the potent voice of Birmingham, speaking the thoughts, the claims and the aspirations of this great community.'[103]

In the 1885 General Election John Bright defeated the Conservative champion Lord Randolph Churchill in the new Birmingham Central constituency, one of seven seats in the town created in the Redistribution Act that year, and headed up a Liberal clean-sweep. He would no doubt have taken real personal satisfaction that he had been elected by working-class, as well as middle-class householders, in a fair ballot, free from pressure, in one of the many new single-member constituencies which comprised a dramatically redrawn electoral map. For if by the end he was the subject of extensive political cosmetic surgery, the abiding truth about John Bright remained that more than any other individual in the nineteenth century he had tended the democratic flame, even in unpropitious times; he had articulated the case for root and branch reform, most notably in that Birmingham speech in 1858; and he had generated the excitement and the popular pressure to carry the day.

George Dawson by Robert White Thrupp.
Albumen *carte-de-visite*, 1860s.

Robert William Dale by Henry Joseph Whitlock.
Albumen *carte-de-visite*, 1865.

George Dawson *was born in 1821 and became a Birmingham preacher (from his base at his own Church of the Saviour) and political activist, with a national reputation. He was a charismatic orator as well as being a successful writer and editor; his message was consistently Radical, for he endorsed campaigns for municipal improvement, the education of the masses, the extension of the franchise, and the importance of civilising people through great literature and through improved accessibility to the visual arts. In 1866 these themes coalesced in his speech (discussed here) inaugurating the new public library in Birmingham. He died in 1876 and his ideas were taken on and developed by* **Robert Dale**. *He too was a minister. Born in 1829 he led the Congregational church at Carr's Lane for thirty-six years up to his death in 1895. He was one of the most prominent nonconformist leaders in England and, like Dawson, was a formidable speaker. He campaigned vigorously for a compulsory national secular state system of education. Like Dawson, he believed in the mission of municipal government to improve the physical and spiritual environment for all citizens, as his speech quoted here from 1881 shows.*

DALE, DAWSON AND THE CIVIC GOSPEL

O ne of the greatest achievements of nineteenth-century Birmingham was to have gifted the civic, or municipal, gospel to the world. During the mayoralty of Joseph Chamberlain (1873-76) the Town Council used powers recently afforded them by central government, in particular the Birmingham Improvement Act of 1852 and the Public Health Acts of 1872 and 1875, to transform sanitation and water supplies. So it dramatically improved the life chances of its populace, funding this by the profits from a bold and astute compulsory purchase of municipal gas provision.[104] It moved on to tackle slum clearance and the creation of dignified commercial and municipal buildings along newly opened boulevards, a scheme designed both to improve health, and give Birmingham a grand centre in keeping with its standing and sense of self-worth. It aimed to provide parks, public spaces, libraries and baths for its people. Chamberlain distilled it in an oft-quoted boast: 'I think I have almost completed my municipal programme. The town will be parked, paved, assised, marketed, gas and watered and improved, all as a result of three years' active work.'[105]

Although other towns had anticipated Birmingham in aspects of this manifesto – Manchester pioneered municipal gas works, and Glasgow town improvement schemes – what was unique about Birmingham was the elevation of municipal action into a mission with a sense of religious purpose, led by committed nonconformists, who were overwhelmingly Unitarians, Quakers and members of the Church of the Saviour. Their interventionism, their deployment of entrepreneurial principles, constituted a revolutionary change from the economical/cost-cutting and *laissez-faire* attitudes prevailing in municipal government up to 1870.[106] Joseph Chamberlain had the energy, drive and business acumen to carry through this transformation, and he took the credit. Yet the story of this chapter is that of the two authors of the municipal gospel, George Dawson and Robert Dale, without whose vision, rhetorical advocacy, and persistence in seeking to draw in the town's brightest and best to civic government, there would have been no Birmingham revolution.

Both were nonconformist ministers leading churches in Birmingham, Dawson one of his own, the Church of the Saviour, where there was no credal definition for membership, and Dale, the foremost Congregational church, that at Carr's Lane. Both were hugely popular and influential among their congregations. A number of Birmingham's most prominent politicians in the mid- to late-nineteenth century, such as William Harris and Jesse Collings, were founder members of Dawson's church and imbibed his ideas there, and Dale was profoundly influenced by the older man, for almost every letter he wrote between

1847 and 1849 contained a reference to George Dawson. Although they later had – respectful and amicable – theological differences, they were for decades close allies in the campaign to make religion relevant to the everyday life of shops, offices and factories in a civic community; above all they were powerful and influential partners in the battle for education reform even if Dawson was to die twenty years before Dale and never saw the progress made on this front.[107]

Other disciples followed Dawson's lead: remarkably, for 31 of the first 33 years of the Free Library Committee of the Town Council, the chairmanship fell to a member of Dawson's congregation.[108] That involvement reflected Dawson's – but also Dale's – belief in the value of churchmen engaging with the world rather than retreating into theological debate; as ministers, they were debarred from serving on Councils, but they could encourage others to get involved. Such a view was a standing reprimand to those evangelicals who, Dale thought, 'became perverted and enfeebled about what constituted "worldliness" when they should have been involved in matters of importance in the world'.[109] Meanwhile, Samuel Timmins, at the unveiling of a statue erected in Dawson's memory on his death in 1876, pithily expressed the dead man's philosophy: 'The great problem of Church and State, politics and religion, was entirely solved with him; they were one and indivisible.'[110] In fairness, they were not the only churchmen who, disturbed by evidence of the working classes' indifference to religion in the 1851 census, like Rev. J.C.Miller of St Martin's, discerned the link between filthy living conditions and resistance to spiritual and moral improvement and determined to do something about it.[111]

Dawson and Dale were both formidable speakers with a national reputation – Dawson, for example, was said by Charles Kingsley to be 'the greatest talker in England', while Dale lost nothing in comparison to the great John Bright, with whom he sometimes shared a platform.[112] Their speeches were printed and had a wide circulation even if – despite his editorship of three Birmingham publications – Dawson on paper could not replicate the vigour and directness of Dawson at the lectern. The two men believed passionately in the overwhelming necessity of education for the working classes, to enable them to climb out of the abject poverty which disfigured so many districts of industrial Birmingham; this manifested itself, in Dawson's case, in a lifelong devotion to the cause of the public library, but both men were also at the very heart of the National Education League, based in Birmingham from 1869, which campaigned for free, compulsory, secular, rate-funded national education for children.

They shared an exalted vision of municipal government which empowered councillors to do God's work in elevating the urban population – spiritually, culturally, and physically. They divined the vital importance of recruiting the able, the talented and the prosperous to the Town Council and its committees, seeing that imaginative management by successful businessmen would channel entrepreneurial methods into municipal projects, to the benefit of all.[113] Dale, for instance, saw the transferable skills of business to municipal governance: 'Should we not acknowledge with gratitude', he asked in 1894, 'the great manufacturer (who) helps to maintain the idea of good workmanship and who by his integrity maintains and elevates the ideal of commercial honour?'[114] Integrity, the recognition of what makes a quality product, business-like methods, were all virtues he, and Dawson, were keen to harness for municipal purposes.

Still, although so similar in outlook, there were differences between the two men. Dawson was the older, and was already fully engaged in his ministry in the Church of the Saviour in the late 1840s when Dale was still an impressionable young man attending his church. Where Dawson was not prescriptive about the creed his church would follow, Dale was a more conventional Congregationalist and determined not to dilute or denigrate the influence of the Church in the world, which he feared was what Dawson was in danger of doing. Where Dawson focused much of his attention on education and the civilising of Birmingham's people, Dale broadened out from education in the 1870s to embrace campaigns for physical improvement piloted by Chamberlain and combatively to champion his friend in the internecine battle over Home Rule in the late 1880s. It is therefore important to treat each as an individual, even if they shared so much of the responsibility for Birmingham's transformation.

Dawson's influence was always founded on his powers of oratory. Within a couple of years of starting out as a minister at Mount Zion Chapel in Birmingham in the mid-1840s he had established a reputation for unorthodox views, trenchantly expressed. With the support of devoted followers he founded the Church of the Saviour, which was to be his base for more than thirty years. Professor A.W.W. Dale, Robert Dale's son, has left a pen portrait of the prophet at his height – 'a mass of iron-grey hair heavily streaked into white, covering his ears; bushy eyebrows beneath which dark brown eyes twinkled and flashed, blazed and melted. His face was lined and seamed, his voice was full and deep and rather husky.'[115] His sermons, and lectures both at the Midland Institute and on the national stage, had a conversational style, a clarity and intensity of perception, but also a familiarity, for he used common-or-garden images: 'Men of business knew what he meant when he talked about honest trading. Women knew what he meant when he talked about the simplicity of living', wrote Robert Dale.[116] He had a formidable reputation even if, as his biographer conceded, some critics thought him prolix, 'his lectures (being) a multitude of different things, good, bad and indifferent, strung together as girls thread beads or boys put buttons on a string'.[117] But their content was protean, often unorthodox and as often, controversial.

In that European Year of Revolutions, 1848, Dawson was prompting the middle classes to meet the challenge laid down by the Chartists. Always interested in politics, he himself advocated a vote for every man, the extension of Free Trade and complete religious equality, and so was closely aligned to John Bright and other contemporary Radicals. That interest extended abroad: Dale wrote that 'he was the first man in Birmingham to study and understand foreign affairs', welcoming Kossuth to his home town, befriending Mazzini and Garibaldi.[118] Yet his particular focus was on the amelioration of the condition of the working classes, for 'everyman had much to fear if his neighbours were unclean'.[119] It was a matter both of security, the avoidance of revolutionary violence; and of morality, overcoming conditions which militated against Godliness. In his speech to the inaugural gathering of the National Education League in 1869 he linked education and squalor: 'Our people are ill-taught, our children die at a rate which is shameful and disgraceful. Our people live in filth and disease. Large parts of our cities are a shame and a disgrace, and the odours of corporeal nastiness interfere even with the propagation of the Gospel.'[120] What did he think was to be done?

George Dawson's importance was that he saw the salvation of the poor as the mission of a civilising municipal government, understood that the old model of civic governance was plainly inadequate for the task, and set out to recruit Birmingham's successful and talented men to the reformative crusade. For him education was at the heart of the matter, and a first step was the establishment of a fine Reference Library, the town's first, a significant municipal project for Birmingham. When it opened in 1866 he was invited – as its foremost advocate – to deliver the address. To Wright Wilson, it was a 'sublime speech'. It was immediately rushed into print. For contemporaries, as for subsequent historians, it distilled the essence of the civic gospel as well as celebrating the moral and intellectual influence of art and literature.

A great library contains the diary of the human race; when the books of mankind are gathered together we can sit down and read the solemn story of Man's history. Here in this room are gathered together the great diaries of the human race, the record of its thoughts, its struggles, its doings. So that a library may be regarded as the solemn chamber in which man can take counsel with all that have been wise and great and good and glorious among the men that have gone before him. (Cheers).

Men are very apt to think that the universe inspired their little creed. When a man has worked himself into an unwise heat, a good place for him to go is a great library, and that will quiet him down admirably. The man who is fond of books is usually a man of lofty thought, of elevated opinion.

One of the greatest and happiest things about this Corporation Library (is that), supported as it is by rates and administered by the Corporation, it is the expression of a conviction on your part that a town exists for moral and intellectual purposes. A great town like this has not done all of its duty when it has put in action a set of ingenious contrivances for cleaning and lighting the streets, for breaking stones and for mending ways; and has not fulfilled its highest function even when it has given the people of the town the best system of drainage...

I had rather a great book or a great picture fell into the hands of the Corporation than into the hands of an individual – a great picture God never intended to be painted for the delight of but one noble family, which may be shut away through the whim of its owner. But the moment you put great works into the hands of the corporate body like this you secure permanence of guardianship in passionless keeping... what a noble thing it would be if the nobility should take to giving their precious collections to the Corporation... and then they would be open to the multitude. I hope in time that this Corporation will be as rich in pictures and works of art as it has already become in books, for I believe that one of the highest offices of civilisation is to determine how to give access to the masterpieces of art and of literature to the whole people. There is no object higher and nobler than that – to make Raphael common, to make Michelangelo intelligible, to the multitudes, to lay open to the workman and the peasant what heretofore only ranks and riches could command. And this freedom from payment is the glory of this library.

There are few places that I would rather haunt after my death than this room, and there are few things I would have my children remember more than this, that this man spoke the discourse at the opening of this glorious library, the first fruits of a clear understanding that a great town exists to discharge towards the people of that town the duties that a great nation exists to discharge towards the people of that nation – that a town exists by the Grace of God, that a great town is a solemn organism through which should flow, and in which should be shaped, all the highest, loftiest and truest ends of a man's intellectual and moral nature. We are a Corporation who have undertaken the highest duty that is possible for us – we have made provision for our people – for <u>all</u> our people – and we have made a provision of God's greatest and best gifts unto Man. (Loud cheers).[121]

Here is a model of Victorian high-mindedness, sublime faith in the beneficial impact of great Art and Literature and of the accumulated wisdom refined from centuries of Man's history. On other occasions Dawson returned to the importance of feeding the mind: 'And when a man has his comfort, his health, his security, the mind and the spirit have needs of their own too, and those needs must be satisfied. This means that the city which really is a city must have parks as well as prisons, an art gallery as well as an asylum, books and libraries as well as baths and washhouses, schools as well as sewers. It must think of beauty and of dignity no less than of order and of health.'[122]

Here, too, in this Inaugural Address, is that hugely influential sanctification of municipal government. As A.W.W. Dale put it, for Dawson, 'a city was a society established by the divine will, as the family, the State and the Church are established for common life, common purpose, common action'.[123] The Town Council was, therefore, responsible for the mind as well as the body and had a duty to provide a healthy and stimulating environment for both. By the 1880s this new way of thinking about the nature, the function, the potential of local government was widely accepted beyond the town itself and Dawson had initiated this transformation.

From libraries he would rapidly come to see that local authorities had a duty to get involved in the provision of schooling, and it is significant how those disciples from the Church of the Saviour, such as William Harris and Jesse Collings, made the running in founding, energising and organising the great Birmingham-based National Education League. Their involvement was the successful culmination of Dawson's other great municipal project – to attract the brightest and best of Birmingham's businessmen to his mission.

As early as 1848 in 'A Letter to the Middle Classes in the Present Crisis', Dawson had chided them with inaction and timidity; 'efficient, active and experienced men are wanted in whom there is life and spirit and who are ready to sacrifice themselves,' he wrote.[124] They were still disappointing him in 1871 when he preached a sermon at his church on the decline of public virtue: 'I mean that public spirit which makes a man to prefer before his own prosperity and well-being that of the town or country to which he belongs... And how many are there who really sacrifice themselves for the good of the town and for whom the affectation of superiority with which they decline to do so, is a simple cover for indifference? By it, the government of the towns sink down into the hands of the vulgar, the self-seeking and the mean.'[125] What he wanted was to secure the services on the Council of those gifted with extraordinary talents, and he succeeded; to Dawson belongs the credit for infusing in some of Birmingham's most talented entrepreneurs the spirit of municipal reform.

It was the interest in education, awakened by the crying need to 'educate our masters', after the 1867 Reform Act enfranchised many working men, which prompted Joseph Chamberlain to get involved in political activity, and campaign for the logical extension, a national system of elementary schools. He had already made a fortune expanding the screw-making business of Nettlefold and Chamberlain, then selling it. Now in the next phase of his life, he joined the Town Council, in the erroneous belief that it would soon assume responsibility for funding the new schools he anticipated emerging from Gladstone and Forster's education reforms in 1870. Yet he stayed after that campaign had run its course and broadened his portfolio to include the reform of utilities and the rebuilding of Central Birmingham. Chamberlain and his friends were of a different order from the small-time businessmen of the earlier municipal regimes, men of lowered horizons, limited imagination and innate conservatism – the Old Guard who had frequented 'The Woodman' pub, where they had conducted their business, and who had a narrow view of investing in, and spending money on, municipal projects. Their achievements amply justified George Dawson's relentless campaign for a different class of councillor.

When it came to the civic gospel, then, George Dawson 'came first. He led the way where others followed.'[126] At a Banquet given for Dawson before he departed for the USA to deliver a series of lectures, Joseph Chamberlain, the mayor, delivered a eulogy: 'It is a great thing to say of a man that he has influenced the life of a great town of 350,000 inhabitants; if it has special characteristics, they are chiefly due to the teachings of George Dawson and the school of earnest fellow-workers, colleagues and friends which he may be said to have founded in this town.'[127] To many historians, however, Robert Dale was an equally important figure. Even more than Dawson, he was deeply engaged in politics. They were part of his vocation; at a dinner held in John Bright's honour in 1864, Dale said: 'The true political spirit is the mind that was in Christ Jesus "who looked not on His own things but also on the things of others".' 'In a country like this where the public business of the state is the private duty of every citizen, those who decline to use their political power are guilty of treachery both to God and to Man.'[128]

For his part, Carr's Lane was never enough: 'He was bent on making Birmingham a very metropolis of liberty, education and courageous municipal government.'[129] So he threw himself into active politics, appearing at pro-Reform rallies in 1866-67 in support of his friend John Bright, where he argued that 'the franchise was not simply a privilege but a necessary check on the legislature by the people'.[130] With reform settled in 1867 he moved on to agitate for 'new and more stringent measures by which every child who is manifestly destined to a life of crime and misery shall if possible be rescued from its doom'. By 1869 he was intimately involved in the battle over education, a committee member of the National Education League as well as vice-president of the Education Aid Society. He articulated the case: 'What we ask for is education, the best education possible, and at any cost, for every child in England.'[131] Yet Forster's Education Act in 1870 was a profound disappointment and roused the nonconformist in him. Why should ratepayers fund denominational (that is Church of England) schools in those areas unable to afford the new schools, which were to be managed by the school boards set up by Forster's act? Indeed, why should schools have any religious teaching at all? Why did these new-fangled school boards manage the schools, rather than local authorities?[132] So Dale, ('in incessant demand' as a speaker) and the National Education League, fought on, unavailingly, against their own Liberal government, to try to overturn this manifest injustice, and Dale and other nonconformists had the wry satisfaction of knowing that their agitation unquestionably did for Gladstone's Liberals in the 1874 election.[133] That agitation over education drew Dale, as it did Harris, Collings and above all Chamberlain, into municipal government.

Dale came to see the Town Council as the guiding force in a Christian polity where 'through human virtue, human self-sacrifice and human patience and sagacity', men worked to improve things for the vulnerable and weak.[134] J.T.Bunce, his friend, and historian of the Corporation, wrote of the way Dale 'helped to raise the quality of the Town Council, to lift its ideals of duty and to mould its progressive policy. When any considerable question affecting the welfare of the town was prominent, he argued it out frankly and boldly by speaking at the ward meetings held for the choice of candidates. For many years he was the chief speaker at the greater political assemblies.'[135] Dale could not stand for Council, but he was a fixture when ward elections were contested in November each year, fighting the cause on behalf of others. That combativeness, and commitment, reflected his belief in the work of the Council. His son quotes at length one illuminating sermon Dale preached.

> 'Two years ago a friend of mine stood for the Town Council. There were two or three thousand voters in that ward. They were a very rough set; we fought hard and we won. Ten days ago he rose in Council. He was able to say that he had visited every street, every court in the ward. He told an appalling story of the condition of the people in that and adjacent wards. He spoke of the squalid homes in which they lived, destructive to health and rendering all high moral Christian life almost impossible. He submitted to Council an elaborate scheme for sweeping all the wretched district away at a cost of four and a half millions. The Council accepted the proposal unanimously. Now, I believe my friend was trying to get the will of God done on earth.'[136]

Here was Dale's ideal: the involvement, the creativity and the doing of the compassionate man, convincing an open-minded and equally compassionate Council. To Dale, 'the man who holds municipal or political office is a minister of God; one man may have just as real a Divine vocation to become a town councillor or MP as another man to become a missionary'.[137] The corollary was that Dale was scathing about those who did not heed the call.

In one of his Week-Day Sermons in 1867, he targeted Birmingham's prosperous men:

"They ought to feel "called of God" to act as "Guardians of the Poor." They ought to work on the Committees of the Hospitals. They ought to be Aldermen and Town Councillors. They ought to give their time as well as their money to whatever improvements are intended to develop the intelligence of the community. They ought to be reformers of local abuses. They ought to see to it that the towns and parishes in which they live are well drained, well lighted, well paved; that there are good schools for every class of the population; that there are harmless public amusements; that all parochial and municipal affairs are conducted honourably and equitably. In nearly every part of the country I hear that prosperous manufacturers and merchants are leaving public duties in the hands of men of lower position and culture than themselves. They shrink from the roughness of local elections... When the prosperous people of a free nation cease to take an active interest in the public life of the towns and cities in which they live, the political greatness and stability of their country are exposed to the most serious dangers. [138]

The imperative to become involved, then, was not simply humanitarian, or to raise the quality and the tone of local government; as so often in Victorian England – and remarked by both Attwood and Bright already in this book – there lurked a dark fear that subterranean working-class frustrations at the squalor and the injustice of it all might just erupt and threaten the propertied classes with an English Revolution, if nothing were done to alleviate the manifest suffering.

That sermon, even on the printed page, conveys Dale's directness and energy. On the platform he was formidable. In an appreciation incorporated in A.W.W.Dale's biography, Bunce wrote of the way 'his manliness and his eloquence materially strengthened his influence. He was literally a power on the platform; his voice could reach to the farthest limits of the largest audience; his robust and rigorous personality impressed all hearers. When he rose to speak there fell upon the assembly the hush which testifies to the recognition of a great orator.' [139] Dale's son colourfully described his father's arrival on the platform of the Town Hall. 'The vigour with which he pulled off his overcoat as he rose to speak was a sure sign of what was coming. His one aim was to instruct and to convince. When the meeting was tempestuous, he ploughed along through the storm with the steady rush of an Atlantic liner as it shoulders its way through blustering seas.' [140] He was necessarily combative, for he had chosen to champion controversial causes, especially free, compulsory, non-denominational education. Above all, he was charismatic. This was the golden age of political oratory – Bright, Gladstone and Chamberlain were contemporaries, and Dale was their equal, with a powerful voice (a necessity in the age before amplification), strong convictions, a physical presence and a magnetic personality, which compelled his auditors. P. Muntz, with the wit and economy of a political cartoonist, caught his essence: 'What a splendid fellow Dale is – he reminds me of the Church militant.' No other Victorian clergyman was quite as involved in the cut and thrust of political bodies, committees and causes as he was.

In many ways he had much to show for his vigorous advocacy, even if in that issue closest to his heart – education – the running sore of public funding for Church of England schools, so painful for nonconformists, would never be satisfactorily resolved. Chamberlain had recognised that perhaps they had got their issues back to front. 'What folly it is to talk about the moral and intellectual elevation of the masses when the conditions of life are such as to render elevation impossible', he said in November 1874 at an Annual General Meeting of the Severn Street Adult School.[141] Largely through his insight, to divine that taking over the private gas companies could generate the funds to pay for sanitation reform, and his drive, in carrying the policy through Council then Parliament, clean water and municipally managed sewage disposal dramatically improved the health of all in Birmingham from the mid-1870s. The Birmingham-inspired Artisans Dwelling Act (1875) of the Conservative minister, R.A. Cross, enabled some of the most toxic slums of Central Birmingham to be cleared, although too little was done to re-house the displaced families in public housing. Birmingham got her grand new Council offices, reflecting the dignity of the Corporation; courtesy of the Municipal Gas scheme it boasted a new civic Art Gallery in the neo-Renaissance style befitting a modern city-state aping its inspirational Italian forebears. Above all, the ablest of the elite had been recruited to the Council, a process underway from the end of the 1860s.

The elite's motivation was no doubt complex. It was social, and the men who belonged to the Council came to feel they were a select and enviable group. It was about power, too, for as Hennock has pointed out, 'the opportunity to conduct wisely the welfare, health and comfort of 400,000 people raised it above the plane on which town councils were regarded as the stamping ground of corrupt, vested interests'.[142] A critic might say that it was unsurprising that rich businessmen would want to be involved at a time when municipal capacities – and budgets – were expanding. For them, it has been argued, 'their chief concern was with cost effectiveness and efficiency and in times of economic depression this meant retrenchment.'[143] This explains the cooling of enthusiasm for town improvement in the recessionary 1880s. In Chamberlain's case there was a potent mix of driving ambition and a strong dictatorial streak; chairmanship of the executive committee of the National Education League, then the mayoralty of Birmingham for three years, developed a pre-existing authoritarian temperament, and decisions were made, projects despatched, with celerity and with an intolerance of opposition.[144] But nevertheless, the motivation of the elite to roll up their sleeves and join in was also a response to a vision of what municipal government should be, and it would be churlish to deny that many of Birmingham's elite responded to the preaching of Dawson and Dale, drawing on a real sense of duty, even of religious mission, to tackle the appalling poverty and filth shockingly displayed in their own town, where unfettered industrial and housing expansion, careless of human consequence, left a squalid legacy.

By 1880 that noble vision had been realised in Birmingham's dramatic transformation and with Dawson gone (he died in 1876) it was Dale who articulated the achievements of the civic gospel. His sermon in 1881 at Carr's Lane, to a packed congregation, was subsequently printed and widely distributed, as well as being reproduced in *The Birmingham Daily Post*, and it serves here, as it clearly did at the time, to encapsulate all that Robert Dale and George Dawson aimed for in their influential ministries spanning over forty years.

Recently I told some American friends that we had come to think it one of the proudest of distinctions to be entrusted with municipal office; that many of the wealthiest, ablest, most cultivated and most honourable of our citizens were inspired with a most generous loyalty to the town which made them willing and eager to accept the tasks of local administration and government; that the great mass of the ratepayers were gradually being penetrated by the same spirit; and that we were resolved to spare no strength and no cost that might be necessary to improve and ennoble the condition of life for the whole people.

The whole condition, the very appearance of the town, has been transfigured during ten years. You have built noble schools, other great schemes of educational reform have been projected, and in a few years the intellectual life of the whole community will be raised to a loftier level. You have erected libraries; you will soon make noble paintings and noble sculpture the joy of the poorest man among us that has the eye to discover their dignity, their grace, and their beauty. The fires of private munificence have been kindled by the fervour of public zeal. If we are true to each other and true to the town, we may do deeds as great as those done by Pisa, Florence, and Venice in their triumphant days. What has been done already has been done by the maintenance of mutual respect among men who have had a common love for the town. We have tried to be generous, we have tried to be fair.'[145]

What Dawson and Dale had aimed for, a reformation of education, the enculturation of the working classes, a purging of Birmingham's life-threatening filth, and the engagement of the town's great and good, had come to pass, and a little un-Christian boasting about Birmingham's civic achievement, which by now had had a national impact, seems in this instance quite forgiveable.

CHAPTER FIVE

Joseph Chamberlain

Joseph Chamberlain *was born (1836) and educated in London before moving to Birmingham to join his uncle's screw manufacturing firm, Nettlefolds. It expanded to take a dominant position in the world market, thanks to his drive and acumen. He went on to become a hugely successful Mayor of Birmingham in 1873, inaugurating a municipal revolution, and creating a local legend, which lasted until his death in 1914. In 1876 he moved into national politics as one of Birmingham's Liberal MPs and quickly assumed the leadership of the Radicals. He was a cabinet minister in 1880, but his opposition to the Irish policy of his own leader, Gladstone, led him to secede from the Liberal Party, and the speech featured here from 1886 represents that moment of a most dramatic upheaval in British politics.*

Joseph Chamberlain and Political Survival

J oseph Chamberlain towers over late nineteenth-century Birmingham; that hegemony lasted over thirty years. Indeed such was the strength of the dynasty he created that for sixty-four consecutive years a Chamberlain represented Birmingham in the Commons.[146] The next two chapters focus on speeches which delineate seminal moments in his career, the first of which, made in April 1886, is concerned with nothing less than a struggle for his very political survival in the greatest crisis of his career, caused by Prime Minister William Gladstone's precipitate commitment to Irish Home Rule. The resultant national upheaval was dramatic, for the Liberal Party, the dominant force of mid-Victorian Britain, was sundered. It subsequently endured a generation effectively out of power. Chamberlain was one of the leading dissidents; indeed to many he was the central figure in the rebellion, 'the man who killed Home Rule', and his subsequent battle to establish a secure political base in Liberal Birmingham was to be prolonged.

Our main speech here marks the beginning of the fight to win over to his cause his Midland constituency. That Joseph Chamberlain survived and, more than that, succeeded, and that Birmingham and the surrounding counties became a Radical fortress with its own distinctive ideology, has national importance. Here was the centre for a new political organisation, the Liberal Unionist party, which until 1906 certainly – and arguably up to the outbreak of the First World War – had a major impact on the shape and character of British politics.

By 1885 Joseph Chamberlain had had several incarnations. He had been a successful businessman; he had led the municipal revolution which had transformed Birmingham into a sanitary, cultivated, well-planned model Victorian town; he had led a revolution in party politics, organising a national campaign for compulsory elementary education, then masterminding a National Liberal Federation to link up, and give a voice and a coherence to, constituency parties, an early exercise in democracy. Finally, he had become an MP in 1876, and by 1880 had been promoted, with what was at the time almost unseemly haste, to a Cabinet post as President of the Board of Trade. He was the foremost Radical in the land, the representative of that wing of the Victorian Liberal Party which espoused social and political reform.[147]

Still, his leader, William Gladstone, was a disappointment to him. Like millions of Victorians he had held the Grand Old Man in veneration; in his First Ministry from 1868 to 1874, Gladstone had disestablished the Church in Ireland, had broken the Anglican monopoly of academic posts at Oxford and Cambridge, had tackled the purchase of commissions in the army, had introduced the secret ballot, and – in sum – he had shown himself a fearless iconoclast. However, his Second Ministry, that of 1880 was beset by difficulties. Gladstone found himself wrestling with Irish issues, trapped into foreign adventures (in the Transvaal, Egypt and Sudan) and therefore distracted from developing any kind of programme of domestic reform, the sort which interested a Radical like Chamberlain. Only in 1884 did Gladstone get round to extending the vote to agricultural labourers (completing the household suffrage Disraeli had instituted for the boroughs in 1867), and even this became a lengthy arm-wrestle with the Conservatives who wanted to control the redrawing of the constituencies.[148] With precious little social reform occurring in these years, Chamberlain was restless and frustrated, and herein lies the key to understanding how the devastating Liberal split came about.

The Third Reform Act's enfranchisement of agricultural labourers was to him a powerful impetus to action; in a letter to Gladstone in 1885 he wrote 'that it was of great importance that these vast masses of people, who have been watching with interest and enthusiasm the efforts made for their enfranchisement, should be assured that their interests are a constant object of concern to the Liberal Party'.[149] He intended to show that concern and in a speech to the Birmingham Artisans Association – an audience of 600 working men, glassworkers, brass workers, jewellers, ironworkers – in the Town Hall at the start of January, 1885, he sketched out what was to become known as the *Unauthorised Programme*. He started by voicing his frustration, but then went on to court notoriety as he assaulted the landed classes.

I have sometimes found it difficult as a Radical member of a Liberal government to reconcile the loyalty I owe to my colleagues and to the party at large with the strenuous and constant promotion of the principles which I am supposed especially to represent. We are about to make a New Departure and I rejoice... Next year two millions of men will enter for the first time into the full enjoyment of their political rights... It is a revolution peacefully and silently accomplished. The centre of power has shifted, the old order is giving place to the new... What will this assembly do with the powers entrusted to it? ... I cannot help thinking it will be more directed to what are called the social subjects than has hitherto been the case.

How to promote the greater happiness of the masses of the people (Hear, hear), *already annexed everything that is worth having, expect everybody else to be content with the crumbs that fall from the table... (All the original) natural rights have passed away, the common rights of ownership have disappeared. Some have been sold, some have been stolen by fraud. Private ownership has taken the place of communal rights, and this has been sanctioned by law. But then, I ask, what ransom will property pay for the security, which it enjoys? Property has obligations as well as rights, but what are the rights of property? Are the game laws a right of property? Is it just and expedient that the armaments of the rich, carried even to barbarous excess, should be protected by a Draconian code of law?... You must look for the cure in legislation which lays the heaviest burden on the shoulders best able to bear them... Legislation which will give a free education to every child in the land.* [150]

Here is the essence of a new Radical prospectus: free schools to allow all to climb a ladder of social mobility out of poverty; land purchase by local authorities to enable labourers to have 'three acres and a cow'; an assault on the landed classes' privileges; and equality of sacrifice in taxation, which implied graduated taxation. In a number of ways this was deeply unwelcome to Gladstone. He disliked the incendiary class-antagonistic language, the threats of 'ransom', the confiscatory implications of compulsory land purchase and – a heresy to the man who had wanted to abolish income tax – escalating rates of taxation. He believed free education unaffordable. More fundamentally still, he saw this as the challenge of an impatient young buck willing the tired old master to leave the stage.

Chamberlain compounded the crime in the summer of 1885 by developing his own solution to the 'Irish Question', unsurprisingly a scheme of local government not dissimilar to that which applied to his beloved Birmingham. It failed to gain traction, being either too little to satisfy the Irish, or too much for his leader. Above all, it showed a temerity and an ambition which threatened Gladstone, and he came actively to dislike his young colleague, who he thought to be ambitious for the leadership. In the middle of the Home Rule crisis Gladstone was to say 'a concession to Chamberlain is treated mainly as an acknowledgement of his superior greatness and wisdom'.[151] For his part, Chamberlain pressed Gladstone to adopt his programme as a way of appealing to the new electorate in the election of 1885; Gladstone largely ignored it. When he became Prime Minister again in January 1886 relations were so fraught between himself and Chamberlain that the latter asked for a letter of contract before accepting an offer of a Cabinet post, and Gladstone humiliated him with the lowliest position, that of President of the Local Government Board.[152] Both knew that – unspoken as yet – there was deep disagreement on what to do about Ireland.

For Gladstone, his 'mission was to pacify Ireland'.[153] In 1868 he had characterised the Irish problem as a poisonous Javan Upas tree with three deadly branches, education, religion and land tenure.[154] He had set out then to treat each in turn but he found it resistant to his brand of sweeping moral force and bold action.[155] In 1880 he had returned to the land issue and instituted tenant rights of security of tenure and fair rents, and had then agreed to the disposal of accumulated rent arrears. These reforms were played out against a background of rural violence courtesy of the Land League, headed by Michael Davitt, who wanted land nationalisation and was prepared to employ physical intimidation and boycotts to achieve the goal. Gladstone found that constructive reform had to be accompanied by coercion, the imposition of curfew and summary arrest. Behind it all lay a fundamental issue, that of the Union of England and Ireland in 1801. Pitt had willed it for security reasons after the Irish uprising of 1798, timed to coincide with a planned French invasion. It meant direct rule from London and the end of an Irish Parliament.

The next eighty years saw repeated Irish campaigns for a revival of devolved powers or for independence plain and simple, from Daniel O'Connell's Repeal (of the Union) movement in the 1830s, to Isaac Butt's parliamentary party, the Home Rule League in the 1870s. Charles Stuart Parnell, fusing this with the Land League organisation at the end of the decade, contrived to create a mass movement for Home Rule. Gladstone found that even after land reforms, rent tribunals, a mix of carrot and stick to deal with rural thuggery, he was still faced in 1885 with Parnell's indomitable and unyielding demand for an Irish Parliament. When the Third Reform Act in 1885 increased the number of Irish seats and gave the vote to thousands of labourers; and when by sheer ill fortune the 1885 election result meant that the balance was held by the 86 seats of Parnell's Irish National Party; then Gladstone, believing that the Irish will had spoken in the election, and believing in any case in national self-determination for small nations, concluded that it was useless attacking the branches of that Upas tree without tackling the roots, the political arrangements of 1801.[156] That meant conceding an Irish Parliament.

His son, Herbert, inadvisedly briefed the press on the way his father's mind was moving in December 1885, and this created turmoil in some parts of his party. The Whig, aristocratic element was solidly unionist and opposed to concessions to what they deemed violent criminals (sections of the Irish National Party), while other Liberals, including a number of Radicals such as Joseph Chamberlain, agreed with that Whig analysis, and also felt that Home Rule would be the start of the disintegration of Empire. When Gladstone came to form his Third Ministry in January 1886 the Whigs under Lord Hartington refused to join; and Chamberlain did so only reluctantly. When, in March 1886, Chamberlain suspected, by Gladstone's secretive manner, that Home Rule was being actively planned, he had it out with him in Cabinet, and resigned. He believed that 'any scheme of the kind attributed to Mr. Gladstone will lead in the long run to the absolute independence of Ireland and Britain would sink to the rank of a third rate power'.[157] From that view he never wavered; but nor did Gladstone himself waver from a personal animosity which the events of the past twelve months had fuelled.

The difficulties for Chamberlain, once the Home Rule Bill was presented that spring, pressed in on him from all sides. He had offended the aristocratic Whigs by talk of 'ransom' and an alliance with them based on defence of the union seemed impossible. The same applied to the Conservatives. Many Liberals thought him motivated by bald ambition. He lost the sympathy and friendship of long-standing friends like John Morley (who later dubbed him Casca for 'assassinating' Gladstone) and Charles Dilke. Even his friends – including Powell-Williams – recognised that 'the people are stark mad about the Grand Old Man and if they get the idea that you are working against Home Rule it would be impossible to hold them'.[158]

This was so nationally; alarmingly for Chamberlain, it was so in Birmingham too. Frank Schnadhorst, Chamberlain's long-time ally and secretary of the Birmingham Liberal Association, pleaded in a sequence of letters that Chamberlain support the principle of Gladstone's bill for Home Rule. 'If it were not for the personal loyalty to yourself, an overwhelming majority of Birmingham Liberals would support the government. I cannot describe to you the distress which many of those who have followed you loyally are in,' he wrote.[159] So it was vital that Chamberlain move quickly to shore up Birmingham support in the 2000, the representatives of the Liberal party there. Already Schnadhorst was working against him, and his very political survival can be attributed to the stalwart work of allies such as Robert Dale, J.T.Bunce and Joseph Powell-Williams. Bunce not only wrote sympathetic editorials in *The Birmingham Daily Post* but also overcame Gladstonian opposition on the management committee to summon the 2000 to a meeting on 21 April and to allow Chamberlain his hearing.[160] Then it was up to Chamberlain.

He was not a born orator, in his early days diligently practising the craft in the Edgbaston Debating Society, where his first contributions 'reeked of the lamp'.[161] He steadily improved; at the height of his powers, he was considered one of the greatest of contemporary orators. Sir Henry Lucy deftly catches the razor-sharp mind, the mastery of detail, the gimlet eye for a weakness and its utterly relentless exploitation. 'Where Mr. Gladstone is often disconcerted by interruption, and is too easily led astray into devious paths, the fiercer the attack on Mr. Chamberlain, the more noisy the interruption, the brighter and the cooler he grows, warding off blows with deft parrying of his rapier, swiftly followed up by telling thrust at the aggressor.'[162] This speech did not quite reach those heights; its importance lies not in quotability but in the substance of what was said and what remained unsaid – and in its consequences.

Fifteen or sixteen years ago I was drawn into politics by my interest in social questions and by my desire to promote the welfare of the great majority of the population. At that time I saw the masses of thrifty hard-working artisans and labourers condemned by bad laws, and the neglect of their rulers, to a life of exacting toil, without the advantages and opportunities which education affords. And I looked to the Liberal party as the means of removing and remedying those grievances. Gentlemen, surely it is the very irony of fate that we should be here tonight to discuss a question which I venture to say never entered our thoughts a few months ago. I was congratulating you upon the hopes that shortly we should see considerable progress made towards the amelioration of the condition of the people. I do not believe there was a man among us at that time who thought that in a few short weeks all these matters would be relegated to the dim and distant future. What has produced this great change in the situation?

(It is) due to the force of character, to the determination and courage of one illustrious man. Mr. Gladstone's scheme is not fully disclosed, but is separation to be conceded at last to violence and menace? That is a cowardly argument and ought not to be addressed by Englishmen to Englishmen... And what Liberal could approve of a proposal that would tax the Irish people to 3/4s of the whole revenue of the country and give them absolutely no representation in the Parliament which

levies these imposts? Do you believe that any free people worthy of the name would submit for long to such miserable restrictions upon their liberty and their representative authority? It will be regarded by the Parnellite party as a man regards his breakfast – an excellent thing in itself but one in no way barring his claim to dinner and to supper... And what of the situation under Home Rule if war were to break out? If this happens, where shall we be? England may be struggling for its very existence but Ireland will be unconcerned... I should like to see the case of Ulster met in some form or other, having regard to the great distinctions of race and religion and politics which I have pointed out. I would be glad if there would be conceded to Ulster a separate assembly.

There could be no effective amendment to this bill unless the representation of Ireland at Westminster were retained on the present footing. And, regarding the Land Purchase Bill, I will not be party to imposing liabilities on the British taxpayer at a time when the proffered security is steadily falling in value. If I am met on these fundamental criticisms I would support Mr. Gladstone with delight on the second reading. But if not then my duty is clear. I shall give an independent but I hope perfectly frank and loyal opposition to proposals which, in my heart and conscience, I believe in their present form would be disastrous, and dangerous to the best interests of the United Kingdom. You would justly despise me now if, for the sake of private interests and personal ambition I were false to my convictions and disregarded what I think are the vital interests of the country.[163]

It is all here. He was convinced that the electorate would not support Home Rule and that the party would be defeated on it.[164] He was sure that Britain and the Empire would be diminished by the policy. He hated the way Home Rule deflected attention from what he thought to be the Liberals' central goal, the amelioration of the lot of the working people for whom he had devised the *Unauthorised Programme*, which Gladstone had diluted and delayed. He thought this particular bill, excluding Irish members from Westminster and confining them to their own parliament, yet reserving many taxation issues to the mother Parliament in Westminster, to be grossly unfair, resurrecting the old cry: 'No taxation without representation'. He disliked concessions to violent Irish criminals and nor did he see why – in the twin track policy of Gladstone's which tried to satisfy Irish tenant demands with a Land Bill at the same time – the English taxpayer should stump up or secure the transfer of lands from an idle, absentee landlord class. He feared for loyal, Protestant Ulster once the majority Catholic South could determine domestic Irish policy. He believed that this Home Rule Bill would not satisfy Ireland more than temporarily; it would in time demand more. Many of these criticisms shaped the Irish debate for decades to come, and the issues of Ulster, Irish representation at Westminster, and perhaps above all, the destructive impact of Irish Home Rule on the Empire, were to remain at the core of Chamberlain's Unionist creed for many years.

He sat down to thunderous applause, and received a virtually unanimous vote of confidence from the 2000. His passionate oratory, and the clarity of his argument wooed many doubters. Schnadhorst tried then to block a further vote to support Chamberlain's views on Gladstone's policy, and only smart thinking, and a charismatic contribution of his own from Dr. Dale, ensured that the vote was put and that the assembly endorsed Chamberlain's stand. The latter was delighted. 'I got through my meeting last night splendidly,' he wrote to Dilke. Garvin, his biographer, was clearly infected by Chamberlain's relief for he concluded that 'for Chamberlain the worst of all dangers was past. Risking all he had saved his citadel. That night he had won the fight for Birmingham.' ... 'For if he had lost Birmingham, all would have been lost.'[165] It wasn't as simple as that.

Certainly the speech was a turning point. His opposition, however carefully framed to avoid assaulting his leader, was now open. Over the next weeks, before the second reading of the bill, colleagues tried to heal the divisions. Henry Labouchere, fellow Radical MP, wrote daily to Chamberlain; right up to the debate in the House, he sought concessions from his Prime Minister on Chamberlain's behalf, and believed he had succeeded. Yet Gladstone proved evasive and unreliable. Chamberlain concluded that Labouchere was 'being bamboozled by an old parliamentary hand', a view confirmed when the Prime Minister, challenged in the House by a Conservative to withdraw the bill and amend it, roared 'Never! Never!', proof of its almost sacred, immutable nature for Gladstone and of the vice-like grip Parnell was exercising over a government which needed his votes to survive.[166] Chamberlain was relieved. 'To satisfy others I have talked about conciliation... but on the whole I would rather vote against the bill.'[167]

Now he had to move very carefully; if he consorted too obviously with Hartington and the Whigs, who completely opposed the bill, but who were long-standing rivals within the Liberal party, Chamberlain risked losing his own Radical supporters. The magnetic pull of Gladstone steadily undermined Chamberlain. Schnadhorst and other loyalists in Birmingham succeeded in wresting his own creation, his power-base, the grass-roots National Liberal Federation from him, only two weeks after that triumphal speech. They then established a Birmingham Home Rule Association. He responded by founding the National Radical Union.

Here was a most significant development. At last there was to be a national structure, based in Birmingham, under his aegis, committed to the sort of social policies he believed in, and which had been too long neglected by the Liberal leadership. In later years it would develop its own particular radical identity within the Liberal Unionist party, the national organisation of all Liberals who rejected Gladstone's Home Rule policy, formed in 1886 under Lord Hartington. By its alliance with Conservative Unionists, it would come to colour and influence government policy to the benefit of the working man. In the immediacy, though, its adherents were few in number.

On the eve of the great debate in May, Chamberlain contrived to pull a rabbit from the hat. He persuaded John Bright to commit his opposition to a letter in which he said he would vote against the bill, and recommend at least abstention to others. Bright's reputation in Birmingham and beyond was such that this intervention proved decisive. He helped ensure Birmingham remained loyal to Chamberlain for 'once Bright sided with Chamberlain, his task in Birmingham eased considerably'.[168] Over ninety Liberals eventually voted against the Home Rule Bill, with Chamberlain contributing a powerful speech ('admirable', thought Bright), securing its defeat. Gladstone asked for a dissolution and called a General Election. To the Grand Old Man, as to the Parnellites, the blame for the *débâcle* lay squarely with Joseph Chamberlain. He was 'the man who killed Home Rule'.

Gladstone lost the General Election as the Unionists swept the country (319 Conservatives, 79 Liberal Unionists, as against 196 Liberals, with 86 Home Rule Irish). In Birmingham, Liberals – despite their rival committees – put on a front of unity, but concerted pressure saw six of the seven seats fall to Liberal Unionists and the last to a Conservative, a rarity in Birmingham. They won despite a strong residual admiration for Gladstone in the town; many, however, disliked his policy of concessions to 'cut-throats who mutilate women and maim cattle'.[169] Many others felt like Rev. W. Tuckwell that 'the energy of a Parliament created for social reform (in 1885) was to be spent on prolonged struggle over a subject which had formed no part of the election programme'.[170] That was certainly Chamberlain's point – he had campaigned on 'three acres and a cow', a Radical programme, and been bitterly disappointed, as our speech illustrates. His, and the National Radical Union's, focus on social matters helps explain the rapid evolution of Chamberlain's impregnable electoral fortress in Birmingham; he quite evidently believed in improving the lot of the working man, and his electorate had faith in his honesty and integrity. One other point: as his biographer Peter Marsh observes, Chamberlain 'discovered the resonances of democratic imperialism' during the campaign, arguing at one meeting in Birmingham 'that if you are going to quail before the dagger of the assassin and the threats of conspirators and rebels, then the sceptre of dominion will have passed from our grasp, and this great Empire will perish …'.[171] That message was to be replayed, and amplified, over the next twenty years with great effect, especially in his home town.

Yet back in 1886 the post-election outlook for Chamberlain and his small group of around thirty Radical Unionists was very uncertain. Was the Liberal Unionist position sustainable? There was a real danger that Liberal opponents of Home Rule would complete the journey across the political spectrum and join the Conservatives. Many of Hartington's Liberal Unionists, the Whig wing of the old Liberal party, 'had not voted down the Home Rule Bill only to have the *Unauthorised Programme* foisted upon dissident Liberalism by... droves of Radical Unionists'.[172] Most soon became indistinguishable from their Conservative allies. In Birmingham those Conservative allies bitterly resented the fact that Lord Salisbury had reached an electoral pact in 1886 with the Liberal Unionists, allowing them a clear run in their 'current' seats. They still smarted under the blows – sometimes literally – inflicted by Liberal mobs at Aston Manor in 1884, when Lord Randolph Churchill had arrived to speak at a Conservative rally, and had realistic ambitions of overturning the Liberal monopoly in the town. Chamberlain indeed had to watch his Birmingham base carefully; when he supported the Conservative government's Irish policy (and coercion and limited reform was the obvious alternative to Gladstone's Home Rule) he ran the danger of uproar in Birmingham, as happened in 1887 when he voted for the Coercion Bill.[173] He shed Radical support he could ill afford to lose as a result.

While his new friend and ally, the left-leaning Lord Randolph Churchill was Chancellor of the Exchequer, Chamberlain had dreamt of a re-alignment of politics and of building a new centre party. It was an all-too-brief conjunction. With Churchill's fall from power in December 1886, having over-reached himself with his Prime Minister, Chamberlain felt more alone, more in limbo than ever. He recognised that to keep the peace with Birmingham Liberals he should offer talks with Gladstonians to reunite the party. After all, 'we Liberals are agreed on ninety nine points and only disagree on one'.[174] The Round Table talks of January/February 1887 foundered on Gladstone's inflexibility and persistent intention of putting Ireland first in his priorities. The gap between Gladstone and Chamberlain then rapidly widened. Chamberlain became vocal on the need for coercion in Ireland to tackle violence, and went to Ulster to assert that 'there are two races in Ireland', meaning that there were Nationalists who wanted Irish independence, and Unionists who wanted to remain part of a United Kingdom. He committed himself to Ulster's defence and re-emphasised the integrity of Empire.[175]

At the end of that year, when Chamberlain was dispatched on a government mission to resolve a Canadian fishing dispute, Schnadhorst, William Harris (architect of the town's caucus system) and other Birmingham Gladstonians, seized control of the 2000 in his absence, and the carefully preserved fiction of Birmingham's Liberal unity was destroyed. Chamberlain had to start again.

The new Birmingham Liberal Unionist Association (BLUA) which resulted was founded on the loyalty of extended family, and close friends like Jesse Collings and William Powell-Williams, men who would be loyal, and key, figures in all Chamberlain's subsequent Birmingham projects. Chamberlain understood politics, how to propagate his cause, how to canvass, how to electioneer, and the BLUA rapidly became a model party organisation. Its programme was that of the National Radical Union, a conscious policy of 'challenging the assumption that support for Gladstone was synonymous with progressive politics'.[176] It also sought to distinguish Chamberlain's Liberal Unionism, with its Radical emphasis on education, land and local government reform, from the reactive, defensive politics of Lord Hartington and his Whig Liberal Unionists.

At his lowest ebb in 1887 when it was difficult to see a way forward, he was assisted and consoled by a burgeoning friendship with Arthur Balfour, Lord Salisbury's nephew and Chief Secretary for Ireland. Balfour admired Chamberlain's selfless courage and integrity in pursuing an Irish policy which had damaged his career and his prospects; he thought Chamberlain's Land Purchase proposals for Ireland at no cost to the British taxpayer, ingenious. He came to see the value to the Conservatives of having an ally who would bring a progressive dimension to Unionism, something to appeal to the newly enfranchised working classes. So it was that Chamberlain was trusted with settling the North American fishing dispute, and came to influence the Salisbury government in policy, prompting and shaping new legislation on tenant rights; on local government (an act to extend Birmingham-style democracy into the counties); and, to Chamberlain's intense satisfaction, in 1890, on free elementary education. He had to accept the Conservative condition, that denominational schools would continue, which caused some anguish in nonconformist circles; but he had won a signal victory, achieving a long-standing goal of providing educational opportunities for all. It was, he said, 'a good measure, thoroughly Liberal'.[177] Ironically, the Conservatives had done more to enact Chamberlain's Radical programme than had Gladstone. These achievements set the seal on the Unionist alliance – it would become closer and closer over the years, and Chamberlain would join the Cabinet in 1895. It was not to be trouble-free but it endured.

Before that, however, came a seminal moment for Chamberlain. As we have seen, the speech he made in April 1886 bought him time in Birmingham, but Schnadhorst's coup of 1888 threatened him with a dangerous rebellion in the heart of his power-base. He rapidly recovered and energetically planned and built the BLUA. Yet the Gladstonians had not been beaten. This is the importance of the by-election in Birmingham Central which took place in April 1889, on the death of John Bright.

It was significant on several counts. Chamberlain had lost an irreplaceable Liberal ally, fearless and direct in his politics, and hugely respected. The Conservatives claimed the vacancy for Randolph Churchill – he had groomed it before 1885, and he had allegedly been promised it by Chamberlain in 1887. Now, Chamberlain denied he had made any such promise, fearful of a powerful rival in his home town; he prevailed on Balfour and Salisbury to persuade Churchill to stand down. Bright's son, Albert, filled the vacancy. This saga went to show the value Balfour, especially, now placed on Chamberlain; he recognised that 'Chamberlain's position in politics largely depended on his position in Birmingham. He was proud of it and it was necessary to him politically', he wrote to Salisbury; so, it was important to help a friend in need.[178] The election was also significant because it represented a straight fight with the Gladstonians. Canvass returns 'indicated a vast support from areas solidly Radical in 1885'.[179] The faithful lieutenant Powell-Williams wrote to Chamberlain that 'the canvass frightens me because it is so good'.[180] In the event Albert Bright won a crushing victory with a 2:1 majority. M. Hurst writes that: 'For the first time the Liberal Unionist Association got to grips with the electorate and was surprised at the strength it found.'[181] Perhaps they had yet to realise that Chamberlain's policy mix of social reform and Imperialism was effective and attractive to the working classes in Birmingham. Indeed, the Unionists never would concede a seat to the Gladstonian Liberals in Birmingham; in 1892 the latter had so hard a pasting that they only fought three seats at the next, 1895, election. Even in the Liberal electoral landslide of 1906, the national victors won nothing in Birmingham.

Others took note. For Hartington and the Whig wing of the Liberal Unionist alliance, it seemed better to make a virtue of Chamberlain's success; Hartington in 1889 ceded to Chamberlain a 'Duchy', an area consisting of Birmingham and the three abutting counties of Worcestershire, Warwickshire and Staffordshire which would become a Radical Unionist base and over which there would be no squabbles between Whig and Radical wings of the Liberal Unionist party. The aim, too, was to hem Chamberlain in and stop him grabbing areas beyond his defined Duchy. 'It became the unquestioned citadel of Liberal Unionism.'[182] By 1892 Chamberlain was the national leader of Liberal Unionism, and infected the whole movement with the energy and the imagination, as well as sheer electioneering know-how, that he had evinced in his Midland fortress.[183] For Balfour, that Bright by-election victory showed how valuable an electoral ally Chamberlain and Birmingham could be; the Unionist *rapprochement* was later marked by an assembly in Birmingham Town Hall of Liberal and Conservative Unionists in 1891, followed by a banquet at which Salisbury and Chamberlain sat side by side.[184]

It is important to observe that Chamberlain was not alone the author of the Liberal split; Hartington and the Whigs never joined the 1886 Gladstone Ministry and made their distaste for Home Rule evident at the outset. There were pockets of Liberal Unionist strength in, among other areas, the West Country and in Glasgow and its environs.[185] However, Chamberlain's role was central. He was the finest speaker on the Liberal Unionist side; his charisma and his courage in taking the fight to Gladstone made him the articulate leader of the revolt, and the April 1886 speech is the start of that. Yet while it won over the 2000 in the short term, it was not for another three years that the Gladstone forces in his home town were finally vanquished – Schnadhorst and Harris had chosen the wrong side. Even back in 1886, the outline of Chamberlain's Birmingham appeal had been discernible: he stood for a coherent, united Empire, and for the pre-eminence of social issues to ameliorate the conditions of the working classes. These were to be the distinguishing elements of Birmingham's Radical Unionism for a generation, and were to be the basis of an electoral hegemony unique in modern British political history – Chamberlain's Duchy.

Lithograph of Joseph Chamberlain, 1900.

Joseph Chamberlain after 1886: *After the split of 1886 Chamberlain became a Liberal Unionist, succeeding Lord Hartington as the party leader in 1892. In 1895 he became a Cabinet Minister under Lord Salisbury, the Conservative and Unionist Prime Minister, choosing the post of Colonial Secretary. He was the driving force for war in South Africa, to take control of an area of great economic potential. The Boer War lasted from 1899 to 1902. It saw the apogee of Imperialist enthusiasm; its cost and its length disabused many people of the glories of Imperial adventure, but Chamberlain remained a convinced Imperialist. His speech of May 1903, featured in this chapter, was partly motivated by a desire to bind the Empire closer together as an economic entity. It failed to convince, it split his party and was instrumental in the Conservative electoral smash of 1906. That year Chamberlain had a paralysing stroke; he lingered on, a broken reed, until his death in 1914.*

JOSEPH CHAMBERLAIN AND TARIFF REFORM

The speech Joseph Chamberlain delivered to his West Birmingham constituents on 15 May 1903 initiated a political earthquake. His biographer, Julian Amery, wrote: 'No speech in British history has ever caused such a sensation…or led to such momentous consequences.' 'We can say of it, as of few other speeches, that after it the world was never the same again.'[186] It had all the heretical impact of a latter-day Martin Luther publishing his *Ninety-Five Theses*.[187] Once again, Joseph Chamberlain split his party, and forced a re-alignment of party loyalties. Where in 1886 attitudes to Home Rule defined allegiance, after this speech in 1903 fidelity to Free Trade came to determine political persuasion, certainly up to 1914. In 1886 Chamberlain's stance had ensured Liberal defeat in the General Election; now his Tariff Reform campaign, launched from Birmingham, so divided the Unionists, demoralising many of the party's Free Trade adherents, that they succumbed in 1906 to their heaviest electoral defeat since 1832. Chamberlain's debilitating stroke later that year didn't paralyse his many followers; they continued to fight for the cause and to endure two more General Election reversals in 1910, prior to the First World War. Only in 1932, with his son Neville's Import Duties Act, could the Chamberlain dynasty claim victory in a fiscal war, which had lasted thirty years.

For Joseph Chamberlain the motivation for this radical policy was primarily Imperial. Twenty years earlier he had been steeled to resist Home Rule by a strong belief in the integrity of Empire, which Gladstone's plans would threaten. In the 1886 election campaign he had said: 'I hope we may be able, sooner or later, to federate all the great independencies of the British Empire into one supreme and Imperial Parliament.'[188] Then again, at least one historian has seen the Imperial debates in the Commons in 1893 as a key to Chamberlain's own Imperialist evolution; there he supported the then Liberal Prime Minister, Rosebery, over plans to 'peg out British claims for posterity'.[189] He had averred: 'I believe in the expansion of Empire.'[190] Two years later, he asked Lord Salisbury for the position of Colonial Secretary in the aftermath to a great election victory, and held the position for eight years. He had been the energetic advocate of a forward policy in South Africa, which culminated in the Boer War between 1899 and 1902, a war indeed of Imperial expansion. He had also been frustrated that his Free Trade government had been unable to respond positively to signals from Canada that she would welcome closer trade links, based on reciprocal trade arrangements.

When the South African War was over in 1902 he was prey to a number of fears, one being that 'the fragile sense of common purpose engendered between Britain and the dominions would be dissipated, and Canada might drift into the economic orbit of the United States'.[191] He would express it thus: Britain's Empire 'is a great potentiality, the greatest that was ever given to man. But for the moment it is a loose bundle of sticks, bound together by a thin tie of sentiment and sympathy but a tie, after all, so slender that a rough blow might shatter it.'[192] 'It is given to this generation to solve the great problem of a United Empire – if we do not solve it, disaster is certain', he would say, for he foresaw the White Dominions such as Canada slipping out of the Mother Country's orbit.[193] The USA by 1900 exported three times what Britain exported to Canada.[194] In a letter to the Duke of Devonshire (formerly Lord Hartington, now President of the Liberal Unionist party) Chamberlain later justified his opposition to Free Trade: 'For my part', he said, 'I care only for the great question of Imperial unity. Everything else is secondary or consequential.'[195] A united Empire was, in his view, essential if Britain was to hold her place in the world. England without an Empire, on the other hand, would be a fifth-rate nation existing on the sufferance of its more powerful neighbours.[196]

That place in the world was already under threat. Britain's percentage share of world manufacturing production had fallen from 31.8% in 1870 to 19.5% in 1900; Germany and the USA's share had risen in the same period. The British portion of the world's pig iron and steel production had more than halved in those thirty years, while Germany and the USA, two countries which protected their domestic industries, had overtaken it; this was the more worrying for what it implied about the capacity to manufacture armaments.[197] At the present rate of decline Chamberlain feared that Britain would be much less an industrial country inhabited by artisans and instead more a distributive country.[198] His pessimism was fuelled by the aggressive naval policy von Tirpitz was pursuing in Germany, a clear threat to British supremacy on the seas.[199] It also gained traction from a fashionable concern for the physical future of the race, for national efficiency, after revelations of malnutrition amongst Boer War recruits. His close association with Birmingham underpinned a darkening perspective.[200]

The town's manufacturers had embraced the Fair Trade movement, founded in 1881, which called for the imposition of duties on foreign manufactures and on food imported to Britain. All seven Conservative candidates had stood on a Fair Trade platform in the 1885 General Election in Birmingham, assured of a warm welcome, and had polled well, though lost. The Birmingham Chamber of Commerce annually called for the imposition of tariffs from the late 1880s onwards. For many years Chamberlain, conventionally Liberal, cleaved to Free Trade orthodoxy, but by the late 1890s his resistance to Birmingham's Fair Traders, especially her embattled metal-working industries, had dissolved. The chairman of Joseph Lucas, cycle-lamp manufacturers, represented many when he complained in 1905 of the way 'inferior-quality' German lamps 'dumped' (sold very cheaply) on the British market, and allowed into the country by current Free Trade policies, stopped him expanding production and 'doubling the number of employees'.[201] That Chamberlain shifted the focus in late May 1903 from imperial preference (the policy of promoting goods imported from and exported to the Empire) to protection of British industries, has been attributed to the successful lobbying of hard-pressed Birmingham constituents.'[202]

There really was a congruence of interest between Chamberlain and his Duchy with regard to things Imperial; Birmingham was proud of its Colonial minister of the crown, and its workers had jobs partly because of the exports of its businesses, BSA, Kynochs, Cadburys amongst many. Enthusiasm for imperial adventures such as the Boer War was unsurprising; David Lloyd George discovered in late 1901 at the Town Hall that to criticise the war, or the integrity of Birmingham's businessmen, was to run the gauntlet of the town's wrath. Chamberlain's Imperial initiative, then, prompted by a deep pessimism about Britain's prospects, and especially her industrial future, answered Birmingham's own very real concerns.

Yet he may never have crossed that fiscal Rubicon by his dramatic public avowal of imperial preference – with all that he knew it entailed in terms of political upheaval – were it not for a growing personal and professional restlessness. The most sensitive political antennae of his generation detected worrying indications of a growing Unionist unpopularity. Even if Birmingham remained devoted to Empire, nationally enthusiasm seemed to be waning, after a costly and protracted war. The Balfour government's Education Act in 1902 by putting Anglican schools on the rates had greatly upset nonconformists, many of whom were numbered in his Liberal Unionist allies. Chamberlain had had to fight hard to convince Birmingham Liberal Unionists to back him, and the government, but he had expended much credit in the effort. He chided Devonshire that: 'The greatest blow struck at the Liberal Unionist influence has been – as I warned it would be – the introduction of the Education Act for which you were to a special degree responsible, and which has driven from our ranks many of our most energetic nonconformist supporters.'[203] His wife confessed to her mother that 'Joe thinks that the party is really on the verge of being broken up by it'.[204] A number of historians concur with E.H.H Green's view: 'Although it is too much to say that without the Education Act there would have been no Tariff Reform, Chamberlain's desire to recover this situation was important in prompting his Tariff Reform initiative.'[205]

Of course, taking the initiative, acting boldly, was completely in character. He sensed drift and passivity in the Balfour administration and chafed at the restraints of the so-called 'dual leadership' with Arthur Balfour, a sop devised to diminish his displeasure at losing out to Balfour on Lord Salisbury's retirement in 1902. Tariff Reform sought to imbue the British people with a sense of purpose (arresting national decline).[206] Beatrice Webb, who had been in love with Chamberlain years earlier, observed him launching his new mission: 'He would make headway… because he had a vision, desired to bring about a new state of affairs and was working night and day for a cause.'[207] That mission would put Chamberlain at the centre of things; it gave him the opportunity to 'pursue additional avenues of power… by creating a unified Empire over which he himself would preside'.[208] If he couldn't be Prime Minister, then he would have global influence instead.

In the spring of 1903 Chamberlain suffered a reversal, which crystallised his thinking both economically, and in terms of politics and power. A year earlier the then Chancellor of the Exchequer, Sir Michael Hicks-Beach, needing to find revenue to fund the Boer War, imposed a corn tax – one shilling a quarter – on imported corn. It provoked an emotional, even hysterical, reaction from many true Free Trade believers. Chamberlain saw this as a heaven-sent chance to initiate a policy of Imperial preference and, before embarking on a tour of the newly defeated Boer territories, he persuaded cabinet colleagues to grant Canada a remission of the corn tax.

In his absence overseas that winter, the new Chancellor, C.T. Ritchie, prevailed on the Cabinet to agree to the abolition of the corn tax in his forthcoming budget. Chamberlain felt bitterly let down and his speech to his West Birmingham constituents on 15 May 1903 was a direct consequence.[209]

It was no surprise that he would initiate policy among his faithful; he would be guaranteed a sympathetic hearing. Beatrice Webb had noted the symbiotic relationship between politician and supporter twenty years earlier: 'The Birmingham citizen adores Mr. Joe, for has he not raised Birmingham to the proud position of great political centre of the universe?' 'The devotion of his electors no doubt springs partly from the consciousness of his deep loyalty and affection for them; but the submission of the whole town to his autocratic rule arises from his power of dealing with different types of men... attracting devotion by the mesmeric quality of his passion and manipulating the rest through wise presentation of their interests.' 'At the first sound of his voice they became as one man. Into the tones of his voice he threw warmth and feeling; the slightest intonation of irony and contempt was reflected in the face of the crowd.'[210]

So, on 15 May 1903 Chamberlain returned to his constituency to deliver his bombshell.

I am proud of being the representative of West Birmingham, an essentially working-class constituency.... It was to me a matter of the greatest gratification that, when I returned (from South Africa), the first to greet me on these shores was a Deputation from you, my friends and constituents assuring me of your welcome home. I could come to no great city in South Africa, hardly to any village or wayside station, but always I was cheered by the presence and enthusiasm of Birmingham men (Cheers)...

Everything that touches Imperial policy, everything which affects their interests as well as yours, has for South Africa, Canada, Australia, as it ought to for us, a supreme importance. And our Imperial policy is vital to them and vital to us. Upon that Imperial policy, and upon what you do in the next few years, depends the tremendous issue of whether this great Empire of ours is to stand together if necessary against all the world, or fall apart into separate states, each selfishly seeking its own interest alone – losing sight of the common weal.

The pervading sentiment of Imperialism has obtained a deep hold on the hearts and minds of our children overseas. The embers (here) are still alight, and in the late war this old country of ours showed it was still possessed by the spirit of our ancestors, to count no sacrifice that was necessary to maintain the honour and interests of the Empire. Is it to end there...with the end of the war? Are we to sink back to the old policy of selfish isolation? I do not think so. (For) the Empire is new. Now is the time to mould that Empire.

It seems to me not at all an impossible assumption that before the end of half a century our fellow subjects overseas may be more numerous than we are at home. Do you wish that, if these ten millions become forty millions, they shall be more closely, intimately, affectionately united to you? Or do you contemplate their going off each in their own direction under a separate flag. Think what it means to your power and influence as a country; to your position among the nations of the world; to your trade and commerce. That question of trade and commerce is one of the greatest importance. Unless it is satisfactorily settled I do not believe in a continued union of the Empire. It is the business of British statesmen to do everything they can to keep the trade of the colonies with Great Britain (Cheers), *to increase that trade, to promote it. In my opinion, the germs of a Federal Union that will make the British Empire powerful and influential for good beyond the dreams of anyone now living, are in the soil; but it is a tender and delicate plant, and requires careful handling.*

Now what is the meaning of Empire? We had no hold over them, but at one time during the (late) war at least 50,000 Colonial soldiers were standing shoulder to shoulder with British troops. If we were face to face with hostile nations, when we had to struggle for our very lives, then it is my conviction there is nothing these self-governing colonies would not do to come to our aid…. (Yet) we have done nothing to encourage an idea of common (financial) responsibility.

My idea of British policy is that at the beginning of this new chapter, we should show our cordial appreciation of the first step taken by the colonies to show their solidarity with us. Every advance they make should be reciprocated. And first among those means is the offer of preferential tariffs (Cheers)… *a policy which comes to us from our children abroad. Last year at the Conference of Premiers they pledged themselves to recommend to their constituents a substantial preference in favour of goods produced in the Mother Country. Canada, the greatest, most prosperous of our self-governing colonies has been the most forward in endeavouring to unite the Empire, by giving us special favour and preference and (in time), if the bonds are drawn closer, the Colonies will be more and more ready to take their share of the burdens of defence.*

The Ministers of Canada have made me a further definite offer. 'We have done for you as much as we can do voluntarily and freely and without return. If you are willing to reciprocate in any way we are prepared to reconsider our tariff, if you will meet us by giving us a drawback on the small tax of 1s a quarter which you have put on corn.' That was a definite and a generous offer we had to refuse. Speaking for the government I am obliged to say that it is contrary to the established fiscal policy of this country; that we hold ourselves bound to keep open market for all the world, even if they close their markets to us (Laughter). *We cannot make any difference between those who treat us well and those who treat us badly. Yes, that is the accepted doctrine of the Free Traders, and we are all Free Traders* (Cries of No,No, and laughter).

Well, ladies and gentlemen, you see the point. You want an Empire. Do you think it better to cultivate trade with your own people, or to let that go in order that you may keep the trade of those who are your competitors and rivals? I say the people of this Empire have got to consider this. They may maintain if they like in all its severity the doctrines of Free Trade; the alternative is that we should insist we will not be bound by any technical definition of Free Trade. We will recover our freedom, resume the power of negotiation, and if necessary, retaliation whenever our own interests or our relations between our colonies are threatened by other people (Renewed cheers).

Make a mistake in your Imperial policy – it is irretrievable (Loud applause)... *For my own part, I believe in a British Empire which, although it should be one of its first duties to cultivate friendship with all the nations of the world, should yet, even if alone, be self-sustaining and self-sufficient, able to maintain itself against the competition of all its rivals.*[211]

Chamberlain had spoken before about binding the Empire more closely, but this speech drew all the strands of his evolving thinking together. His very real fear of national decline, of imperial dissolution, and of future international conflict, are here, as is an open challenge to the rigid orthodoxies of Free Trade. At this stage that challenge takes the form of imperial preference but, soon enough, other fronts against Free Trade were to be opened up, as the implications sank in. Within a fortnight he was conceding in a Commons debate that there was an inevitable corollary to colonial preference – food taxes on foreign, non-colonial produce. In a defiant tone he said: 'there, I make the honourable gentlemen opposite a present of it'; however, he would come to rue the ceding of this gift, as he admitted to the King in September 1903.[212] 'The unscrupulous use which has been made of the Big Loaf cry (the accusation was that imperial preference would inevitably mean less bread for one's money) has prejudiced this policy so greatly that for the moment it is politically impossible.'[213]

In that Commons debate he had tied tariffs to social reform; taxes could be used to fund his old pet project of Old Age Pensions. By late June he had recognised working-class indifference to this offer and promised instead that to compensate for higher bread prices, 'they may be fully relieved by a reduction of a similar amount in the cost of their tea, their sugar, their tobacco. There is no working man in the kingdom who need fear under the system I propose.'[214] As the year advanced, Tariff Reform, as it became known, expanded to embrace protection for embattled farmers, and for manufacturers; it was to be, for converts, a cure for all evils, and by

1910 it was, once again, seen as a means of raising money from the foreigner (who imported to Britain) to pay for social reform, an alternative to Lloyd George's confiscatory tax plans on the rich. What it shows is that Chamberlain embarked on this campaign without thinking through all the consequences and the possibilities; it evolved as others saw its potential.

He was quick to see the logic of protecting British industry from unfair competition. Given his industrial background, formerly the dynamic director of the leading screw manufacturing business, he intuitively sympathised with manufacturers and judged the country's health by the success of its industries. He had little truck with those who argued that, because Britain's invisible exports (insurance, shipping, profits and dividends from foreign investments) outweighed deficits in balance of trade in manufactured goods, consequently all was well with the economy. He conceded Britain might continue to become richer through these invisible earnings, but he worried about jobs if industry succumbed to foreign competition.[215]

At Bingley Hall in Birmingham on 4 November – usually remembered for his theatrical production of two identical loaves of bread which he dubbed the Big and the Little Loaves to show how exaggerated were the fears of a return to the Hungry Forties (the depressed 1840s) under Tariff Reform – he spelt out the dangers to local businesses.[216] Jewellery imports exceeded exports by more and more each year, and the trade was hindered from selling abroad by prohibitive tariffs there. A 60% tariff impeded the export of brass manufactures. The pearl-button trade used to employ 6000 men and now employed 1000. The cycle industry's exports had fallen vertiginously in the previous decade, because foreign tariffs ranged up to 45%, and because the USA dumped their cycles on the British market.[217]

This latter iniquity would be a constant refrain for him; in the 1906 election he said: 'We have also endeavoured to regulate the importation of sweaters (*unskilled alien workers*) but we have done nothing to regulate the importation of sweated goods (*produced by cheap labour*)'. He found the attitude of the trade unions baffling; they campaigned for action to stop alien immigration but they remained resolutely opposed to addressing foreign competition through tariffs.[218] By 1906, indeed, his pitch to the working class had been refined; he now saw tariffs as the answer to the scourge of unemployment. He had supported the government's Alien Immigration Act of 1905, responding to a long-standing Birmingham concern about foreign workers taking jobs.[219] He also saw tariffs, stopping foreign dumped goods, as the means to reviving employment prospects. 'To get you more employment, end one-sided Free Trade', he said in the 1906 Election campaign in Birmingham, under a banner across the proscenium arch which read 'Work for the Unemployed'.[220]

These arguments were developed in a series of speeches in 1903 and 1904 across the country, 'a unique campaign in British politics – a single-handed attempt by an ex-minister to convert the nation to one man's dream of the future', wrote one biographer, Richard Jay.[221] Indeed, no British politician before or since has ever matched Chamberlain's speech-making tours made over twenty years from 1886. They formed part of a series of coordinated activities which showed Chamberlain to be a master of the political campaign.

Within weeks of that first great speech he had his own Tariff Reform Committee in Birmingham, staffed by his loyal allies from the Birmingham Liberal Unionist Association. Its

Congreve Street warehouses dispatched pamphlets, posters and cartoons all over the country.[222] Postcard reproductions of Joe Chamberlain proliferated, as did cartoon images of John Bull beating off the attentions of the dastardly Herr Dumper. John Bull was the hero of a pro-tariff film with a national distribution, while sound recordings of Joseph Chamberlain arguing the protectionist case were released in 1905.[223] A national sister organisation, the Tariff Reform League, well-funded by sympathetic businessmen, distributed the most material, its financial muscle allowing it to overshadow the efforts of the Free Food Union and the Cobden Club. A former sales manager with an eye for packaging and product placement, Chamberlain understood better than any contemporary politician how to project the argument visually and it helped that much of the press was sympathetic – apart from *The Post* all the important Birmingham organs, and nationally, the majority of papers, backed some fiscal reform.[224] To provide authoritative evidence on the case for Tariff Reform he later set up the Tariff Reform Commission, staffed by academics, especially economists, a sort of private civil service.

In truth, all Chamberlain's organisational and promotional talents were needed, for to win over a majority of the electorate was an uphill battle. Most contemporaries did not see the economic crisis that Chamberlain discerned; it did not help his case that just as he launched his crusade there was an upturn in trade, though this was largely due to increased coal and cotton exports and not in the metal-working and heavy manufacturing industries which really concerned him. The prevailing narrative, cleverly replayed and amplified by the Free Trade establishment, credited Free Trade with dispelling the 'Hungry Forties', with emancipating hitherto enslaved workers, and with promoting international harmony and trust rather than secrecy and envy. Free Trade was unselfish and fostered public and private morality. *The Economist* in a different historical context in 1843 had distilled that moral dimension: 'Free Trade itself is a good, like virtue, holiness and righteousness, to be loved, admired and honoured.'[225] Tariff Reform, critics argued, would bring a return to the starvation suffered before Peel rescued the working classes by abolishing the Corn Laws. Tariff Reform implied exploitation of the consumer by the producer; housewives and their families would face higher prices and be able to buy less. Unwittingly that Bingley Hall speech of Chamberlain's with his Big and Little Loaves gave his opponents a memorable image, which they exploited right through to the election of 1906; dear bread was a vote loser.[226]

Free Trade had notable, and determined, advocates among politicians. For the Liberals, it was an unquestioned article of faith. A party which was demoralised in 1900 (it failed to contest over 160 seats in the Khaki Election that year, and was deeply divided about the advisability of war against South Africa) found a new unity and sense of purpose in reaction to Unionist policies. Nonconformists (almost invariably Liberal) hated Balfour's Education Act. Liberals almost to a man rushed to denounce tariffs and protection in 1903 after Chamberlain's speech. So, his initiative invigorated the opposition. It also inflicted on his own side years of in-fighting and division.

From the first it was a gauntlet thrown down to challenge Ritchie and Cabinet Free Traders. Through the summer of 1903, two factions in Cabinet conducted an increasingly acrimonious war of words. Arthur Balfour's talents were not suited to a firm and decisive resolution of the differences. In September he agreed to Chamberlain's proposition that he resign and take his case to the country; that resignation was a neat way of ensuring that the most partisan Free Traders in the Cabinet – Ritchie, Balfour of Burleigh and Hamilton – also resigned.[227] Balfour tried to limit the appearance of a party, and a Cabinet, at sixes and sevens by devising a middle path of selective retaliation in September and through a concerted effort to keep a sceptical Duke of Devonshire inside the Cabinet, but the next months and years revealed the depth of the fissure that Chamberlain had opened. A significant number of Unionist MPs, including Winston Churchill, abandoned the party and joined the Liberals.

The divisions within the Liberal Unionist party were especially bitter. Chamberlain worked hard through the autumn of 1903 to win local branches to Tariff Reform. He put up protectionist candidates in by-elections that winter with encouraging success. Funds were diverted from central Liberal Unionist coffers to help publicise Tariff Reform in the regions. Through the spring of 1904 he manoeuvred to wrest control of the national Liberal Unionist Association out of Devonshire's Free Trade grasp and had succeeded by the summer. He restructured it, to the consternation of ousted Liberal Unionists like Arthur Elliot who, in a letter to *The Times*, wrote of 'the persistent efforts recently made to alter the character of the old organisations and turn them into a machine for promoting the old Birmingham doctrine of preference and protection'.[228] Chamberlain's combativeness and his ruthlessness in pursuit of his political goals were as evident as they had been in that fight for survival over Home Rule. Now he went after free-food opponents, determined to have them deselected, with sympathetic protectionists nominated in their stead. This fate befell an outspoken critic, Lord Hugh Cecil, who wrote to the Prime Minister: 'The truth is that all along Joe has been the aggressor and has striven to drive us out of the party. At present he is making war.'[229]

Two years after that Birmingham speech the situation had clarified. Chamberlain recognised that it would take more than one election before Tariff Reform could be introduced. Balfour had announced that, after any future Colonial Conference (summit of British Empire leaders) and any subsequent proposal for imperial preference, a mandate would have to be sought from the electorate. Chamberlain, nearing seventy, would probably not be in active politics by then. In any case, the chances of a Unionist victory were increasingly slim. Electorates do not like divided parties and many relationships on the Unionist side had been poisoned, none more so than those between Chamberlain and his leader. Chamberlain despised the languor and indecisiveness of his leader; Balfour resented Chamberlain's unrelenting scheming, his palpable lust for power, and his advocacy of a policy of food taxes, which were manifestly unpopular. By the autumn of 1905 Balfour had had enough; he sought and found an opportunity to resign.

In many ways the 1906 General Election result, which saw a sweeping Liberal victory and a crushing defeat for the Unionist party was a commentary on Joseph Chamberlain's policy initiative of May 1903. There were other explanations for that defeat, including resentment at the cost and futility of the Boer War ('Joe's War'), dislike of the policy of importing Chinese labour into the South African mines after the war, nonconformist outrage at the Balfour Education Act and working-class anger at the Taff Vale Judgement, which rendered trade unions liable for the strike actions of their members.[230] Yet the overriding issue across the country seems to have been that of food taxes and protection. In Lancashire, where the Liberals gained 33 seats, *The Manchester Guardian* reflected that 'a candidate only had to be a Free Trader to get in, whether he was known or unknown, semi-Unionist or thorough Home Ruler, Protestant or Roman Catholic, entertaining or dull. He had only to be a Protectionist to lose all chance of getting in, though he spoke with the tongues of men and angels.'[231] If the cause Chamberlain espoused was electorally damaging, so too was the impact of the internecine fighting he had provoked. Even the press reflected that disunity. *The Daily Telegraph* and *The Times* were Balfourite and retaliationist, whereas *The Standard* and *Morning Post* supported Chamberlain's 'whole hogger' policy.[232] The state of the party's national electoral machine reflected the way many party members were distracted by policy disputes. *The Times*, in conducting its post-mortem on the election, concluded that 'sheer bad management, neglect of the constituencies by their representatives, and slackness of organisation and resulting apathy' explained the result.[233]

Yet Birmingham emerged unscathed. All eleven seats in Chamberlain's Duchy (Birmingham and the abutting seats) returned Unionists. It was a unique phenomenon in the country in 1906. It reflected a complete identity of interest between Chamberlain and the town he had served for nearly forty years. Where nationally enthusiasm for Empire seems to have dulled, there are numerous indications in street parties, popular demonstrations, support for Empire Days and for voluntary, Imperial organisations, to suggest that Birmingham's middle and working classes still responded zealously to Chamberlain's Imperial lead. It was the printing and distribution centre for the hundreds of thousands of pamphlets, placards, flyers and posters emanating from the Tariff Reform Committee's warehouses. It was also the acknowledged hub for a national tariff movement. So it is unsurprising that in Birmingham – a metal-working centre, suffering from foreign competition, with a long pedigree of Fair Trade agitation – Chamberlain's ideas should find support.[234]

When Chamberlain spoke at Saltley in the most working-class, and the most marginal, of seats, East Birmingham, in January 1906, he promoted his policy of tariffs as the answer to the constituency's unemployment problems. That, and a plea that the men 'show generous loyalty to old friends and causes', won the day.[235] So in Birmingham, a policy after all influenced by its businessmen and its workers, where even trade union officials sympathised, probably had the effect of consolidating Unionist control over the area. Certainly this is the case, too, with the neighbouring Black Country where Henry Pelling concluded: 'Chamberlain's distinctive influence obtained not merely a new lease of life – it also widened in its extent ...(for) finished metal goods could clearly benefit from Protection.'[236]

Birmingham was a loyal, Chamberlainite fastness; the further away from Birmingham, the more his force and attraction markedly faded. Indeed, Unionists were defeated in all the constituencies he visited on his national speaking tour in 1903/4, excepting Birmingham. The hard truth was that for all the passion, the energy and the political courage he showed in 1903 by embracing imperial preference and Tariff Reform, it proved to be a disastrous gamble, which consigned his party to opposition until after the First World War. It was little consolation that from 1906 the Unionist Party was overwhelmingly protectionist – even a generation later, in the 1923 General Election, to espouse the cause was to invite electoral defeat.

© National Portrait Gallery, London

Oswald Mosley by Bassano Ltd. Whole-plate glass negative, 28 October 1922.

Oswald Mosley *was born in 1896, the scion of a family of Northern gentry. After Winchester and Sandhurst he fought in the Great War with distinction. He returned to a considerable inheritance, which made him financially independent. He became a Conservative MP in 1918, at 22 the baby of the House. He left the party over the employment of Black and Tan irregulars in Ireland, revolted by their violence. He became an exotic and wealthy recruit for the fledgling Labour Party. The speech considered in this chapter reflects his deep concern for the unemployed, and his espousal of radical economic policies to tackle Britain's stagnation. He became a Labour minister in 1929, but thought the leadership hide-bound. He resigned in 1930, founded his New Party in 1931, which was routed in the 1931 Election, and went on to form the British Union of Fascists. He was imprisoned from 1940 to 1943 as a Nazi sympathiser and died in 1980.*

OSWALD MOSLEY –
A SOCIALIST IN BIRMINGHAM

Beatrice Webb was prescient when she reflected in 1923 on the twenty-seven-year-old Oswald Mosley, near the start of his political career. 'Tall and slim, this young person would make his way in the world without his adventitious advantages which are many – birth, wealth, a beautiful, aristocratic wife. He is an orator in the grand old style and an assiduous worker in the modern manner. So much perfection argues rottenness somewhere.'[237] He was indeed one of the most charismatic politicians of his generation, with film-star looks that earned him the sobriquet 'Valentino', and he was probably its foremost orator; he was also far-sighted in the imaginative plans he had to tackle the scourge of the age, mass unemployment. However, his frustration at unimaginative, dunderheaded economic conservatives, unwilling to think creatively in a time of national emergency, brought out his imperious and dictatorial character. His affiliations reflected that restless search for the executive power to act, and so he boxed the political compass, rapidly moving from the Conservative, past Asquith's Liberal, to the Labour Party and thence out of the historic parties to his own New Party, before settling on a fascist organisation, the British Union of Fascists (BUF), whose activities from the 1930s onwards ensured his reputation for 'rottenness' and his enduring notoriety.

Mosley's Labour phase was located in Birmingham, where he first ran Neville Chamberlain agonisingly close in the Ladywood constituency in the October 1924 General Election, then secured the seat at Smethwick in an ill-tempered by-election in 1926. He had consciously chosen Birmingham from among 70 offers from local Labour parties in 1924 for, as he wrote in his autobiography: 'I wanted to give some striking service to the party, and the Chamberlains and their machine had ruled Birmingham for 60 years; their party machine was at that time probably the strongest in the country.'[238] He succeeded in extensively, but not permanently, damaging that Unionist fortress, for in 1929 Labour won 6 seats in what had been overwhelmingly a Conservative monopoly. Birmingham afforded Mosley a platform, as it did for our other speakers in this book. Up to the point when he abandoned the party in 1931 Labour supporters, especially in Smethwick, were markedly loyal to him, and enthusiastic about his policies, even when the Cabinet Old Guard rejected every one of his proposals and precipitated his resignation from office early in 1930.

So it was logical that he should first set out his unorthodox solutions to Britain's grave post-war economic crisis in Birmingham, and that they should be known thereafter as 'The Birmingham Proposals'. To the historian of the inter-war period they are of the first importance. Along with their later manifestation, the Mosley Memorandum in 1930, they constitute one of the only radical attempts in the whole period to challenge the prevailing Free Trade orthodoxies; in a sea of mediocrity, as A.J.P. Taylor wrote, 'only Mosley rose to the height of the challenge… His proposals offered a blueprint for most of the constructive advances in economic policy we have seen today… They were an astonishing achievement.'[239] It was entirely fitting that such a trenchant and articulate assault on *laissez-faire* and Free Trade should originate in Birmingham, where Joseph Chamberlain had launched the crusade for Tariff Reform twenty years earlier. Mosley's prescription will be examined later in the chapter.

The exotic figure who descended on Ladywood in 1924 was profoundly shaped by his youthful experiences. Oswald Mosley was born in 1896, his parents separated early and he was largely brought up by his grandfather at Rolleston-on-Dove in Staffordshire, the Mosley family seat, and absorbed there a deep sense of feudal obligation to tenancy and estate workers which, in time, informed his eccentric and personal interpretation of socialism.[240] Winchester inculcated in him a sense of public service; more precisely, in some of its pupils (Lord Parmoor, William Arnold-Foster, Hugh Gaitskell and Lord Chelmsford) that developed sense of social conscience and duty took the form of joining the nascent Labour Party. Mosley was later derided in Birmingham, by the local Press and by Conservative opponents, for stepping out of his aristocratic class to join Labour, but the evidence there, and of these Old Boys, is that Labour benefited from the influx of talent and money, and with such recruits was better enabled to deflect accusations of a lack of competence for government.[241] Mosley did not go on from Winchester to one of the ancient universities, instead joining Sandhurst in 1914; the lack of formal university education meant that he was, according to his biographer, unencumbered by the Free Trade orthodoxies taught there, and the more original for all that.[242]

The First World War proved formative for him in many ways. He had seen that victory was achieved by submitting the individual to the collective will. Indeed, he had been powerfully affected by the sight of serried ranks of German troops below him as he flew over the Ypres lines near Poperinghe – the discipline, the control informed his later love of military order in the BUF. Paradoxically for a man not averse to 'the good old English fist' when fighting the Communists in the 1930s, the war made him a life-long advocate of peace, a supporter of the League of Nations and a friend of its most powerful advocate, Lord Robert Cecil. He wrote: 'I went into politics to prevent any recurrence of the war that inflicted such losses on my generation, and in place of that senseless destruction, to build a fair way of life.'[243]

He also felt a deep responsibility for the working-class soldiers with whom he had served, to ensure that the state fulfilled those promises glibly made that they would return to a 'land fit for heroes'. He saw himself as a representative of that war generation, and was conscious for many years of the division between those who had fought and experienced the horrors, and those from an older generation who had stayed at home.[244] The war affected him in another, familial way: Rolleston was sold, and he inherited the considerable proceeds. On the one hand he repined the loss of an historic role as manorial lord, but on the other hand it gave him the wealth and the independence to pursue both a political career and London's eligible heiresses, one of whom, Cynthia Curzon, he married in 1920.

Through the early 1920s, the youthful Conservative MP became convinced that, far from the political classes setting out to realise the promises of that 'land fit for heroes', there was an establishment conspiracy to do nothing, to let the natural laws of the free market take their course. Visits to Liverpool and Birmingham slums powerfully reinforced that sense of a betrayal. 'Birmingham gave vivid proof of the execrable housing conditions that all the pledges given to the war generation had betrayed. This more than any other single factor was the motive power which took me into Labour,' he wrote.[245]

He rolled his sleeves up, and organised and spoke with a will (up to 22 speeches in a day) during the General Strike in Birmingham in 1926, making friends and allies in the trade unions and especially among the miners, and importantly, learning about the volatility of their working lives. One final influence in these years was his visit to America. He witnessed for himself the systemic threat posed to the livelihoods of Britain's skilled craftsmen by Ford's mass production techniques at Detroit; and he observed approvingly the huge scale of America's single market, insulating itself in a self-sufficient and burgeoning economy, suggesting to Mosley parallels with the British Empire and the revival of ideas of imperial preference. How Chamberlain would have approved!

By the time Mosley applied to join the Labour Party in March 1924 he had abandoned any affiliation to the Conservatives, for he had fallen out badly with the party leadership and many of his backbench colleagues. At issue were the brutalities of the Black and Tans, which he exposed, though his peers derided him, and Mosley's disapproval of the government's foreign adventures, in Russia and in Chanak.[246] He was passing through his pro-League of Nations, peace at all costs, phase which aligned him temporarily with the Liberals before, in a nice instance of historical irony, he embraced the socialist party, because 'it was the dynamism of the Labour Party at that time which attracted me.'[247]

The gifts and attributes he brought to it were protean. In the most material sense, he had money and connections. He funded the agent's salary, the hire of the Labour hall and municipal expenses in Ladywood, even after he relocated to Smethwick; there too he paid his agent. He also subsidised other Labour candidates in Erdington and Sparkbrook, as well as paying for campaign literature for all the party's candidates in the 1929 election.[248] His socialist brethren appear to have welcomed these infusions of cash; without trade union money, it was very necessary. As for his connections, although savagely assaulted in the right-wing press, especially in the Smethwick by-election campaign, for the perceived disparity between the candidate's aristocratic background and the industrial grimness of his constituency, it would seem that many working-class people felt flattered by the attentions of upper-class candidates; 'a link with powerful, wealthy and glamorous men and women appealed strongly to those who endured humdrum and deprived lives,' wrote Martin Pugh.[249] One contemporary account described the Mosleys' arrival at a Labour meeting, Mosley 'with the gait of Douglas Fairbanks, followed by a lady in heavy costly furs'. 'The song "For he's a jolly good fellow" greeted the young man from two thousand throats. One of the armleted stewards, excited, whispered in my ear, 'Lady Cynthia Mosley', and later, as though thinking he had not sufficiently impressed me, he added (proudly), 'Lord Curzon's daughter.'[250]

Certainly the results seem to bear out the conclusion; the local Labour weekly, *The Town*

Crier, excoriated the 'bitterness and unscrupulousness of Lords Rothermere and Northcliffe'. whose newspapers had created 'such a position in Smethwick that if, on the eve of the poll, Mosley had committed bigamy or murdered his wife, nobody would have believed the story, such was the barrage of mud from the Tory press'. [251]

More important than his wealth were his personal qualities. Edon Wertheimer, a socialist contemporary, wrote: 'He is willing to earn power by unsparing energy and sleepless devotion to the task in hand; the secret of his advance was that he was a hard worker'. [252] That energy, his love of action, and his sheer passion expressed itself in his public speaking. From the early 1920s his glamour and his controversial views made him a compelling orator; *The Westminster Gazette* judged him 'the most polished literary speaker in the Commons. Words flow from him in graceful, epigrammatic phrases that have a sting in them; to listen to him is an education in the English language'. [253] He could be less mellifluous – he himself writes of how constant barracking toughened him up and forced him to develop a method of 'direct, often brutal, personal attack with every available sarcasm, satire and invective. I became a master of flouts and jeers and jibes'. [254] Whilst such assaults enflamed opponents, he enthralled audiences of the faithful; *The Town Crier* commented, of the Ladywood contest in 1924, how 'his power over his audience was amazing'. [255] At the Llandudno Labour Party Conference in 1930 he electrified the delegates and even a Conservative journalist conceded that 'the throng was hypnotised by the man, by his audacity, as bang! bang! bang!, he thundered directions. The thing that got hold of the Conference was that here was a man with a straight-cut policy, here was the Moses'. [256] In truth, this was not the style adopted in the speech we examine from 1925, but the content of that speech, as of everything else he articulated in these years, was indicative of a deep seriousness and an urgent desire to act.

The words 'act' and 'do' pepper his speeches: one thrilling performance at Birkenhead in 1930 after his resignation from the Cabinet can stand for a decade of political rhetoric, when he spoke of hearing men calling, 'Lift us out of the mud; give us practical remedies here and now'. He concluded by intoning, 'Let us do something'. [257] What he wanted to 'do', to execute, was an agenda framed in 1918 – of high wages, full employment, decent homes, reduced hours, increased production – and subsequently little changed. It was a patrician concern for the men he had led, who had fought to defend the country. He was no aristocratic dilettante playing at economics – he had read deeply, talked with Keynes, thought and observed, and his ideas were coherent and at least as practical as any alternative nostrum. But his rash impatience in their pursuit gave rise to theatrical and passionate declamation, which swept his audiences along but also led him to sacrifice a career within Westminster in favour of the seductive, but ultimately destructive, attractions of independence, demagoguery and outlawry.

Mosley himself was immodest about his Birmingham achievement. 'My territorial strength was in Birmingham, which I found a Conservative stronghold and which in five years under my leadership was turned into a Labour fortress throughout the central area'. [258] His money and his enthusiasm nearly stole Ladywood in 1924; he revelled in the evidence of a Labour surge he'd inspired. 'It was a joyous day when, in the courtyards running back from the streets in the Birmingham slums, we saw the blue window cards coming down and the red going up'. [259] He loved the fright he had given Neville Chamberlain, who got home by 77 votes; 'a downpour from heaven washed the lifeless body of the last of the Chamberlains back to Westminster'.[260] Still without a seat, he threw himself into local Labour politics, and took a leading part in the Birmingham strike committee to show his sympathy for the workers in the General Strike of May 1926. When Smethwick's seat became vacant in December 1926 he fought a campaign that drew national attention. For Labour he symbolised renewal after the difficulties of that General Strike; to the Conservatives he was a class traitor 'playing shamelessly on the passions and cupidity of a moronic electorate'. To the generally hostile press (both nationally and in Birmingham) he was a *poseur*, an idler born with a silver spoon in his mouth.[261]

The Town Crier recognised that his crushing majority of 6,582 (a nine-fold increase on the previous Labour majority) in Smethwick represented not just that 'he happens to be a well-to-do man who has thrown himself and his resources on the side of the worker', nor that 'he was the outstanding personality, (but that) he has a policy that will bring hope to the masses'. 'He fought on a straight socialist platform in a manner which would have gladdened the heart of Keir Hardie, against the Tory policy of wage reductions, setting out the socialist alternative of a living wage for all workers.'[262] *The Birmingham Daily Post* could only fulminate about 'his infamous wages lie', and (foreshadowing the 1930s) 'his countenancing of hooliganism and meeting-wrecking tactics'. The town may, as it suggested, have been 'disgusted by the rowdyism of the irresponsible', but the workers voted for Mosley; it would seem that any violence was in reaction to that meted out to Mosley by opponents bent on disrupting his meetings.[263] Certainly, by the time Mosley founded the BUF in 1932, he and his allies had realised that his greatest asset was his oratory, and any means was justified to protect him as he sought to get his message across.[264]

Although a political opponent, Mosley admired Joseph Chamberlain and aped his methods and policies. Like Chamberlain in 1903, he sought to unite the country under his leadership at a time of perceived national emergency. They both revolted against complacent *laissez-faire* assumptions, they both doubted the capacity of Britain to win the battle to export enough goods to sustain full employment and they were both critical of financiers and *rentiers*, instead championing manufacturing industry. Nor did the parallels end there. Mosley's style of politics in the city was similar to Old Joe's; 'personalised appeals and patronage backed by generous amounts of cash'.[265]

His electioneering echoed the master's: 'Herculean canvassing, largely on foot, and superb organisation, made possible Labour's successes in the 1929 General Election.'[266] Of the earlier Smethwick campaign, *The Times* special correspondent had written: 'The organisation is one that would gratify any candidate; one only has to walk through the borough to see the results of the intensive work and almost every house displays a portrait of the Labour candidate.'[267]

Pugh points out that a number of wealthy ex-Conservative socialists fought in 1929 in Birmingham and the Black Country and that they built on that Chamberlain legacy in which working-class voters respected their social superiors.[268] Men like Etonian John Strachey, and Oliver Baldwin, were indeed close and supportive allies as Labour secured a base here. In the heady aftermath to the General Election result Mosley claimed an historical significance: 'The father's fortress has been seized from the nerveless grasp of the sons. Birmingham once followed a man and has now dismissed his plaster effigies.'[269] It was merely a temporary aberration; in the 1931 Election – after the Labour Government broke up – Birmingham reverted until 1945 to its old Unionist monopoly.

Mosley's appeal in Birmingham was very much located in the fact that his prospectus echoed Chamberlainite, and protectionist Fair Trade, policies championed in the city for decades. He did not believe that the country's 1.65 million unemployed in 1925 would be rescued by a sudden revival in trade. He was pessimistic about British manufacturing prospects in the face both of Ford's mass production techniques, and of cheap labour in India and China. He thought it the function of government to secure full employment and decent conditions for the people and was consequently appalled that Baldwin's Conservative government should choose to do the single most damaging thing it could do to an ailing economy, return to the Gold Standard and revalue sterling. J.M.Keynes, the great economist, and a strong influence on Mosley, concluded that by returning to the pre-war exchange rate the Chancellor of the Exchequer, Winston Churchill, had overvalued British currency by 10%, and to remain competitive, deflation, price and wage reduction, was inevitable.[270] It was to *do* something that Mosley had joined the Labour Party, for socialism envisaged the state managing the economy. Unfortunately for him, the Labour leadership by 1931 had proven to be pusillanimous and hide-bound, trapped by liberal economic orthodoxies and unwilling to use its powers to act boldly.

The speech he made to his Ladywood constituents on 3 May 1925 was to be a distillation of ideas he would later publish in '*Revolution by Reason*'. What he said that day would be dubbed the 'Birmingham Proposals'. *The Town Crier* described the queues of people outside the Town Hall, extending round the building and into Paradise Street; the numbers, some 5,000, were double what the Hall could accommodate. Once underway, the meeting first heard from Miss Ishbel Macdonald, the Labour leader's daughter, an indication that at this time and indeed right up to 1930, Mosley was a close friend and protégé of Ramsay Macdonald. Then it was Oswald Mosley's turn to speak and he started by moving a resolution that:

This meeting condemns the inaction and lethargy of the Conservative Government in face of problems causing bitter distress to the people. The best hope of an early improvement in employment, and securing living wages for the workers, rested in socialisation of the banks and the use of national credit resources, not for the profit of the individual but for the benefit of the nation. Mr. 'Original' Churchill had been called in as 'the brain' specialist of the Unionist Party and the country was told to expect wonderful things to happen when the Budget box of mysteries was opened. But instead of the big lion of constructive thought, out crept a poor little silkworm. He agreed with Mr. Snowden – it was the worst rich man's Budget in history. It was a rich man's Budget only camouflaged by a sham and stolen pension scheme. Everybody knew that Philip Snowden intended this year bringing in a pension scheme but with this difference; it was not contributory, the workers didn't have to pay for it but the rich taxpayer. Mr. Churchill stole it, with the inevitable

Chamberlain was a master of political propaganda. He links the dream of Imperial free trade with the coat of arms of Birmingham in one of the souvenir postcards, thousands of which were distributed.

In the 1906 election Birmingham alone survived the Liberal landslide. The voters remained steadfastly loyal to Chamberlain and all seven tariff-reforming Unionist candidates won their seats.

Although remembered for the controversial Munich Agreement, Neville Chamberlain was a distinguished and successful Chancellor of the Exchequer and a reforming Minister of Health.

© Cadbury Research Library: Special Collections

© Cadbury Research Library: Special Collections

Neville Chamberlain addresses reporters at Heston aerodrome after his return from negotiations with Hitler in Munich in 1938. He famously proclaimed that there would be "Peace in our time". A year later Britain was at war.

The Chamberlain political dynasty pictured in the garden at Highbury. Joseph (right) with his sons – Austen (centre) and Neville (left). Joseph's third wife, Mary Endicott (right), and his daughter Beatrice (left) are seated.

During the Smethwick by-election campaign of 1926, the Press satirised
the apparent gulf between Oswald Mosley's aristocratic connections
and the Socialist cause he was advocating.

Mosley's charismatic, passionate and persuasive style of oratory can be glimpsed in this sequence of
images taken in Smethwick during the by-election.

Protest against Powell. Enoch Powell did not anticipate, or understand, the revulsion many felt at the way he couched his arguments about immigration and integration.

Enoch Powell was a powerful orator, whose precise language and orthodox style reflected his love of the Classics.

Malala Yousafzai has become the articulate voice arguing for education of all the world's children, and especially for the education of girls and women.

Prime Minister David Cameron chose Birmingham to deliver a critically important speech, laying out a new approach to counter radicalisation in 21st-century Britain.

difference that he made the workers pay. Not one penny was provided towards the scheme. Let us be careful; make it the special duty of Labour to watch that the pensions of the ex-servicemen were not being harshly cut down as they, the workers, were being cut down.

There is unemployment today because the people haven't the power to buy goods and so I propose to put money into the hands of the people to buy goods. That would create demand, which would bring all the idle machines, and all the men that were idle, into the production of goods for the use of the people in this country. Critics said 'issue more money and up would go prices and nobody would be a penny better off.' That would be so if they could not produce any more goods in response to that demand, but if they did produce more goods, as well as the additional money that was put out, then prices would remain exactly as they were. This proposal differs greatly from ordinary suggestions for the simple issue of more money, to be distributed anywhere, through the big banks. I say – send that money direct to the necessitous areas, give it to the poor whose demand was for commodities that mattered to this country, and so would stimulate employment in the great staple trades. Thus, do away with the poor law and the dole. Give your producers credits to be used on the unemployed. Make the working-man no longer the object of the dole and the Tory jeer, but a free man able to stand up and borrow money upon his own future productive capacity. Then you will have fresh production of goods to meet the demands of that fresh production of money and you will have broken out of that vicious circle of destitution and unemployment. This policy emanated from Birmingham. It was a policy for which in all its details approval had not yet been won by the labour movement in its entirety, but it was not the first time an unauthorised programme had gone out from Birmingham. I believe that such a scheme would at one stroke lay the foundations of a socialist Commonwealth.[270]

It was not the fiery, combative, rhetorical Mosley, jibes against Churchill and the Conservative rich men aside. Its importance lay in the novelty of its approach. 'This revealed, for the first time, a political originality of the highest order.'[272] He dared to attack the Budget and, elsewhere, advocated a floating exchange rate, which would settle at a level that would enable British industry to compete. He wanted the banks to be nationalised, deeply distrusting their motives. His ideas are rooted in the notion of planning the economy, planning demand, and rejecting the fetish and the chimera of export-led recovery. He prioritised the home market instead. It was a direct attack on free market orthodoxy, which was anathema to Conservatives and – surprisingly – many Labour frontbenchers too.

He would later amplify this by proposing an Economic Planning Council, staffed by union and business experts, to direct credit, manage supply in order to avoid inflation, and even to bulk-buy food and materials from abroad to get a better price. The idea of deficit budgeting, of borrowing to direct money to the poor and unemployed, and thus to create demand, reflected the influence of his discussions with Keynes, who had argued in 1923 that government spending was needed to overcome business pessimism in the post-war slump and to get the economy going again.[273] He differed from conventional socialist thinking in that, where he focused on 'creating additional demand, to evoke our unused capacity', it prioritised redistribution and nationalisation. One could say that he was more interested in planned wealth creation prior to any later sharing of the spoils. A further development in the light of his American visit in 1926 was that Chamberlainite vision of an imperial market protected by tariff barriers, within which British industries could secure their markets.

This contribution established Mosley as a serious thinker on the economy; by 1930, with unemployment by July breaking through the 2 million barrier, he was the foremost expert on unemployment and how to tackle it.[274] The immediate reception of his ideas, by the Ladywood constituency members, was positive, and they were endorsed for presentation at the National Labour Party Conference. He continued to be the darling of the unions and of Labour delegates through the 1920s, was voted three times onto the National Executive Committee in national ballots, and his appointment to a ministerial post as Chancellor of the Duchy of Lancaster in 1929 after Labour victory was his reward. He was to assist the Lord Privy Seal, J.H.Thomas, to devise schemes to counter unemployment. In Thomas, and in Philip Snowden, Mosley was to encounter, incarnate, the dead hand of orthodox economic thinking. Churchill wrote: 'We must imagine with what joy Mr. Snowden was welcomed at the Treasury by the permanent officials. Here was the High Priest entering the Sanctuary. The Treasury mind and the Snowden mind embraced each other with the fervour of two long separated lizards.'[275]

Snowden was terrified of inflation, having seen it rampant in Weimar Germany. He welcomed the Gold Standard and its handmaid, deflation, seeing this as a reward for the thrift and foresight of the saver. Far from ushering in a socialist revolution, Snowden tended the sacred flame of nineteenth-century liberal/free market economics, with its core principles of Free Trade, a minimum of government intervention and low taxation. Whilst Snowden effectively blocked his ideas at Cabinet level, Mosley found J.H. Thomas, a railwayman and trade unionist, skilled only in union negotiation, no sort of ally or advocate either. 'He was utterly incapable of understanding the subject (unemployment)', he wrote; 'he did not know whether he was going or coming.'[276] Mosley's ideas foundered; he was unable to convince Cabinet of the merits of a scheme to pay old age pensions to men of sixty, to encourage them to retire, so vacating jobs for younger men. Nor could he persuade an unimaginative Minister of Transport, a bitter enemy, Herbert Morrison, to envision and then expedite a national road scheme to employ thousands of the jobless.

Frustrated, and still believing, as he had in his 'Birmingham Proposals', that the duty of government was to act, especially in the hurricane-force economic conditions of early 1930, Mosley set about pulling his ideas together in what became known as the Mosley Memorandum. It was designed to appeal over J.H.Thomas's head to Macdonald himself. The Memorandum proposed a small war cabinet serviced by experts led by Keynes, an idea which reflected Mosley's conviction that a small executive team empowered to act could rapidly execute policy. He envisaged a protected home market and a long-term plan to restructure the staple industries whose technologies, working methods and management sorely needed reform. Finally, to tide the unemployed over in the short term while this major restructuring occurred, there would be an imaginative programme of public works financed by borrowing.

Depressingly for Mosley, opposition in Cabinet came not just from the usual suspects, fearful for their positions if there were to be a powerful inner cabinet, but from Macdonald himself. The Prime Minister wrote privately of his despair as 'the flood of unemployment flows and rises, and baffles everybody'.[277] He was appalled at Snowden's 'hard dogmatics'. Still, he was also unconvinced by the idea that prosperity could be restored by borrowing, and terrified of doing anything which would allow critics to call Labour irresponsible. Macdonald gave the appearance of preferring to talk rather than to act, and so inevitably took the Treasury's part. To Mosley, the government's acceptance of Treasury *laissez-faire* principles was a betrayal of what Labour should be about. 'It seemed terrified of acquiring or using power.' He resigned from the government in May 1930: 'I felt quite simply that if I lent myself any longer to this cynical harlequinade I should be betraying completely the people to whom we had given solemn pledges to deal with the unemployment problem.'[278] It seemed precipitate to Macdonald, as it has done to colleagues and historians ever since. Macdonald wrote in his diary that the 'test of a man's personality is his behaviour in disagreement. In every test he failed.'[279] Mosley would never hold office again. His resignation speech saw his reputation at its zenith; Bob Boothby, the Conservative MP, considered it 'the greatest parliamentary *tour de force* this generation will hear', and *The Daily Herald* faithfully recorded 'the long and continuous cheering from every section of the House'.[280] That temporary government embarrassment did not change its policy a jot and he now started the journey out of conventional party politics, happiest to make the populist appeal over the heads of the old, conservative, generation.

He drafted the Mosley Manifesto in December 1930, reprising his conviction that only a focus on the home market, protected by tariffs, with State intervention through loans and stimulus for the construction industry, would suffice to meet the economic catastrophe facing Britain after the Wall Street Crash. Seventeen Labour MPs signed, half from the West Midlands, and Mosley formed a 'ginger' organisation, the New Labour Group, to coordinate a campaign for a new approach to galloping unemployment. In one last sally in February 1931 he caustically assaulted Snowden's cheese-paring Budgetary retrenchment as quite inadequate for the task facing the country: 'These suggestions to put the nation to bed on a starvation diet are those of an old woman in a fright.' But with generous support from William Morris, the motor-car manufacturer, and convinced that the country demanded action now, Mosley and five other MPs from that ginger group resigned to form the New Party in March 1931. Oswald Mosley, having sampled what all had to offer, now abandoned mainstream party politics.[281]

Smethwick had remained conspicuously loyal to him. Activists strongly supported his Manifesto policy. The *Smethwick Telephone* reflected their frustrations. 'They could not get legislation in the face of the present methods: the wind-bag representative of a minority, or a representative of a fashionable seaside resort who passed his opinion on industrial proposals affecting the working population. That was what was called democracy.'[282] They were prepared to support Mosley the backbencher and agitate as an awkward squad within the Labour Party, but were hurt and offended by reading in the Press of Mosley's defection. He did not come to Birmingham to explain. Instead, the local Labour Council chairman was summoned to London to hear of the cutting of the ties. To his loyalist argument that 'as long as the ship was afloat it was everyone's duty to keep it so', Mosley rehearsed his bitter feeling that the Labour Party was going to 'rack and ruin'.[283] Later in the year he explained his reasoning at a Trafalgar Square rally:

> 'Spokesmen of the late Labour Government saw in the crisis (of August 1931) that collapse of capitalism which they had prophesied with religious fervour…. (Yet), the great day dawned and Labour resigned; cleared out, just when they had the realisation of their greatest wish. What must we think of a Salvation Army which takes to its heels on the Day of Judgement?'

It was the Labour government's lack of courage which most upset him; 'I had come to the deliberate conclusion that in a real crisis Labour would always betray both its principles and the people who trusted it.'[284] However, his own resignation precipitated a long march into the wilderness. The timing of his abandonment of Labour was woeful. In the summer of 1931 the full force of an economic hurricane hit Britain and Europe. The Labour government fractured over the rigorous application of Snowden's retrenchment policies to the benefits of the unemployed. This might have been the defining moment for the prophet who had thought more seriously than any other party politician about how to stimulate an ailing economy and bring hope to the millions of its casualties. Instead he had to watch from the sidelines, and when a National Government was formed of which he was no part, and a General Election called in October 1931, his New Party was annihilated. Against the national, patriotic appeal of a Coalition formed in dire emergency, even Mosley's formidable platform oratory was hopelessly inadequate. He came bottom of the poll at Stoke-on-Trent and the New Party was wiped out as a parliamentary presence.

The General Election campaign had taught Mosley a lesson he never forgot. Faced with wild disorder from howling mobs of betrayed Labour supporters wherever he spoke, Mosley rapidly concluded that he needed organised, disciplined security. In the saddest of conclusions to his close association with the city, Mosley's arrival at the Birmingham Rag Market prompted a violent disturbance, a battle of bottles and chairs as bodyguards fought with impassioned opponents. *The Birmingham Post* blamed the provocation of his stewards.[285]

The New Party, with its confrontations with the Reds, and its attraction to the militant right wing, led Mosley seamlessly into Fascism. The British Union of Fascists adopted his economic solutions from the 1920s, married them to a military discipline he admired from his war years, and from meeting Mussolini, and focused on the idea of 'Mosley the hero', the saviour of a nation in the last throes of disintegration. A country which could laugh so readily at Roderick Spode, P.G.Wodehouse's ridiculous parody of the fascist leader of the Black Shorts, was never going to convert in significant numbers to Mosley's Fascism.[286] As his views hardened, and became more objectionable, Mosley metamorphosed into a peripheral eccentric, and the great promise, the creative and visionary thinking, of his Birmingham years was all but forgotten, until a new generation of historians, led by Robert Skidelsky in the 1970s, produced a more nuanced portrait of his life.

CHAPTER EIGHT

Neville Chamberlain

Neville Chamberlain *was born in 1869, son of Joseph Chamberlain and his second wife, Florence. Like his father he became a successful businessman and Mayor of Birmingham. Lloyd George recognised his organisational talents and appointed him Director-General of National Service in the War. He became Conservative MP for Birmingham Ladywood in 1918, and was a very successful Minister of Health in Baldwin's ministry (1924-29). As Chancellor of the Exchequer, he balanced the books and was the driving force in the National Government formed in 1931. Such was his influence that it seemed completely natural that he would succeed Baldwin as Prime Minister in 1937. He then took an especial interest in foreign affairs. The speech featured here marks the failure of his policy of appeasing Adolf Hitler. He announced that a state of war existed against Germany in September 1939, falling from power and dying soon after in 1940.*

NEVILLE CHAMBERLAIN AND APPEASEMENT

I t was Neville, Joseph Chamberlain's second son, who fulfilled the family destiny and became Prime Minister in 1937. He had built a formidable reputation as Mayor of Birmingham, then as a social reforming Minister of Health in the 1920s who did much for the unemployed, the widowed, the orphaned and the old. He was then an iron Chancellor of the Exchequer, who restored a sickening economy to a semblance of good order in the 1930s. While at the Treasury, to his intense satisfaction, import duties were enacted, so consummating the Tariff Reform campaign initiated thirty years earlier by his father (Chapter 6). The sum of these solid achievements should have ensured both popularity and high regard, but the ingenious and constructive legislation he fostered has for seventy years been overshadowed by a seemingly imperishable notoriety as arch-appeaser, the man who cravenly surrendered to Hitler at Munich.

Cato's *Guilty Men*, written in the aftermath to Dunkirk, was a savage indictment of inter-war governments, particularly that of Chamberlain, in which British armaments had been neglected, Hitler's intentions had been misjudged, and blind capitulation had fed the dictator's voracious appetite.[287] When Winston Churchill wrote *The Gathering Storm* soon after the Second World War, he reinforced the idea that Chamberlain had pursued a dishonourable policy, miscalculating and misreading Hitler's 'predetermined deadly course', all the while naturally highlighting the author's own prescience.[288] There was a reaction to this interpretation from the late 1960s to the 1990s; revisionist historians living through the Cold War, experiencing attempts at *détente*, witnessing the long Imperial sunset as Britain withdrew from her colonies, saw Chamberlain's realism, his recognition of the limits on British power in the face of global threats from Germany, Italy, and Japan, in a more sympathetic light.

Latterly, however, the pendulum of historical approbation has swung back again; counter-revisionists have focused on Chamberlain's manipulation of the media, his suppression of unorthodox and critical thinking in his own party, and his arrogant disregard of public opinion, in pursuit of a profoundly misguided policy towards the dictators.[289] His weekly letters to his sisters Ida and Hilda – unique insights into the mind of a Prime Minister – unfortunately only augmented a by now settled judgement, when they were published. In writing unblushingly that Hitler 'had been very favourably impressed' – 'I have had a conversation with a man', (he had said), and 'one with whom I can do business', the extent of his dangerous self-delusion at Munich in September 1938 was manifest.[290]

On balance, many historians would now concede that up to Munich there was a case for Appeasement; Chamberlain's crime was to carry on into 1939 believing in Hitler's trustworthiness and in the possibility of disarming and settling grievances. The speech Chamberlain made in Birmingham on 17 March 1939 was of enormous importance, therefore. Late in the day, Chamberlain appeared to alter course; we will look at the extent to which he himself had undergone a conversion. To others in government, in wider politics, in the military, that speech was a line in the sand and it precipitated a number of decisions, which betokened Britain's preparation for war. It was, however, too late to rescue Chamberlain's reputation. His stock remains low; indeed the public's view has little changed in seventy years, and nor has the commonly accepted lesson of Munich for latter-day statesmen that, whether he be Nasser, Khrushchev or Saddam Hussein, bullies must be confronted and faced down.

His business and political career before 1937 developed in him that distinctive set of character traits that made him controversial later. From his father he inherited a strong sense of the duty owed by the privileged to the working classes. That paternalistic outlook extended into his behaviour as an employer at Hoskins and Sons, the Bordesley firm manufacturing ships' berths he owned from 1897, where he devised production bonuses, strove to retain his workers in recession and encouraged trade union membership. As a reforming chairman of the town planning committee, he prioritised working-class housing and pioneered the first two town planning acts through Parliament to enable the city to tackle the issue of slums. As Mayor during the First World War he initiated, then realised, the plan for a Birmingham Symphony Orchestra to bring music to the people of the city, and he fought the Treasury to allow a Birmingham Municipal Bank to be created, to encourage war-time saving.

When he had a national canvas on which to operate, as Minister of Health, his unglamorous reform of poor-law administration and of the funding of local government, and his Widows, Orphans and Old Age Pensions legislation, comprised some of the most effective social reform of the century. Underpinning all he was doing, then, was a strong commitment to the lives and welfare of ordinary people; that obligation was heightened by the knowledge of what they had gone through in the Great War, and that informed his abhorrence of war and his commitment to do all in his power to avoid another conflagration.[291]

Even before he became an MP for Ladywood (later switching to Edgbaston) in 1918 his achievements in Birmingham had commended him to Lloyd George, the Prime Minister, as 'a man of push and go', someone who could help administer and lead a war-time organisation. His Director-Generalship of the National Service was unhappy, and developed in him a life-long aversion to Lloyd George, but the point is that his efficiency and decisiveness had already established a proven track record. With the Chancellorship under his belt in the 1930s, the man who became Prime Minister was a formidable figure: 'He was relentless, sanguine, a most efficient dispatcher of business, impelled always to act and to decide, and never afraid of taking an unwelcome decision.'[292] His earliest biographer, Keith Feiling, writing soon after Chamberlain's unmourned death in 1940, wrote of how he was 'masterful, confident and ruled by an instinct for order. He would give a lead and impart an edge on every question. His approach was arduously careful, but his mind, once made up, was hard to change.'[293] It is unsurprising, then, that he should contemplate personally resolving the Czechoslovakian crisis in 1938 face to face with Hitler, for Plan Z (as he called his dramatic flight to Berchtesgaden) was merely one more example of his desire to be brisk, business-like, controlling and decisive.

There was an unattractive obverse to the skills of executive authority he had refined by the late 1930s. His confidence in his own abilities led him to the certainty that he was right, and to some contemporaries an irritating smugness. Consequently he had little but contempt for those who opposed him; 'they must be crushed'.[294] That contempt embraced Parliamentary critics and public opinion, of which he had a very low regard, seeing the people as 'too easily swayed by emotion'.[295] As much as anything, it was his appearance and his manner which did him few favours; corvine, dubbed 'The Coroner' by his backbenchers, glacial and severe, he looked like a Victorian actuary or a provincial undertaker, and his speeches reflected that image, for they were precise, orderly, correct but also occasionally sneering and sarcastic.[296] He had charisma and presence – Sir John Simon, Chamberlain's Chancellor, wrote of a magnificent speech in February 1938 that it was 'perfect in manner, disarming in frankness, so powerful in argument' – but it was sometimes unalluring.[297]

Even when he was Chancellor he was involving himself in foreign policy. He first became interested because his brief encompassed issues such as reparations, war debts, and affordable levels of military spending and of rearmament. His attritional campaign as Chancellor to bring stability to the economy had by the 1934 Budget produced sufficient dividends to allow him to speak of a country moving from *Bleak House* to *Great Expectations*, but up until the Second World War he would remain vigilant and solicitous of the economy. On its eve he was urging that skilled labour not be deflected from factories producing consumer goods into munitions factories, for fear that exports might fall away and the country be faced with another terrifying sterling, and balance of payments, crisis.[298] He even shared his concerns with Mussolini, stressing that 'he had been obliged to suffer the disappointment of seeing the result of his careful finance over many years dissipated in building up armaments, instead of making improvements in public health and in the condition of the people'.[299] As a result of this perhaps understandable preoccupation, he tried to ensure that when rearmament came, and as we will see, he was prominent in determining its timing, it did not threaten the stability of recovery; economic health would be an important element in any future war.

With an ageing Baldwin tiring visibly in No. 10, Chamberlain wrote: 'I am more and more carrying the government on my back.'[300] He was more than a Chancellor; he signalled the need to rearm in 1934 (at an economically responsible rate) and was the most influential figure in the framing of the Defence White Papers in 1936 and 1937. He above anyone else determined the subsequent scale of the investment in arms (£1.5 billion over a five-year period), and the strategy, which was to prioritise the RAF (especially bombers which were to be a deterrent) and the Navy, and to relegate the Army to a few divisions, incapable of acting as a Continental expeditionary force. He spelt the end to sanctions against Mussolini, calling them 'the very midsummer of madness' in 1936 and so ensuring both the ceding of Abyssinia to Italy and the end of the League of Nations as an international peacekeeper with any utility. When he came to succeed Baldwin he believed himself to be both capable and expert in foreign affairs.

A number of elements coalesced to determine that the new Prime Minister would pursue a policy of Appeasement. In essence it had been at the heart of British foreign policy throughout the inter-war period. One historian has written that 'both as an attitude of mind and as a policy it was not a silly or treacherous idea in the minds of stubborn, gullible men, but a noble idea rooted in Christianity, courage and common sense'.[301]

Given a widespread feeling that the Versailles Treaty was fundamentally flawed, that Germany had been harshly punished, that France had been unnecessarily vindictive, vengeful, and positively unhelpful, and that another war was unthinkable, to be avoided at all costs, it is entirely understandable that politicians would seek to negotiate with those who had a grievance, notably the Germans.[302] The Anglo-German Naval agreement in 1935 casually rewrote the Versailles Treaty to allow a sizeable German surface fleet, and indicated that Hitler was perfectly prepared to come to an agreement in what was for him an inessential area (he wanted Continental hegemony and was prepared to let Britain have her sea power as long as she did not interfere) and that therefore Appeasement could be an effective policy. The signals from a pacific public – in the infamous Oxford Union debate in 1933, in the East Fulham by-election in 1934 and in the impressive endorsement for sanctions rather than physical force in the 1935 Peace Ballot sponsored by the League of Nations Union – all directed politicians towards negotiated rather than military solutions.[303] The 1935 General Election campaign, in which Baldwin had soft-pedalled rearmament ('there will be no great armaments', he had promised) to ensure victory, showed the lack of appetite for a bold and courageous stand against the dictators, even when the Führer ordered the invasion of the demilitarised Rhineland in March 1936. Chamberlain, like almost all other leading British politicians, was relieved that France showed no willingness to stop Hitler, so releasing Britain from any obligation to help. In addition to all this, Britain felt vulnerable; it seemed impossible to fulfil commitments stretching from the South Seas to the Mediterranean and the English Channel against determined enemies, especially with such a fragile economy.

Prime Minister Chamberlain's method of conducting foreign policy was at once more active and energetic, and more personal.[304] The League of Nations he thought largely irrelevant. His attitude to the Foreign Office has divided historians. He certainly railed against the pedestrian pace at which it conducted its diplomacy, but John Charmley has emphasised how scrupulous he was in listening to the intelligence from ambassadors round Europe before embarking on Plan Z.[305] Still, he preferred using private emissaries. His Foreign Secretary, Lord Halifax, was dispatched to Germany to hunt with Goering and to establish good relations with the Nazi regime; sister-in-law Ivy was used as a personal envoy to Mussolini. Sir Nevile Henderson, ambassador in Berlin and a fully paid-up appeaser, was employed to establish a constructive, friendly tone in Anglo-German communications, while Horace Wilson, a civil servant absolutely in Chamberlain's confidence, was entrusted during the Munich Crisis with the most sensitive of missions to Hitler. These personal contacts, short-circuiting official channels, yielded little and contributed to Foreign Secretary Sir Anthony Eden's resignation in February 1938; as a corollary, the burden Chamberlain placed on himself made him often feel isolated and melancholic.[306]

Mussolini undermined Chamberlain's position by discovering every detail of the British negotiating position from a spy in the British embassy in Rome and, even when an agreement (the Anglo-Italian Agreement in 1939) was made, it was ineffectual.[307] Hitler became increasingly irritated by Britain's busy-body pretension to be involved and to order international affairs. When Henderson presented Hitler with the outlines of a general settlement in March 1938 (the only time such a settlement was offered to the German government) the Führer bluntly rejected the offer. Chamberlain had thought that offers of colonies, and of economic partnership, would open the way both for a deliberate, negotiated and peaceable re-ordering of Central Europe to satisfy German grievances, and for agreement on air disarmament.[308] Hitler's advance into Austria a week later demonstrated how little he needed a negotiated settlement.

After the *Anschluss* in March 1938 the year was dominated by leaks, rumours and then the reality of suffocating German pressure on Czechoslovakia to yield the Sudetenland, the western border area of the country, which had a majority German population. For Chamberlain, the important issue as the crisis grew in late summer was that any transfer of land should be peaceful. He would need to release France (alongside whom Britain would be obliged to stand) from her commitments made to Czechoslovakia – Edouard Daladier, the French Premier, overcame his qualms about leaving an ally in the lurch with embarrassing alacrity. Chamberlain used a personal emissary, Lord Runciman, to soften up the Czechs for concession.

Underpinning his own conviction that Britain must avoid entanglement were many factors. First was his own aversion to another World War, which is what a German invasion implied. Then there was his belief – from erroneous military intelligence – that the Germans were far stronger in the air than they actually were (and far more capable of a truly destructive bombing campaign on Southern Britain), and that the Czechs were far less capable of meaningful resistance than they might have been. Much more accurate SIS intelligence that the German army had expanded to a frightening 90 divisions from an earlier estimate of 36 spooked the British, who were consequently aware of the impossibility of physically helping Czechoslovakia in the event of a German invasion.[309] He wrote to sister Ida in early September 1938: 'Again and again Canning (*whose biography he was reading*) lays it down that you should never menace unless you are in a position to carry out your threats.'[310] As the tension grew, he determined to fly to see Hitler: 'The plan should be tried just when things looked blackest.'[311]

Munich has become synonymous with national disgrace; at the end of Chamberlain's third flight in a fortnight to see Hitler, Czechoslovakia was dismembered, on a tight ten-day timetable, and the Sudetenland was absorbed – Britain had more than acquiesced.[312] Her Prime Minister had pressurised first France, then Czechoslovakia, into submission. Chamberlain's eagerness to avoid war convinced Hitler that Britain had absolutely no intention of resisting; 'Our enemies are worms', Hitler later said, 'I saw them at Munich.'[313] Chamberlain profoundly misread Hitler; his naïve belief in honour, trust, reason and gentlemen's agreements was wholly misplaced with a man such as Hitler.[314] Critics such as Churchill saw a golden opportunity missed to stop Hitler in his tracks in 1938. The indictment of Chamberlain is reinforced by the ruthless way his government managed public opinion, suppressing the doubters in the Press; as remorselessly it silenced critics in his own party.[315] Here was no innocent, but a calculating and intolerant man bent on driving a policy based on personal conviction. That arrogance and conceit was exemplified in his letters that autumn. There are shades of an eager suitor in comments such as 'Hitler definitely liked me' and 'he has been very favourably impressed', while Chamberlain shows guileless complacency when writing 'all the world seems full of my praises'.[316]

On the other hand, defenders of Munich recognise Chamberlain's courage, persistence (Hitler was furious that his chance of a military campaign was thwarted and came to hate Chamberlain 'with his silly umbrella') and, above all, his realism.[317] 'Chamberlain recognised that we have not the means of defending ourselves and he knows it,' said General Ironside.[318] Alec Dunglass (later Lord Home) witnessed the popularity of Munich on Chamberlain's announcement of his third, desperate visit to the Führer, when all seemed lost – 'There were a lot of appeasers in the House that day'. His remark implied that much of the ardour cooled on mature reflection later.[319] Undoubtedly, as Chamberlain hoped, if Hitler now reneged it would be crystal-clear to Dominion, American and world opinion who was responsible for war, and this was indeed a valuable benefit of Munich. Others have justified Munich for the breathing space to allow Britain time to rearm; it is certainly true that the new commitment to building fighter planes for defence ensured that by June 1940 Britain outmatched the Luftwaffe in this area, although it is also the case that the year's grace before September 1939 allowed the Nazis to continue their relentless build-up of arms.

What is unquestionable is that across the course of that Munich fortnight attitudes to Appeasement changed. Halifax, the Foreign Secretary, became convinced that a line must be drawn and Hitler resisted if he continued to bully. Subsequently he was cynical about any prospect of negotiated peace with the Führer; his new resolution was important for he had real standing in the party, the Cabinet and the country, and because Chamberlain lost a close ally. Yet if he, and the public, and men hitherto appeasers like Sir Samuel Hoare, the Home Secretary, rapidly cooled towards Appeasement, shocked by Nazi violence against the Jews on Kristallnacht in November, and by Hitler's speeches rejecting any prospect of disarmament, Chamberlain did not. This was the result of his tight management of the media; he and his tight-knit circle were unaware of the strength of public revulsion growing against Hitler. 'The only thing I care about is to be able to carry out the policy I believe, indeed I know to be right,' he wrote self-importantly to his step-mother Mary.[320]

He still believed that the Munich Agreement he had signed with Hitler, vowing that Britain and Germany would consult and cooperate to remove differences, was the foundation of future amity. So, he dragged his heels on calls to accelerate rearmament and direct labour, and in a speech in January 1939 he declared British rearmament to be strictly defensive, and Britain's motto to be 'Defence not defiance'. He refused to bring Churchill into his Cabinet for fear of upsetting the dictators. He insisted on reading into the relative mildness of some of Hitler's speeches in the New Year a sign that he wanted peace and friendship, and he continued to woo a patently untrustworthy Mussolini (a possible counter-weight to Hitler), visiting Rome to sign the Anglo-Italian Agreement in February. He persisted in believing that Hitler was susceptible to a general resolution based on economic agreement over food and raw materials, and over the colonies.

Fittingly for a man steeped in the works of the Bard, there is an almost Shakespearean quality to the tragic shattering of Chamberlain's illusions in March 1939. Secret Service warnings were ignored, as a euphoric Chamberlain addressed the lobby correspondents on 9 March, confidently predicting that Germany had been given pause by British rearmament, and that economic cooperation beckoned. It reflected his private view that 'we have at last got on top of the dictators'.[321] Hitler evidently did not agree; on 14 March German forces started the invasion of the rest of Czechoslovakia, comprehensively undermining Hitler's claim at Munich only to be interested in territories where Germans were in a majority.

For a few days at least Chamberlain was seriously out of step with his fellow countrymen. Even *The Times* and Nevile Henderson, hitherto uncritical advocates of Appeasement, denounced the invasion, the latter appalled by German 'cynicism and immorality'.[322] 'The occupation of Prague was the turning point of our times,' wrote a prominent backbencher, Page Croft.[323] Chamberlain's abandonment of the 1938 guarantee to the Czechs to stand by them were they to be invaded seemed Jesuitical; he argued the country had fallen apart rather than been invaded. In his Commons statement he said he was unmoved by Czech tragedy or German betrayal and added that 'the object we have in mind is of too great significance to the happiness of mankind for us lightly to give it up'.[324] The crass insensitivity jarred. The gravest questions were now raised about his judgement. Many thought like the MP, Harold Nicholson: 'The feeling in the lobbies is that Chamberlain will either have to go or completely reverse his policy.'[325]

Even Chamberlain recognised his error: 'As soon as I had time to think I saw that it was impossible to deal with Hitler after he had thrown all his assurances to the winds.'[326] One mandarin observed that 'throughout Whitehall it was possible to detect the strange sound, as if of the turning of the worms'.[327] A meeting of the Birmingham Unionist Association two nights later was to be his chance of redemption. 'It will give me a great opportunity to speak to the world', he wrote, for the speech was broadcast to the country, the Empire, the USA and to Germany. He had planned to devote this occasion to the economy and social services, among friendly constituents who would appreciate a prospectus first enunciated by his father, Joseph; on Halifax's advice he drastically amended it, as he sat on the train from Euston to Birmingham. Halifax had warned that unless Chamberlain got it right he would face an insurrection in the Party and in the Commons.[328]

He was, then, under great pressure when he rose to speak:

I had intended to talk upon trade and employment, upon social service and finance. But the tremendous events taking place this week in Europe have thrown everything else into the background; you will want to hear some indication of the views of His Majesty's Government as to the nature and implications of those events.

Public opinion in the world has received a sharper shock than has ever yet been administered to it. Last Wednesday (in the Commons) I was obliged to confine myself to a very restrained and cautious exposition; perhaps naturally that cool and objective statement gave rise to a misapprehension that my colleagues and I did not feel strongly on the subject. I hope to correct that mistake tonight. It has (also) been suggested that this Czech occupation was the direct consequence of the visit I paid to Germany last autumn. When I decided to go I never expected to escape criticism. I went there in what appeared an almost desperate situation, this seeming to offer the only chance of averting a European war. Not a voice was raised in criticism; everyone applauded the effort. Only when the results fell short of expectations did the attack begin.

After all, the first and the most immediate object of my visit was achieved (Cheers). *The peace of Europe was saved; and if it had not been for those visits, hundreds of thousands of families would today have been in mourning for the flower of Europe's best manhood. What was the alternative? Nothing we could have done, nothing France could have done, or Russia, could possibly have saved Czechoslovakia from invasion and destruction. But I had another purpose, too - to further a policy called European appeasement. If that policy were to succeed it was essential that no Power should seek to obtain a general domination of Europe. I hoped in going to Munich to find out by personal contact what was in Herr Hitler's mind. At my second visit he repeated with great earnestness what he had already said at Berchtesgaden, namely that this was the last of his territorial ambitions in Europe and that he had no wish to include in the Reich people of other races. ... And then in the Munich Agreement itself there is this clause: 'The final determination of the frontiers will be carried out by international commission.'*

Well, in view of those repeated assurances I considered myself justified in founding a hope upon them that once this Czechoslovakian question was settled it would be possible to carry further this policy of appeasement. Notwithstanding, I was not prepared to relax precautions and so our defence programme was actually accelerated (Cheers). *I am convinced that after Munich the great majority of the British people shared my hope and ardently desired that that policy should be carried further. But today I share their disappointment, their indignation* (Cheers) *that those hopes have been so wantonly shattered. Surely I was entitled to that consultation provided for in the Munich Agreement? Instead Herr Hitler has taken the law into his own hands and within hours German troops were in the Czech capital. What became of this declaration, 'No further territorial ambition', of that assurance 'We don't want Czechs in the Reich?'*

The Rhineland, Austrian Anschluss, severance of Sudetenland – all these things shocked and affronted public opinion. Yet there was something to be said on account of racial affinity, or just claims too long resisted, for the necessity of change. But the events this week fall into a different category. They must cause us all to be asking ourselves: 'Is this the end of an old adventure or the beginning of a new?' 'Is this the last attack upon a small state or is it to be followed by others?'

We must all review the position with a sense of responsibility which the situation's gravity demands. Every aspect of our national life must be looked at from the angle of national safety. I do not believe there is anyone who will question my sincerity when I say there is hardly anything I would not sacrifice for peace (Cheers). But there is one thing I must except, that is the liberty that we have enjoyed for hundreds of years and which we will never surrender. It is only six weeks since I spoke in this city and I pointed out that any demand to dominate the world by force was one the democracies must resist and I added I could not believe such a challenge was intended. And indeed with the lessons of history for all to read it seems incredible that we should see such a challenge. I feel bound to repeat that, while I am not prepared to engage this country by unspecified commitments, yet no greater mistake could be made than to suppose that – because it believes war to be a senseless and cruel thing, this nation has so lost its fibre that it will not take part to the utmost of its power resisting such a challenge if it were ever made.[329]

This career-saving speech was a robust defence of Munich and the Appeasement policy designed to avoid bloodshed. It talked of German promises made and broken. Chamberlain articulated a personal hurt, that he should have been side-lined, treated as irrelevant. The speech emphasised the new departure in German foreign policy, represented by the devouring of the Czech people, and it posed the worrying question, who and what next? Most importantly, it put down a marker. It made it clear that Britain could and would contemplate war, however distasteful that was, if challenged. *The Times* reported: 'Mr. Chamberlain had a remarkable ovation at the end of his speech.' Birmingham party members recognised this as a Rubicon crossed, and critics were at least temporarily silenced. Yet Chamberlain himself remained equivocal. He could write in successive letters to his sisters that 'I am proposing another appeal to Mussolini rather in the hope of putting on a brake. I want to gain time for I never accept the view that war is inevitable.' 'It (*the crisis*) has convinced me that our present plans are too slow.' [330] He told the Irish leader de Valera that he did not feel he had really changed his policy, which was 'securing peace by the removal of reasonable causes of war, whilst pursuing a policy of rearmament'.[331]

His actions up to the outbreak of war in September 1939 in the face of sequent provocations reflected that ambivalence. The Italian invasion of Albania in April was a blow to his faith in Mussolini ('he behaved like a sneak and a cad'); Nazi occupation of Memel in March was similarly disheartening. In appearance, British foreign policy became more assertive as the country contemplated war. Guarantees to threatened Poland, Greece and Romania were made in the aftermath to the Prague *débâcle*, despite these countries being no easier to assist militarily than Czechoslovakia. The Polish guarantee 'was momentous', writes D.C. Watt, for 'the decision war or peace had been voluntarily surrendered into the nervous hands of Colonel Beck (*The Polish Foreign Minister*)'.[332] It also ignored the bald judgement of his brother, Austen, the architect of the Locarno Treaties when Foreign Secretary in 1925: 'The Polish corridor is something for which no British government ever will or ever can risk the bones of a British grenadier.'[333]

Chamberlain at the same time conceded both the establishment of a Ministry of Supply to direct production and labour towards military goals and conscription for 20- to 21-year old men, a principle he had resisted for months. Tortuous negotiations were opened with Soviet Russia in hopes of building an Eastern alliance system capable of resisting German bullying, despite the overwhelming distrust of Russia shown by Poland, which had so recently bloodily fought the Bolshevik regime.

Yet Chamberlain's heart was not really in it, a fact obvious to many observers. The evidence that the Birmingham speech did not really represent a conversion at the deepest level is compelling. Days after the Polish guarantee he was qualifying it to his sister – 'What we are concerned with is not boundaries but attacks on independence, and it is we who will judge whether their independence is threatened or not.'[334] He felt it important not to provoke the dictators and so he contacted them privately to explain that the conscription introduced in April was only defensive in intent. Similarly, though he had yielded over a Ministry of Supply, he appointed not Churchill but a nonentity, Leslie Burgin, to the job (the announcement of which produced a 'deep gasp of horror and pain' in the House).[335] Just three weeks after the Albanian invasion he was renewing overtures to Mussolini believing him winnable to a further alliance.[336] He continued to misread Hitler: in late April he conjectured that 'he has now touched the limit and has decided to put the best face on it'.[337]

Where many in his party were prepared to sup with the devil, in the shape of Stalin, to stop Hitler, Chamberlain did all he could to be obstructive. 'I must confess to the most profound distrust of Russia,' he wrote. 'I distrust her motives.'[338] Fearful of Bolshevik expansionist ambitions, he clung to a condition that Russia should only help a country which requested assistance; then he baulked at Russian troops crossing Polish soil to help resist an invading German army. Perhaps Molotov, Russia's Foreign Minister, never did intend to ally with Britain and France, and had long coveted a Nazi-Soviet Pact, but perhaps Chamberlain's lack of enthusiasm communicated itself too readily and scuppered what chance there was. Strategically, the removal of a potential second front was a German triumph, and a British and French disaster.

Through August 1939 the pressure built on Poland. Chamberlain cast around desperately for ways of avoiding war. He even seemed prepared to consider an offer from Hitler to be allowed a free hand in Poland, in return for guaranteed peace thereafter. He and Halifax still toyed with the idea of an international conference hosted by Mussolini, just as German storm troopers overran Polish borders on 1 September. To widespread condemnation in the Commons,

Chamberlain delayed issuing an ultimatum to Germany for two days after that Polish invasion, at the behest of the French government, which wanted to prepare the French people for war; to all appearances here was a man too desperate to find a way out of doing the honourable thing, stopping Hitler in the only way he would understand, by declaring war. At root he was temperamentally unsuited to be a war leader – the ruination of his plans for a lasting, negotiated international peace all but broke him.

That Birmingham speech in March 1939 had marked the start of a new policy in the country – active preparation for what now seemed to most an inevitable war, and a recognition that in Hitler there was a leader bent on using violence to establish a new European order. The man who delivered it, one of Birmingham's favourite sons, a municipal leader and social reformer of the first order, had seriously misjudged affairs in an area he thought he understood but did not; even now, he never really committed himself to the post-Prague realities on which he felt compelled, by the weight of opinion, to enunciate that day. He remained wedded to a conviction that so unthinkable, so horrific, was the prospect of war that any rational man must surely be motivated, as he was, to try and ensure its elimination. Birmingham, Whitehall and the Treasury were no adequate preparation for dealing with the amorality and brutality of Adolf Hitler and Benito Mussolini. He survived unhappily as Prime Minister through the first few months of a Phoney War after the declaration of war in September 1939. Defeat in Norway in May 1940 brought him down, to be replaced by a belligerent Winston Churchill. Chamberlain served him loyally, but already sick, he died shortly after his fall from power in late 1940.

So, the mature judgement of history indicts him, not for trying, up to Munich, to find a peaceful resolution to understandable grievances, but because in the authoritative words of R.A.C. Parker: 'After Munich he attempted tenaciously but with varying degrees of concealment from increasingly disillusioned colleagues and from worried public opinion, to renew and extend his supposed success. He persisted even after Prague. Whenever he was free to choose he opted for conciliation rather than confrontation. It seemed impossible for him to think himself mistaken.'[339]

CHAPTER NINE

Enoch Powell

Enoch Powell *was Birmingham-born in 1912, educated at King Edward's School and at Cambridge. A distinguished classicist, he went on to become Professor of Greek at Sydney University at the age of 25. He returned to Europe to fight Hitler. He rose from the other ranks to be a brigadier; no one else in the British army rose further in the war. He joined the Conservative Party in 1945 working in its research department. He represented Wolverhampton South-West from 1950 to 1974. He held ministerial posts in the Treasury (1957-58) and was an imaginative Minister of Health (1960-3). He fell out with his leader, Edward Heath, after 1965, and his anti-European, monetarist and immigration views widened the gulf between them. The notorious speech of April 1968 studied here made him a pariah and remained extremely controversial till his death in 1998, by which time he had left the Conservative Party to become an Ulster Unionist MP.*

ENOCH POWELL AND IMMIGRATION

E noch Powell was born in Birmingham in 1912, and went on to become MP for nearby Wolverhampton South-West and the most charismatic politician of his generation; as it happens, he was the biographer of Birmingham's most famous son, Joseph Chamberlain.[340] There are many echoes of Chamberlain in Powell's political career. Both developed a formidable power base in the West Midlands; Powell, like Chamberlain, was an industrious and effective political campaigner, and he was one of the last serious politicians in Britain to imitate Chamberlain's populist method, delivering 'a programme of public speeches as the prime means of appealing to the electorate'.[341] They were both Unionists, and for a while Conservatives of a distinctive sort, though each defied the orthodox party line and sought to ginger up their parties to make them more dynamic. This approach would lead in each case to open rebellion, and to division.

They both had a public reputation usually accorded to prime ministers, and so influential were they that many consider them responsible for the results of whole General Elections, Chamberlain in 1906, and Powell in 1970, when the swing to the Conservatives in the West Midlands delivered a Heath government, and in 1974 when his savage criticism of Edward Heath's policies ensured a Labour victory. Most pertinently to this book, their reputations were shaped by famous speeches delivered in Birmingham. Robert Rhodes James has noted the parallel: 'It is doubtful whether any British speech in peacetime has had an immediate effect comparable to that created by Powell's Birmingham speech (in April 1968), since Joseph Chamberlain flung down the gauntlet of Tariff Reform.'[342] Certainly, Enoch Powell's 'apocalyptic prediction of disaster remains the most notorious speech by any British politician of the sixties', concludes a recent historian of the period; perhaps he undersells it, for it is certainly arguable that no political speech anywhere in Britain since 1945 has rivalled it for infamy.[343]

Powell's speech in April 1968 was about the dangers of immigration; his justification was that he was merely reflecting the concerns of West Midlands constituents, and here too he echoed Chamberlain, who had agitated at workmen's behest – successfully – in the 1890s, for limitations on alien immigration.[344] It was an issue which, as will be seen, had only lately struck Powell as being of central importance. However, what was consistent, throughout his career, was his formidable intellect, his clarity of focus and of thinking, his determination, and an unbending stiffness which made him an uncomfortable colleague. Schooled by an ambitious and demanding mother,

Powell was a prodigiously gifted classical scholar at King Edward's School, Birmingham and then at Trinity College, Cambridge, where he took a first in Classics, then became a very youthful Fellow, before at twenty-five years old being elected to a chair as Professor of Classics at Sydney University.

Within short order he had volunteered to fight Nazism, joining the Royal Warwickshire regiment as a private soldier; his intellect marked him out, and he was commissioned and became an intelligence officer, with the Eighth Army in the Desert, and later in India, reaching the rank of brigadier. He fell in love with the Raj, and – believing the British were there to stay – he conceived an ambition to be India's viceroy. Attlee and Mountbatten's plan for a hasty scuttle shocked the young Conservative Party researcher in 1947.[345] It not only forced a reassessment of career goals; in one of those moments of absolutist conviction and logical clarity, which marked his political decision-making, he concluded that without the jewel in the crown the British Empire was finished, and that the ambition to maintain a British presence East of Suez was absurd, a notion that would become germane to later arguments about immigration. Unlike his peers he felt no obligation for a former mother country to welcome her erstwhile subjects to settle – a notion that would become germane to later arguments about immigration. After all, if a colony voted for independence, the contract was ended, Britain's liability over.

Powell voted Labour in 1945 in sheer disgust at the Appeasement policies of Neville Chamberlain; soon enough his deeply held antipathy towards socialism, to nationalisation, to government planning and controls, convinced him he was a Conservative, notwithstanding the presence in the party of the flotsam of Appeasement enthusiasts from before the war. He became member for Wolverhampton South-West at the 1950 General Election, by the slim margin of 691 votes; until 1974 he represented this West Midlands seat, steadily increasing his majority (winning by 14,467 in 1970), and becoming a much respected voice for his people.

By 1955 he had been appointed (by Anthony Eden) Parliamentary Secretary to Duncan Sandys, the Minister of Housing. Powell's tenure reveals something of his redoubtable capacity for analysis, technical mastery and hard work, overseeing measures on slum clearance and for decontrolling rents, here allowing him to free a sector of the economy from the dead hand of government administration.[346] Those skills were needed in his next post, that of Chief Secretary to the Treasury, to which he had been elevated in 1957 by the new Prime Minister, Harold Macmillan. Faced with a seemingly intractable case of inflation, Powell, Peter Thorneycroft, the Chancellor of the Exchequer, and the Economic Secretary, Nigel Birch, each separately concluded that its cause was an excess of money in circulation, and the solution was a dramatic reduction in public spending. Powell proved to be the most forceful and articulate advocate of proto-monetarist policies, which would later be adopted by Margaret Thatcher, Keith Joseph and Geoffrey Howe. His analysis would mature and develop into an increasingly individualist rather than corporatist vision, which had no time for National Economic Development Councils, or Price Commissions (which were 'nonsense and would not work') for pay policy, or regional relocation. All these fashionable nostrums embraced by Conservatives (especially under Edward Heath), as well as by Harold Wilson's Labour Party, were anathema to him.

In 1958, budgetary policies which involved a credit squeeze, an increase in the Bank Rate, and cuts in expenditure were opposed by Macmillan whose world view had been shaped by a profound fear of the return of the unemployment he had witnessed in the North East in the 1930s, and by department ministers wedded to increased expenditure. The three treasury ministers saw this as a matter of principle, and resigned in January 1958. Powell's opinion of Macmillan, 'an actor manager', was unflattering; he despised his feebleness and inability to take tough decisions, and his tendency to scheme and to plot, epitomised by the secrecy, half-truths and evasion he employed to ensure Sir Alec Douglas Home's succession as Prime Minister in 1963.[347]

Still, Macmillan could not easily do without a man of Powell's evident talent and he appointed him Minister of Health in 1960, with a seat in the Cabinet in 1962, where Powell's ferocious, fanatical appearance disconcerted him: 'Powell looks at me in Cabinet like Savonarola eyeing one of the more disreputable popes.'[348] Macmillan was unsettled by Powell's all-too-transparent disdain for his leader's methods. Powell was a successful Minister of Health. His biographer concludes that he 'unquestionably laid the foundations of a modern health service; he was the first to see the need for the NHS to be an evolutionary beast. He made the ministry one of immense political importance.'[349] His legacy also encompassed a ten-year hospital building programme, and the demolition of Victorian lunatic asylums, as well as the promotion of campaigns of fluoridisation and against smoking. He had mastered his brief thoroughly, partly the dividend from relentless hospital and health authority tours to note deficiencies: 'In general he took the view that there was too great a tendency to operate the service for the benefit of those who run it.'[350] He pioneered a now fashionable emphasis on the need for government services to respond to the needs of the consuming public. It was an unfortunate irony that Powell's final months in office were dominated by a battle over health workers' pay as he loyally stuck to a government policy of pay restraint in the face of nurses' industrial action, even though philosophically he had no time for such government interventionism.

He resigned from a post he loved in 1963 over his perception that Macmillan had dissembled and manoeuvred to ensure Home succeeded him. He never held office again. He would be a shadow cabinet member under Home, then under Heath, but like Chamberlain there is a keen sense of wasted talent, of an unfulfilled career. Soon enough his trenchant views on the economy, reviewed above, and on Europe (for he believed that Britain would surrender her sovereignty if she joined the Common Market) opened up a gulf with Edward Heath, who found it impossible to get Powell to accept shadow cabinet discipline. That gulf would become unbridgeable once Powell turned his attention to immigration.

There were few indications in the first two decades of his political career that Powell feared the imminent racial apocalypse, about which he would later be so exercised. His speeches were largely concerned with economic policy and with the health service. He eschewed giving support to local Birmingham or Wolverhampton Immigration Control associations in the 1950s when importuned by constituents to do so; the Birmingham chairman publicly highlighted 'the menace of coloured infiltration and a piebald population'.[351] When *The Wolverhampton Express and Star* advocated immigration control in 1956, Powell pointedly ignored it. As a minister he seems to have acquiesced in the settled Treasury view of immigration as a valuable source of much-needed labour in the economy; at the Department of Health he paid tribute to the work of foreign doctors and nurses.[352]

The man labelled 'racialist' in 1968 by both Edward Heath and *The Times*, won universal acclaim in a passionate and forceful speech ('the greatest parliamentary speech I ever heard', wrote Denis Healey) from the Commons backbenches in July 1959, savaging the British colonial authorities for their brutality towards Mau Mau prisoners at the Hola camp.[353] He attacked the moral relativism that justified beating Mau Mau to death because they were 'sub-human'. 'We cannot say we will have African standards in Africa, Asian standards in Asia, and perhaps British standards at home. We must be consistent with ourselves everywhere. We cannot, we dare not, in Africa of all places, fall below our own highest standards in the acceptance of responsibility.'[354] That speech established Powell's reputation as one of the great rhetoricians of his generation and as a politician brave enough to criticise his own party in government. It also contradicts the notion that Powell viewed those who were, at the time, thought of as the Empire's coloured subjects, as intrinsically racially inferior.

Nevertheless, his interest in immigration unquestionably quickened in the early sixties, around the time that he started to articulate a deeply held love of England in its post-Imperial incarnation, expressed in an idyllic, romantic vision of its history and its culture. In a speech in 1961 in the City of London he talked of England: 'the nationhood of the mother country remaining unaltered, with a continuity of existence which was unbroken... (under) a kingship which embraced and expressed the qualities that are peculiarly England's: the unity of England... the homogeneity of England, so profound and embracing that the counties and the regions make it a hobby to discover their differences and assert their peculiarities; the continuity of England, which has brought this unity and homogeneity about by the slow alchemy of centuries.'[355]

Here are revealed clues to Powell's thinking about what was happening to his country and which explain the hardening of his attitudes. He said later in a *Tyne Tees* documentary that it was the sheer numbers of immigrants, which awakened him: in Birmingham the figure rose from 8,000 in 1953 to 30,000 in 1958.[356] Such numbers, he feared, threatened England's 'unity and homogeneity'; he forecast ghettoisation, influenced by contemporary images from America, especially Chicago and Detroit, and worried whether integration was ever really possible.

He was later to outrage liberal opinion when he talked of 'immigrants remaining integrated in an immigrant community which links them with their homeland overseas. The West Indian or Asian does not, by being born in England, become an Englishman. In law he becomes a United Kingdom citizen by birth; in fact he is a West Indian or an Asian still.'[357] In areas where immigrants predominated he was apprehensive for the native Briton who was made to feel 'the toad beneath the harrow', a stranger in his own country, where the Labour government's new Race Relations Bill in 1968 would introduce reverse discrimination.[358]

A crucial moment for Powell had been the Smethwick General Election contest in 1964. Here, an industrial town in the Black Country where between 8% and 10% of the 70,000 population were recent immigrants, the local paper, *The Smethwick Telephone*, ran a relentless campaign against the effect of immigration on housing allocation for indigenous white locals. Enough of the voters of Smethwick recorded their distress in October 1964 to defy national

trends and ensure the rejection of the Labour candidate, Foreign Secretary Patrick Gordon
Walker, in favour of the controversial local Conservative, Peter Griffiths. He had proposed an
absolute ban on unskilled immigrants. Party leaflets provocatively stating that 'If you want a
nigger neighbour, vote Labour' betray the depth of local feeling.[359] The language and the tone
of a dirty campaign disgusted many, both at Westminster and locally, and the Prime Minister,
Harold Wilson declared that Peter Griffiths 'will serve his time here (in the Commons) as a
Parliamentary leper'.[360]

Smethwick reinforced Powell's belief that immigration was becoming the key issue in the
West Midlands, a view also shaped by warnings of the menace of coloured infiltration made by
members of the British Immigration Control Association based in Birmingham.[361] The episode
epitomised for him a liberal establishment antipathetic to the views and interests of ordinary
people. 'We are told in terms of arrogant moral superiority that we have got 'a multi-racial
society' and had better like it.'[362] He saw a dangerous fissure opening up between the native
inhabitants of the West Midlands, and the unsympathetic denizens of Whitehall.[363] His populist
appeal is echoed by latter-day UKIP candidates, who capitalise on feelings of resentment about
a self-obsessed Westminster.

Many observing Powell's new-found interest in the immigration issue concluded that it was
motivated largely by political opportunism.[364] After the Conservative election defeat in 1964,
Powell had observed how Peter Griffiths had found an issue which appealed to the electorate.
One of Powell's first immigration speeches of note was coincidentally only a few months later
when, at Wolverhampton in May 1965, he called for Commonwealth immigrants to be treated
the same as aliens, and for dependants to be denied any automatic right of entry. Although
Powell failed ignominiously when he ran for Tory leadership in 1965, he could see in
immigration an issue, set alongside his increasingly trenchant monetarism, and a 'Little
Englander' foreign policy, which could form the basis for a dynamic prospectus, startlingly
different from Heath's corporatist and internationalist orthodoxy. Powell undoubtedly was
ambitious, and dreamt of displacing a visibly struggling leader in the late 1960s; immigration
would be an issue connecting Powell to broad swathes of the country in a way no other
politician could contemplate.

The timing and tenor of the speech he made in Birmingham was determined by the
coalescence of several factors. The shadow cabinet – in which he was Shadow Defence
Secretary – had agreed a relatively conciliatory response to Labour's Race Relations Bill, debated
in the Commons in early 1968, and Powell had succeeded in getting Heath to adopt assisted
repatriation among policy proposals. Yet he felt the shadow cabinet did not understand the
deep unhappiness of people, represented in some of his constituents, on the receiving end of
immigration policy blithely determined in Westminster. He revolted at the implications of the
Bill – it was, in his eyes, to put the native white Briton in the dock for justifiable resentment
against incomers. Beyond that, he concluded that his constituents felt 'hopelessness, trapped
and imprisoned' in areas of intense immigrant settlement.[365]

Meanwhile, the government in early 1968 wrestled with the issue of persecuted Kenyan
Asians wishing to settle in Britain; Powell in a speech in Walsall in February 1968 called for a

voucher system to control what might be a flood of immigrants. At the same time he urged strict limits on dependants wishing to join immigrants already settled in Britain. That speech drew hundreds of positive letters of support in his constituency postbag.[366] Contemporaneously, television screens broadcast frightening images of race riots in Detroit, only underlining his conviction that such scenes would be replicated in multi-racial cities in Britain unless a dramatic change in policy ensued. As he saw the Labour government adopt his voucher proposal in the Commonwealth Immigration Act of spring 1968, and as he drove a reluctant Heath right-wards over voluntary, assisted repatriation and over the Race Relations Bill, Powell appeared to be putting down his own marker.

Lord Lambton, the Conservative MP, writing in *The Express and Star* believed that what Powell 'was saying in effect' (in his Birmingham speech) was 'I am the man to lead you. I am alone of the Conservative leaders today who understands what people in this country want.'[367] So when he came to speak at the Midland Hotel to the eighty-odd guests at the West Midlands Area meeting of the Conservative Political Centre on 20 April his tone reflected his own, and some of his constituents' anger, at the way – he argued – right-thinking liberals ignored or patronised ordinary British people, at the sharp end of an experiment in multi-culturalism about which there had never been any consultation.[368] As Peter Jenkins later wrote in *The Guardian*, 'he exploited the feeling that politicians are conspiring against the people, that the country is led by men who have no idea what interests or frightens the ordinary people in the backstreets of Wolverhampton'.[369]

There was more than a touch of devilment too; Powell did not respect a leader who had tried to curb his own tendency to stray into areas outside his brief. Powell could argue that he was speaking in his West Midlands political base and and there the collective responsibility of shadow cabinet did not apply. He could also plead that what he said was firmly based on agreed shadow cabinet immigration policy. Yet he knew he was going to be controversial; he told his friend Clem Jones the editor of *The Wolverhampton Express and Star* that his speech 'would fizz like a rocket'.[370] Why otherwise would *ATV* have been alerted in advance of the speech? What he then said fizzed every bit as pyrotechnically as he anticipated.

The discussion of future grave, but avoidable, evils is the most unpopular and the most necessary occupation for the politician. A week or two ago I fell into conversation with a constituent, a middle-aged, quite ordinary working-man employed in one of our nationalised industries. After a sentence or two about the weather, he suddenly said: 'if I had the money to go, I wouldn't stay in the country. I have three children. I shan't be satisfied till I have seen them all settled overseas. In this country in fifteen or twenty years time the black man will have the whip hand over the white man.'

I can already hear the chorus of execration. How dare I say such a horrible thing? How dare I stir up trouble and inflame feelings by repeating such a horrible conversation? The answer is that I do not have the right not to do so. Here is a decent, ordinary fellow-Englishman, who in broad daylight in my own town says to me, his Member of Parliament, that this country will not be worth living in for his children. What he is saying thousands, and hundreds of thousands, are saying and thinking – not throughout Great Britain perhaps, but in the areas that are already undergoing the total transformation to which there is no parallel in a thousand years of history.

In fifteen or twenty years on present trends there will be in this country 3 ½ million Commonwealth immigrants and their descendants, a figure given by the Registrar General's office. There is no comparable figure for the year 2000 but it must be in the region of five to seven million, approximately one-tenth of the whole population and approaching that of Greater London. As time goes on the proportion of this total, who are immigrant descendants, who are born in England, will rapidly increase and by 1985 would constitute the majority. It is this fact above all which creates the urgency of action now. How can its dimensions be reduced? By stopping further inflow, and by promoting the maximum outflow, both answers which are the official policy of the Conservative Party.

Those whom the gods wish to destroy they first make mad. We must be mad, literally mad, as a nation to be permitting the annual inflow of 50,000 dependants, who are, for the most part, the material of the future growth of the immigrant-descended population. It is like watching a nation busily engaged in heaping up its own funeral pyre. A third element of the Conservative Party's policy is that all who are in this country as citizens should be equal before the law and that there shall be no discrimination or difference made between them by public authority. This does not mean that the immigrant and his descendants should be elevated into a privileged or special class, or that the citizen should be denied his right to discriminate in the management of his own affairs between one fellow-citizen and another or that he should be subjected to inquisition as to his reasons and motives for behaving in one lawful manner rather than another.

There could be no grosser misconception of the realities than is entertained by those who vociferously demand legislation 'against discrimination', whether they be leader-writers of the same kidney and sometimes in the same newspapers which year after year in the 1930s tried to blind this country to the rising peril which confronted it, or archbishops who live in their palaces, faring delicately, with the bedclothes pulled right over their heads. They have got it exactly and diametrically wrong. The discrimination and the deprivation, the sense of alarm and of resentment lies not with the immigrant population but with those among whom they have come and are still coming. That is why to enact legislation of the kind before Parliament at this moment is to risk throwing a match onto gunpowder.

(For) the existing population found themselves made strangers in their own country. They found their wives unable to obtain hospital beds in childbirth, their children unable to obtain school places, their homes and neighbourhoods changed beyond recognition; at work they found that employers hesitated to apply to the immigrant worker the standards of discipline and competence required of the native-born worker. On top of this they now learn that a one-way privilege is to be established by Act of Parliament: a law to be enacted to give the stranger, the disgruntled, and the agent provocateur, the power to pillory them for their private actions.

What has surprised and alarmed me in the hundreds upon hundreds of letters I have received (since his Walsall speech) *was the high proportion of ordinary, decent sensible people omitting their address, because it was dangerous to have committed themselves to paper to a Member of Parliament. The sense of being a persecuted minority is growing among ordinary English people. I am going to allow just one to speak for me. She was writing from Northumberland about something which is happening in my own constituency.*

'Eight years ago in a respectable street in Wolverhampton a house was sold to a negro. Now only one white (a woman old-age pensioner) lives there. This is her story. She lost her husband and both her sons in the war. So she turned her seven-roomed house, her only asset, into a boarding house. Then the immigrants moved in. With growing fear, she saw one house after another taken over. The quiet street became a place of noise and confusion. Regretfully her white tenants moved out.

Immigrant families have tried to rent rooms in her house, but she always refused. Her little store of money went. She went to apply for a rate reduction. It was suggested she let part of her seven-roomed house. When she said the only people she could get were negroes, the girl said 'racial prejudice won't get you anywhere in this country.'

The telephone is her lifeline. She is becoming afraid to go out. Windows are broken. She finds excreta pushed through the letterbox. When she goes to the shops, she is followed by children, charming wide-grinning piccaninnies. They cannot speak English, but one word they know. 'Racialist', they chant. When the new Race Relations Bill is passed this woman is convinced she will go to prison. And is she so wrong? I begin to wonder.'

To be integrated into a population means to become for all practical purposes indistinguishable from its other members. But to imagine that (integration) *enters the heads of a great and growing majority of immigrants and their descendants is a ludicrous and dangerous misconception. The cloud no bigger than a man's hand has been visible recently in Wolverhampton where* (he quotes John Stonehouse MP) *'The Sikh community's campaign to maintain customs inappropriate in Britain is much to be regretted. Working in Britain they should be prepared to accept the terms and conditions of their employment. To claim special communal rights leads to a dangerous fragmentation within society.' For these dangerous and divisive elements the Race Relations Bill is the very pabulum they need to flourish.*[371]

As I look ahead I am filled with foreboding. Like the Roman, I seem to see 'the River Tiber foaming with much blood'. That tragic and intractable phenomenon which we watch with horror on the other side of the Atlantic is coming upon us here by our own volition and our own neglect. Only resolute and urgent action will avert it even now. All I know is that to see and not to speak would be the great betrayal.[372]

The speech's impact came from Powell's controlled passion and anger, from both its clarity and precision and its prophetic character. The extent to which he anticipated the subsequent furore has been much debated. That famed lucid rationality may have blinded him to the hurtfulness and offensiveness of how he framed his message. Perhaps it was a lack of emotional intelligence when he said innocently that he was merely reiterating agreed Conservative policy. He rehearsed again his concerns about the numbers of immigrants, about their resistance to integration (implicitly a threat to the English identity he held dear) and about legislation, which criminalised white citizens.

What was new was, firstly, the premonition of a racial Armageddon, reinforced in references to funeral pyres, to matches thrown on gunpowder, and most notoriously in that phrase from Virgil to 'the River Tiber foaming with much blood'. Secondly, it was the language and use of specific anecdotes, from the old man and the old lady, to make his point, which struck listeners; if it did not upset the audience of the Midland Hotel that day, it appalled others nationally. Some felt he had given credence to urban mythology, of which these anecdotes were an example.[373] The 'Birmingham Speech', as it was known ever after, divided the nation. Edward Heath considered the speech 'racialist in tone and liable to exacerbate racial tension', and – encouraged by senior Conservative colleagues – immediately sacked Powell from the shadow cabinet. As much as anything, he did so because it was a strike against his authority, its language and tone being quite at odds with official Conservative immigration policy. This would herald open war between the two men, culminating in Powell's savage diatribes against Heath's economic U-turns and European policies in the early 1970s, when Powell electrified the

Commons, asking whether Heath 'had taken leave of his senses'.

The press was largely antipathetical, exemplified by an Olympian leader in *The Times* which said that:

'... the Birmingham speech was of course disgraceful... because it was racialist, calculated to inflame hatred between the races, not only of white against black, but also of black against white. The language, the innuendoes, the constant appeals to self-pity, the anecdotes, all combine to make a deliberate appeal to racial hatred. Within a few weeks of the murder of Martin Luther King and the burning in many American cities, it is almost unbelievable that any man should be so irresponsible as to promote hatred in the face of these examples of the results that can follow.' [374]

Senior politicians echoed this; Humphrey Berkeley, the Conservative MP, called it 'the most disgraceful public utterance since the days of Oswald Mosley', while the Labour peer, Lady Gaitskell, thought it 'a direct incitement to racial hatred and ultimately to racial violence'.[375] Such critics blamed Powell for the racist feeling which grew in Britain in the late 1960s. Powell touched a raw nerve in those who hated, and felt ashamed about, Imperial exploitation and felt the urgent need to make reparation, and in those who believed passionately that there was no difference between peoples whatever the colour of their skin.[376] Yet there were some at Westminster who took a different line: Michael Foot, for example, and Anthony Crosland, another senior Labour politician, who was sickened by the self-righteousness of many in the Westminster elite, who on encountering sympathisers with Powell, labelled them 'fascist'. This was, thought Crosland, 'libellous and impertinent', because such sympathy 'reflects a genuine sense of insecurity and anxiety for a traditional way of life'.[377]

Support for Powell, from those who feared immigration or saw it negatively, in terms of pressures on housing or jobs, rather than seeing the wider economic benefits or a great social potentiality in new and invigorating cultures, materialised dramatically in the days after the speech. Hundreds of London dockers marched from the East End to Westminster protesting about his victimisation, shouting: 'Don't knock Enoch!' Smithfield meat porters petitioned Parliament days later. Many smaller factories in the West Midlands experienced walk-outs; men at the Wolverhampton and Dudley Brewery marched on Wolverhampton town hall. Powell received over 43,000 letters of support.[378] His own constituency party remained determinedly loyal. Indeed so strong became his local power base that Cummings in *The Daily Express* in February 1971 could caricature him as a very English de Gaulle and it as 'Wolverhampton Les Deux Eglises'.[379] A Gallup opinion poll in the speech's aftermath found 74% agreeing with Powell; roughly the same percentage thought Heath wrong to sack him. In a sign of just how significant the speech was to be in establishing Powell's reputation, a poll for the same organisation in 1969 found Powell 'the single most admired politician in the country'.[380] The truth appeared to be that – as Richard Crossman, the politician and diarist observed – Enoch had 'stirred up the nearest thing to a mass movement since the 1930s... the illiterate industrial proletariat... have revolted against the literate'.[381] This neatly expressed the elitism that Powell attacked.

That Birmingham speech was a defining moment for Powell himself and for the politics of race in Britain. He later said: 'I realised how significant it all was for me. I was never expected to hold office again.'[382] He had not anticipated the relentless, often violent, protests he faced on university campuses and in public meetings. For all that he was a profound and radical critic of conventional economic and foreign policy, he found it hard to shake off his association in the public mind with race and to throw off Heath's characterisation of his racialism. 'I would take a racialist to mean a person who believes in the inherent inferiority of one race to another,' he told a Birmingham newspaper the next month. 'So the answer to the question of whether I am a racialist is, 'No'.[383] The speech isolated him within his own party, and made it unlikely, however incompetent the Heath government became, that he would ever become Conservative leader. Instead his deep disillusion with a Heath government, which had abandoned economic promises, and forced through EEC membership, led to his leaving the party for the Ulster Unionists in 1974.

That is not to suggest that his wider reputation suffered a similar diminuendo. His biographer, Patrick Cosgrave, concluded that by 1970 Powell 'had a moral authority akin to Churchill's in 1940' for both men had defied received opinion yet had implacable public support for their views. 'By June 1970 Powell had established himself as far and away the most powerful speaker in politics.... one who regularly generated massive explosions of enthusiasm.'[384] Powell's reputation rested on the fact that he was the foremost public speaker of his generation; his performances could be electric, and his message was limpid, forceful, severely logical, direct and, for all that it often relied on statistical weight, it was coloured and made vivid by allusion and by imagery (frequently classical). Powell was thought to be authentic and courageous, prepared to tell it as it was, willing to take on convention. He was the harbinger of a new orthodoxy of denationalisation, of privatisation, of abandoning exchange controls and of a free market approach to wages and prices; equally, he was the prophet who articulated the patriotic resentment of many who thought joining the EEC would entail the sacrifice of British sovereignty.

This raises the question as to the importance, and the value, of Powell's contribution to the issue of immigration. Although his predictions of future immigrant numbers were pilloried at the time, even as early as 1970 the Runnymede Trust, with a reputation for scholarly objectivity, reported that Powell was more right than wrong.[385] He was eventually proved prescient; in his Birmingham speech he had predicted immigrant descendants would form 6% of the population by 2000; the 2001 census reported it to be 9%.[386] In highlighting the way that successive governments, and Whitehall, were developing a multi-racial society without a national debate or electoral consent he anticipated arguments still deployed by UKIP sympathisers. He was, however, spectacularly wrong in his extravagant doom-mongering about the inevitable civil disorder stemming from race issues.[387] Furthermore, the irony was that Powell may well have unwittingly encouraged the very violence of which he warned, for far-right groups, made up of white working-class men, held him up as a hero; they drew succour from his comments, chanting 'Powell, Powell,' or 'We want Enoch', when engaged in gang brutality. As a corollary, 'most immigrants regarded him as an implacable enemy'.[388] Yet, racial violence largely became a thing of the past; were he to return in 2015, he might be struck by the diversity of races and cultures in much of urban Britain achieved peacefully.

In some ways his intervention made it more difficult for the government to act – Bill Deedes, veteran politician and journalist, felt at the time that by speaking as he did, Powell made it impossible for the Government to take the necessary action, because to do so would make it look as though it was supporting him.[389] Indeed an expression of sympathy with Powell's views on immigration was still to invite obloquy, as Nigel Hastilow found when deselected as Conservative candidate for Halesowen in 2007.[390] Late in December 2014, prompted by an incautious remark by Nigel Farage, the UKIP leader, a *Daily Telegraph* editorial underlined the enduring impact of Powell's contribution, for it argued: 'The problem of the Birmingham speech is that Enoch Powell used language that alienated many and made it impossible to have a sensible debate on immigration without the person raising it being excoriated.'[391] It is a sadness that so notorious is the speech that its author will forever be remembered for that day in the Midland Hotel, rather than for his vital and unquestioned, if largely unremarked, contribution to the Thatcherite revolution. Like his great Birmingham predecessor, Joseph Chamberlain, one speech in his native city effectively consigned him to the political wilderness.

THE TWENTY-FIRST CENTURY

F or all Mary Beard's pessimism about the future of oratory, noted in the Introduction, two important speeches delivered in Birmingham in the twenty-first century demonstrate the continuing force and influence of this form of communication. Speeches made by Malala Yousafzai in September 2013 and by Prime Minister, David Cameron, in July 2015 show many of the best oratorical qualities explored in the other examples in this book. Attwood, Bright and the Chartist leaders spoke to, and wooed, huge crowds. Latterly our orators addressed more manageable assemblies of the enthusiastic and the already converted. A common feature to all was that of the charisma and the personality of the speaker, expressing itself in the theatrical medium of the platform. The oration was intended to persuade through the logic of the argument, the earnest passion of the speaker, but also through its distillation in a memorable and arresting phrase; as we have seen, in many cases the cause espoused was one of reform or radical change. Nineteenth- and early twentieth-century speakers did not have the benefit of instant visual communication, of television news and YouTube dissemination, but Malala and David Cameron were conscious that telling soundbites lifted from their speeches would reach a wide audience instantaneously. That reach would be more effective, and lasting, than by simply setting out the ideas on paper in an article.

Both chose Birmingham as the location for delivering speeches embodying seriously important ideas which echo issues and preoccupations from Birmingham's past. For Malala the context was straightforward. Shot by the Taliban in Pakistan in retribution for her outspoken criticisms of their negative attitudes to women's education she herself had experienced in her native Swat, she was flown to Birmingham, where doctors saved her.[392] Asked to open the new Library of Birmingham in September 2013, she was presented with a wonderful opportunity to propagate two linked central arguments.[393] In celebrating the preciousness of books in a 'great library' ('a city without a library is like a graveyard'), she stayed true to the pioneering civic ideas of George Dawson over a century earlier. Beyond that, she understood that reading, knowledge and education have a central role in combating extremism – 'pens and books are the weapons that defeat terrorism'. She appealed to all who would listen that children in Nigeria, Syria, Somalia, Pakistan, India and Afghanistan should be helped 'to read and to go to school'. In a ringing, memorable conclusion she pleaded: 'And let us not forget that even one book, one pen, one child and one teacher can change the world.' Again, there are suggestive links back to Birmingham's past, for Chamberlain, Dale and Dawson had made the city the national campaign headquarters for the movement for free elementary education for all in the late 1860s, the National Education League, seeing in education the means to elevate and civilise the working classes.

In Malala's case, the Library was but one element in a wider global struggle, and the significance of what she said in highlighting the educational deprivation of '57 million children (who) are out of school' worldwide resonated beyond Britain. They were part of a personal and heartfelt campaign which demanded that all girls, and indeed children everywhere, be freely educated. This contributed in December 2014 to her being awarded a Nobel Peace Prize.

That the Prime Minister, David Cameron, should come to Birmingham to make one of the most significant speeches on what he termed 'the struggle of our generation', the battle against Islamic extremism, showed both careful calculation and an appreciation of the symbolism of the event.[394] Birmingham had been the site of Enoch Powell's notorious speech in 1968, and has since gone on to play its part in making Britain a 'beacon to the world', exemplifying multi-racial and multi-faith democracy, diversity and opportunity, as the Prime Minister himself put it.

Before Cameron's visit, Birmingham education had been in the spotlight. Some schools had been tainted by association with 'Trojan Horse' infiltration, identified in an inquiry for the government by the former counter-terrorism chief, Peter Clarke in 2014.[395] Clarke had presented evidence that in some schools 'children were being encouraged to accept unquestionably a particularly hardline strand of Sunni Islam'. Other manifestations of extremism he observed included anti-western, anti-US and anti-Israel rhetoric, a segregation dividing the world into 'us' and 'them', a perception of a worldwide conspiracy against Muslims. This report evidently informed some of what David Cameron would say in Birmingham in 2015. Even in the year or so since Peter Clarke published that report, alarm at extremism had grown, as 700 British-born Muslims, some from Birmingham, travelled to Syria to fight for ISIS, the Islamic State of Iraq and Syria, which employed beheadings, bombings, defenestrations and torture in the fight to establish itself. Only a fortnight before Cameron's speech, over thirty British holidaymakers had died in a terrorist atrocity on a beach at Sousse in Tunisia. It was against this background that David Cameron delivered his address. It was presented, like Malala's, at an educational institution, but in this case in a school, Ninestiles Academy, rather than the Library of Birmingham.

His speech exemplified the oratorical qualities already seen in Joseph Chamberlain and Enoch Powell's speeches: a detailed argument, logically and remorselessly delivered. Like those forerunners, and like Bright, this was a long speech (over 35 minutes in duration), demanding concentration and engagement from its listeners. As in the best speeches, that argument was made the more persuasive by intonation and inflexion, for this was, just as it was for Dawson and Dale, for Joseph Chamberlain and for Powell, a performance, designed to convince. For what Cameron said challenged a number of assumptions about Islam and was designed to set government policy on a markedly more proactive course in addressing the causes of radicalisation in Britain.

He condemned from the outset Islamist extremism, seeking to distinguish 'the cultish world view' of people who posed a real threat 'to basic liberal values such as democracy, freedom and sexual equality', from many Muslims in Britain who welcomed those self-same British values. Strong, moderate Muslim voices were drowned out by extremists 'who set the tone of the debate'. He was determined that the government should support Muslim progressives. What was also striking was a new directness on the subject of the dangers of extremism, and about its character. 'To deny (Islamist violence) has anything to do with Islam means you disempower the critical reforming voices', he said. Here the Prime Minister was stretching out the government's hand to those Muslims who wanted to repudiate a religious justification for violence.[396] That directness of approach could be seen when he challenged the misguided notion that out of a surfeit of cultural sensitivity society should soft-pedal on its abhorrence of female genital mutilation, forced marriage, and child sex abuse: 'It sickens me to think that nearly 4000 cases of FGM were reported in our country last year alone, and that there were 11000 cases of honour-based violence over the last five years'. As bluntly he spoke to young Muslims tempted to join the extremists: 'If you are a boy, they will brainwash you, strap bombs to your body and blow you up. If you are a girl, they will enslave and abuse you.'

This, argued *The Spectator*'s Douglas Murray, was a major shift in tone, for the UK government's 'previous warnings about joining ISIS have sounded like a sort of beseeching, a sort of we're better together plea. Much better, as the PM has done, to explain the unvarnished truth.'[397]

In his speech, David Cameron committed his government to challenging the extremists and their rhetoric, partly by a new Extremism Bill and partly through empowering moderate Muslim groups to seize back the initiative, in defining the meaning of Islam, from the 'self-claimed Islamic voice' of extremists. He demanded that 'the ludicrous conspiracy theories' that, for example, blamed Mossad for 9/11, and the British intelligence services for 7/7, and finally alleged that the West is out to destroy Islam, be tackled head-on. He rejected what he called 'the grievance justification' for extremism and the violence it spawns. By banning certain extremist groups, and dealing with those non-violent extremists who helped young people along the journey to radicalisation; by encouraging Internet providers to be much more vigilant of on-line extremist activity and universities to be more discriminating about who they permitted to address students, the Prime Minister signalled his desire to confront the influence of extremists who convert young people to the paths of terror. He finished his speech by arguing that a great deal more needed to be done to address segregation in housing, and in schools, of certain ethnic groups: 'It cannot be right that people can grow up and go to school and hardly ever come into meaningful contact with people from other backgrounds and faiths'. It was for government and local authorities to promote integration and employment, opportunity and through this a greater cohesion.

Political observers concluded that this was a notable speech and although it attracted praise it inevitably drew some criticism, for it challenged the presumption that Islam was invariably a religion of peace, and it called for an end to any misguided indulgence of those different cultural mores which were repellent to British values.[398] In differentiating between the many Muslims who feel attached to British values, and those who have become alienated and espouse violence, and in seeking to involve the peaceable majority in a much more positive way than hitherto, he was suggesting that the defeat of terrorism was as much in the hands of Muslim communities themselves as in those of government.

That a Pashtun schoolgirl should do the honours in opening the splendid new Library of Birmingham and speak to a peaceable multi-ethnic crowd would in all probability have seemed inconceivable to Enoch Powell a generation earlier. His dire prognostications of race violence and spilled blood were evidently wildly inaccurate. David Cameron recognised in his speech the immense success with which communities in Birmingham such as Ninestiles Academy had welcomed different races and religions and made them, in Malala's homely phrase, 'fellow Brummies'. Powell in his 'Rivers of Blood' speech had been concerned that some ethnic groups might remain unintegrated and become alienated and unassimilated. Those problems may have helped foster the extremism that David Cameron sought to address in his own Birmingham speech in 2015. The fullness of its coverage in the media, the degree of scrutiny to which it has been exposed, suggest that many observers sensed in this latest example of Birmingham oratory another watershed moment.

With a couple of honourable Chamberlainite exceptions, the speeches in this book have reflected a provincial voice at times railing against metropolitan myopia. This manifested itself in the nineteenth-century campaigns of Attwood, the Chartists, and Bright for adequate representation for the great conurbations of the industrial Midlands and the North. Later it can be seen in the crusade for Tariff Reform, a particular hobbyhorse of the West Midlands manufacturing classes. Enoch Powell's frustrations owed much to his feeling that the Establishment in London understood nothing of the everyday lives of his Midlands constituents. Yet by 2015 there was a marked difference; Malala was an international figure, arguably the most famous schoolgirl in the world. Her speech enunciated a universal rather than a provincial message, that peace and above all education and books should be the right of every child in even the poorest, and the most unenlightened, countries of the world. Birmingham was her platform.

Whilst it is true that another Prime Minister, Neville Chamberlain, anticipated David Cameron by coming to Birmingham to announce a significant new policy (the reluctant decision to abandon Appeasement in March 1939), in a sense that was perfectly understandable; he spoke in his own Edgbaston constituency, and was fulfilling a Conservative Party engagement long in the diary. What was especially important about David Cameron's Prime Ministerial speech was that he quite deliberately chose to make it in Birmingham, a city with a long history of building multi-racial and multi-faith communities, and yet also a city with the experience of the difficulties and challenges which needed to be addressed to sustain that achievement. Much of this book tells the story of Birmingham's forceful provincial voice seeking to convert the metropolitan Establishment to a series of radical causes; in a recognition of the city's continuing significance and relevance it ends with the country's Prime Minister coming to Birmingham and using it as a platform to launch a major national policy initiative.

TIMELINE OF EVENTS

1829   Foundation of the Birmingham Political Union – Thomas Attwood prominent.

1830   Death of George IV, accession of William IV, and resignation of Wellington's government. Grey becomes PM.

1831   First Reform Bill, in March, rejected by the Lords in October.

1832   Thomas Attwood's speech on Reform at Newhall Hill, May; Days of May after Lords again reject new Reform Bill; Reform Bill passed June.

1837   Accession of Queen Victoria.

1838   Charter drafted by London Working Men's Association; Attwood addresses Reform meeting in Glasgow. BPU revived. Speeches at Holloway Head, Birmingham by Attwood and Feargus O'Connor.

1839   Chartist Convention moves to Birmingham, May; Bull Ring protests and riots - speech by Edward Brown.

1841   Robert Peel becomes Prime Minister; Anti-Corn Law League campaign underway in Manchester led by Cobden and Bright.

1846   Peel's administration repeals the Corn Laws.

1847   George Dawson founds the Church of the Saviour in Edward Street.

1848   Last phase of Chartism.

1853   Robert Dale becomes Minister at Carr's Lane Congregational Church.

1854   Britain goes to war in the Crimea until 1856.

1855   Lord Palmerston, John Bright's *bête noir*, becomes Prime Minister.

1857   John Bright is defeated in Manchester but elected in Birmingham at the General Election.

1858   John Bright makes his inaugural speech, on parliamentary reform, to his new constituents in Birmingham.

1866   George Dawson's speech at the opening of Birmingham's Library; Gladstone's Reform Bill precipitates Liberal Party rebellion and fall of the Liberal government. Derby/Disraeli now head a Conservative Government.

1867   Disraeli's Second Reform Bill passed; Robert Dale's sermon on the obligation of Birmingham's rich and influential to show civic leadership.

1868   William Gladstone becomes Prime Minister for the first time.

1869   National Education League founded in Birmingham.

1873   Joseph Chamberlain becomes Mayor of Birmingham, presiding over a dramatic programme of civic improvement.

1876   Chamberlain becomes a Liberal MP for Birmingham.

1877 Chamberlain and other local Liberals found the National Liberal Federation in Birmingham.

1880 William Gladstone's Second Ministry; Chamberlain becomes President of the Board of Trade.

1885 Chamberlain announces his Unauthorised Programme of Radical reform. Gladstone's government falls; Lord Salisbury succeeds with a Conservative minority government. Liberal General Election victory, December.

1886 Gladstone forms a Third Ministry; Chamberlain a reluctant and short-lived member. Gladstone's Home Rule Bill; Chamberlain announces his opposition with his Birmingham speech. Home Rule Bill defeated; Liberals split between Gladstonians and Liberal Unionists.

1888 Chamberlain creates the Birmingham Liberal Unionist Association.

1889 By-election in Birmingham Central on the death of John Bright sees victory for Chamberlain's Liberal Unionists, confirming his control over the West Midlands 'Duchy', which is to be his power base until his death.

1895 Chamberlain becomes Colonial Secretary in Salisbury's government.

1899 Boer War to 1902.

1901 Death of Queen Victoria.

1903 Chamberlain announces his commitment to Tariff Reform in Birmingham in May, precipitating his resignation from the Cabinet, and the start of deep Conservative Party division, Free Traders v. Tariff Reformers.

1906 Liberal landslide in the General Election in January; Birmingham remains a Unionist stronghold. Chamberlain's stroke ends his active political career.

1914 – 1918 First World War.

1918 Oswald Mosley becomes a new Conservative MP.

1924 Mosley joins Labour Party and fights Neville Chamberlain in Ladywood in the General Election.

1925 Mosley's Birmingham speech outlines a new and vigorous approach to unemployment, the essence of his *Birmingham Proposals*. The Locarno Treaties, greatly stabilising Europe, were signed in December by which Germany recognised its frontiers with France and Belgium, along with the demilitarised Rhineland. This was guaranteed by Britain and Italy. Germany was readmitted to the League of Nations.

1926 Mosley active and influential in Birmingham trade unions' strike committee in General Strike. Mosley elected in Smethwick by-election in December after an acrimonious press campaign.

1929 Mosley becomes Chancellor of the Duchy of Lancaster, in Ramsay Macdonald's new Labour Government, sharing responsibility with J.H. Thomas for solving unemployment.

1930 Mosley resigns from government over Labour Government paralysis over unemployment.

1931 Mosley leaves the Labour Party to found the New Party, which is annihilated in the October General Election.

1932 Neville Chamberlain, now Chancellor of the Exchequer in Macdonald's National (Coalition) Government, introduces Import Duties Bill to complete his father's unfinished Tariff Reform business.

1933 Adolf Hitler comes to power in Germany.

1937 Neville Chamberlain becomes Prime Minister committed to a policy of Appeasement.

1938 Hitler achieves *Anschluss*, German union with Austria. Chamberlain flies three times to Germany (lastly to Munich) in September to negotiate a peaceable transfer of Sudeten Czech territory to Germany.

1939 Hitler invades the rest of Czechoslovakia and takes Prague in March. Chamberlain makes his speech in Birmingham abandoning Appeasement. In September war is declared on Germany.

1945 End of the Second World War; Labour government in power under Clement Attlee.

1957 Enoch Powell becomes a Treasury minister under Conservative Prime Minister Harold Macmillan.

1958 Powell resigns over the Prime Minister's economic policy.

1960 Powell becomes Minister of Health.

1963 Powell resigns when Macmillan is replaced by Alec Douglas-Home.

1968 Powell makes his notorious 'Rivers of Blood' immigration/race relations speech in Birmingham.

1974 He urges the electorate to vote Labour.

2012 In October Malala is shot by Taliban gunmen in North West Pakistan and flown to Birmingham's Queen Elizabeth Hospital for surgery and recuperation.

2013 Malala makes her speech on the universal right to education for children everywhere at the Opening of the Library of Birmingham.

2014 Malala is awarded a Nobel Peace Prize.

2014 Report on 'Trojan Horse' infiltration of some Birmingham schools.

2015 Prime Minister David Cameron's speech on Muslim extremism at Ninestiles Academy in Birmingham.

GLOSSARY OF POLITICAL TERMS

Appeasement: a term with several connotations. For many years after 1918 it was seen as constructive negotiation with disaffected countries, to endeavour peaceably to ameliorate a justifiable sense of grievance. Under Neville Chamberlain in the late 1930s it came to be a term of opprobrium, seen as craven and ignoble surrender to the bullying of foreign powers.

Boroughmongers: rich and influential men (usually aristocratic) who to all intents and purposes owned boroughs with small or corruptible electorates, allowing them to nominate their own candidates for election.

Charter (whose proponents were **Chartists**): a programme of six points for the reform of Parliament. They were: universal manhood suffrage; vote by secret ballot; equal electoral districts; payment for MPs; an end to the property qualification for MPs; and annual Parliaments.

Civic gospel: a philosophy of municipal activism propounded and developed in Birmingham. The great town or city was thought of as a moral and improving entity whose responsibility was for the physical and cultural well-being of its citizens.

Conservative Party: Sir Robert Peel sought in 1834 with his Tamworth Manifesto to signal a shift in his party from simple Tory opposition to all political and constitutional change. He gave the Tory party a new name. He called then for the 'reform of proven abuses', and his brand of Conservatism in his Ministry from 1841 to 1846 exemplified that willingness to adapt, change and improve according to necessity and circumstance. This was seen most notably in his recognition that the Corn Laws protected the landed classes, whilst consigning everyone else to expensive food and often to hardship – he repealed them in 1846. Disraeli, another Conservative leader illustrated that openness to reform when he pushed through a dramatic and extensive Parliamentary Reform Act in 1867.

Distribution of seats: constituencies were either borough or county seats; many of the boroughs had gained representation in the Middle Ages or in the reign of Elizabeth I. Every county had at least two seats. From 1832, Reform Acts began to address the inequitability of small (often corrupt or aristocratically controlled) boroughs representing a handful of voters whilst large new towns were unrepresented; by 1885 the process of equalising electoral districts was well advanced.

Duchy: a term applied from the late 1880s to Joseph Chamberlain's West Midlands sphere of political control, the seven Birmingham constituencies and those constituencies from neighbouring Warwickshire, Worcestershire and Staffordshire which abutted Birmingham. This fiefdom became an impregnable Unionist fortress up to 1914 and beyond.

Enfranchisement: the granting of the right to vote to those hitherto excluded.

Fair Trade: a movement from the early 1880s calling for an end in Britain to Free Trade (the import of goods without customs and excise); supporters of Fair Trade wanted tariffs on imported goods from countries which penalised British exports, and an end to the dumping of cheap foreign goods on British markets.

Fascism: a movement of radical, authoritarian, nationalism after the First World War, originating in Italy as a reaction to the failure of the liberal democracies in bringing about the war in 1914. Fascist governments would be totalitarian dictatorships. In Britain in the 1930s Oswald Mosley founded a fascist party which echoed continental fascist movements, notably those of Hitler and Mussolini.

Franchise: the right to vote.

Home Rule: the demand, taken up by Gladstone in 1886, that rather than be allowed full independence, Ireland be permitted to have its own Parliament and govern herself, whilst remaining ultimately subject, in the key areas of foreign policy and defence, to the Imperial Parliament at Westminster. Gladstone failed to carry his proposals into law. In the end in 1922 Southern Ireland gained complete, unfettered independence.

Householder suffrage: granting the vote to those who either owned or rented houses of a defined annual value.

Jacobin: a supporter of the Leftist French Revolutionaries who inaugurated the Terror. In English politics the term was usually applied to those holding extreme anti-monarchy and anti-property views.

Keynesianism: an economic theory developed by the Cambridge economist John Maynard Keynes during and after the First World War, which held that the imperfections in an economy should be corrected by government action; for example, in a recession the government could stimulate demand by welfare payments or employment schemes, for as individuals start to earn money their spending will stimulate an increased demand. The government would borrow to finance these schemes.

Labour: the Labour Party was founded in 1900 bringing together early socialist parties with many trade unions, which recognised the wisdom of having a voice in Parliament. The fledgling party made rapid strides – 40 seats in Parliament in 1906, and by 1924 it had sufficient to allow it to form its first (minority) government under Ramsay Macdonald.

League of Nations: an inter-governmental organisation set up by the Paris Peace Conference in 1920 with a mission of promoting and establishing world peace. Its permanent headquarters was in Geneva. It was weakened from the outset by the refusal of the USA to join and by lack of support from Russia and Germany; whilst it could apply sanctions, its lack of a military capability rendered it impotent in some of the major inter-war crises.

Liberal Party: created in 1859 bringing together Whigs, Radicals and Peelites (the remnants of Robert Peel's followers after the Conservative Party split in 1846 over Corn Law Repeal), it was a formidable electoral force appealing especially to those who sought a high-minded moral programme and to those who felt themselves unjustly excluded from the Victorian establishment; it dominated politics until 1886 and the split over Home Rule. It achieved much for nonconformists by undermining the Anglican monopoly at Oxford and Cambridge and in Ireland, as well as attacking privilege in the Civil Service and the Army. For much of the last half of the nineteenth century the Liberal Party followed followed the goals of its charismatic leader, William Gladstone, for example, in his mission to pacify Ireland.

Liberal Unionist: in 1886 the Liberal Party split over its leader's (William Gladstone's) support for Home Rule for Ireland. The Liberal rebels were led by Lord Hartington, an aristocratic Whig, and Joseph Chamberlain, leader of the Radicals. Rebels were united by the idea of preserving the Union of Ireland with the rest of Britain, fearing Home Rule was the first stage in the dissolution of the Empire. The Liberal Unionists formed a significant fourth (or indeed, in light of the 80 or so seats of the Irish Nationalists – third) party in the Commons with over 70 MPs in the 1895 General Election. By 1914 they had merged with the Conservative and Unionist Party to fight the Home Rule Act passed in that year.

Manhood suffrage: (often called universal manhood suffrage). A vote for every man, whether he had property or not. Despite the campaigning efforts of Mary Wollstonecraft in the 1790s and John Stuart Mill in 1866 on behalf of women, universal manhood suffrage continued to be a demand made solely for all men, until late in the nineteenth century.

Multiculturalism: a state of cultural diversity with a cultural mosaic of different ethnic and religious ideas and values co-existing in society.

Multiracism: a society where a number of races co-exist.

Nonconformists: (sometimes dubbed Dissenters). They were non-Anglican Protestants, worshipping in churches without bishops and the diocesan organisation of the Established church – the foremost nonconformist churches were Baptist, Congregationalist, Methodist and Unitarian.

Radicals: often linked to the nonconformists, Radicals campaigned for fundamental reform to Britain's institutions – reform of Parliament, of education, of national economic policy, of taxation, and of social legislation (on Poverty and on Slavery).

Secret ballot: until 1872 votes in British elections were conducted openly, in many cases therefore being open to 'suasion' (persuasion), or simple bribery. John Bright was the foremost campaigner for the vote to be conducted in secret, which would make the process of election more seemly and less open to bribery and corruption.

Tariff Reform: was the campaign for an end to Free Trade, at the start of the twentieth century, framed and articulated by Joseph Chamberlain in Birmingham and taken up nationally by a significant number of enthusiasts, who feared British industry and agriculture was suffering a possibly terminal decline, in a world where other countries were erecting tariff barriers against our exports.

Whig: a party of aristocrats and moneyed middle classes representing the desire of industrialists and Dissenters in the eighteenth and nineteenth centuries for political and social change through reform of Parliament, and to tackle the monopoly and privilege of the Anglican church. After 1860 the Whigs formed a prominent part of the Liberal Party.

NOTES

Introduction

1. Briggs, A., *Victorian People* (London, Odhams, 1954), pp. 205-239.
2. Reekes, A., 'Birmingham Exceptionalism, Joseph Chamberlain and the 1906 General Election', (unpublished M.Res. thesis, University of Birmingham, 2014). See also Lawrence J., *Speaking for the People* (Cambridge, CUP, 1998), esp. p. 181 on the 'use of physical force, a central and widely tolerated element in popular politics'.
3. Bryman, A., *Religion in the Birmingham Area: Essays in the Sociology of Religion* (Birmingham, University of Birmingham Institute, 1975).
4. Beard, M., 'Have Modern Politicians Lost the Art of Rhetoric?' *BBC* Politics, www.bbc.co.uk/news/uk-politics31128840, 6 February 2015.
5. Chase, M., *Chartism – A New History* (Manchester, MUP, 2007), pp. 41-45.
6. *Birmingham Daily Mail*, 18 January 1906; Thackeray, D., *Conservatism for the Democratic Age* (Manchester, MUP, 2013), pp. 19-25.

Chapter 1: Thomas Attwood and the Birmingham Political Union

7. Quoted by Briggs A., 'Thomas Attwood and the Economic Background of the Birmingham Political Union', in *Collected Essays Volume One* (The Harvester Press, Brighton, 1985), p. 138; on Grey and Attwood see Moss, D., *Thomas Attwood* (McGill-Queen's University Press, Canada, 1990), p. 210.
8. Briggs, A., *op.cit.*, p. 138.
9. For George Edmonds, see Thomas, S.'s entry on George Edmonds in *Oxford Dictionary of National Biography*, OUP, 2013; quote on Attwood, Briggs, A., 'The Background of the Parliamentary Reform Movement in Three English Cities', in *Collected Essays Volume One* (The Harvester Press, Brighton, 1985), p. 187.
10. See: Moss, D., *op.cit.*, pp. 34-50; Behagg, C.'s entry on Thomas Attwood in *Oxford Dictionary of National Biography*, OUP, 2013; Briggs, A., *op.cit.*, pp. 142-149.
11. Hurd, D., *Robert Peel* (Weidenfeld and Nicolson, London, 2007), pp. 50-51.
12. See Moss, D., *op.cit.*, pp. 57-59.
13. *Report of the Proceedings of the Town's Meeting in Support of Parliamentary Reform*, 13 December 1830.
14. Briggs, A., *History of Birmingham, vol. ii* (OUP, Oxford, 1952), pp. 31-86.
15. Evans, E., *Parliamentary Reform, c. 1770-1918* (Longman, London, 2000), pp. 1-18.
16. Moss, D., *op.cit.*, pp. 77-99; Thomas, S., George Edmonds.
17. Pearce, E., *Reform! The Fight for the 1832 Reform Act* (Jonathan Cape, London, 2003), p. 209.
18. Moss, D., *op.cit.*, pp.,152-161; Briggs, A., *op.cit.*, p. 187.
19. *Report of the Proceedings at the Meeting of the Inhabitants of Birmingham Monday 25th January 1830 for the Establishment of a General Political Union*.
20. Brock, M., *The Great Reform Act* (Hutchinson, London, 1973), pp. 230-267.
21. Brock, M., *op.cit.*, pp. 77-79.
22. Moss, D., *op.cit.*, pp. 201-211.
23. LoPatin, N., 'Ritual, Symbolism and Radical Rhetoric: Political Unions and Political Identity in the Age of Parliamentary Reform', *Journal of Victorian Culture* 1998, vol.,3 i, pp.,1-16.
24. *Report of the Proceedings of the Great Meeting of the Inhabitants of the Midlands Districts held at Birmingham, May 7th 1832*.
25. Vernon, J., *Politics and the People* (CUP, Cambridge, 1993), p. 108.
26. LoPatin, N., *op.cit.*, p. 16.
27. Brock, M., *op.cit.*, pp. 296-7.
28. Moss, D., *op.cit.*, pp. 215-226.
29. *Report of the Proceedings of the Inhabitants of Birmingham held at Newhall Hill on May 16th 1832 to present an Address to Earl Grey on his Reinstatement to Office*.

Chapter 2: Birmingham and the early Chartists

30. Gammage, R.G., *History of the Chartist Movement* (this edition, Routledge, London, 1970), p. 9.
31. For the social and economic interpretation see Briggs, A., *Chartist Studies* (Macmillan, London, 1959), pp. 1-28; for the political interpretation see Stedman Jones, G., 'The Language of Chartism' in *The Chartist Experience* ed. Epstein, J., and Thompson, D., (Macmillan, London, 1982), pp. 3-58; for an historiographical overview see Taylor, M., 'Rethinking the Chartists. Searching for Synthesis in the Historiography of Chartism', *The Historical Journal* 39, 2 (1996), pp. 479-495. Thompson, D., *Early Chartists*, (London 1971), pp. 12-13.
32. *Hansard*, 12 July 1839.
33. Briggs, A., *op.cit.*, pp. 22-24.
34. Chase, M., *Chartism: A New History* (MUP, Manchester, 2007), p. 63.
35. Behagg, C., 'An Alliance with the Middle Class: the Birmingham Political Union and Early Chartism', in *The*

Chartist Experience ed. Epstein, J., and Thompson, D., (Macmillan, London, 1982), p. 65.

36 Behagg, C., *op.cit.*, p. 74.

37 Chase, M., *op.cit.*, pp. 1-22.

38 Hovell, M., *The Chartist Movement* (Manchester, MUP, 1918), p. 107.

39 Chase,M., *op.cit.*, p. 32.

40 *Birmingham Journal*, 11 August 1838.

41 *The Times*, 8 August 1838.

42 *Birmingham Journal*, 11 August 1838.

43 Tholfsen, T.,'The Chartist Crisis in Birmingham', *International Review of Social History* 1958 vol.3, issue 3, pp. 461-480.

44 *Borough of Birmingham Report of the Committee Appointed by the Town Council to Investigate the Causes of the Late Riots*, (Birmingham 1840), p. 4.

45 *Northern Star*, 18 May 1839, quoting a report 'From the Sun'.

46 Chase, M., *op.cit.*, pp. 61-62.

47 *Northern Star*, 8 May 1839.

48 *Northern Star*, 30 March 1839.

49 Cited by Tholfsen, T., 'The Chartist Crisis', *op.cit.*, p. 467.

50 Edsall, N.,'Varieties of Radicalism', *The Historical Journal* 1973 vol.16, no.1.

51 Behagg, C., *op.cit.*, p. 66.

52 Taylor, D., 'To the Bull Ring! Politics, Protest and Policing in Birmingham During the Chartist Period', (unpublished M.Res thesis, the University of Birmingham, 2014). p. 50.

53 Belchem, J., 'Radical Language and Ideology in Early Nineteenth Century England: the Challenge of the Platform'. *Albion*, vol.20, no.2, Summer 1988, p. 257.

54 Taylor, D., *op.cit.*, p. 6.

55 The Municipal Corporations Act of 1835 was designed to break the historic organs of local government, often corrupt and generally inadequate in fast-growing industrial towns, by creating democratically elected corporations. Towns had to apply to Parliament for the necessary enabling legislation and the franchise was exclusive, confined to the payers of the poor rate, in Birmingham but 1/8th of the adult population.

56 Behagg, C., *op.cit.*, p. 79.

57 Tholfsen, T., *op.cit.*, p. 466.

58 Ward, R., *City State and Nation – Birmingham's Political History 1830 – 1940* (Phillimore, Chichester, 2005), pp.43-47.

59 Chase, M., *op.cit.*, p. 4.

60 Pearce, E., ed., *The Diaries of Charles Greville* (Pimlico, London, 2005). This entry, 1 January 1839, p. 178.

61 Chase, M., *op.cit.*, p. 97.

62 See Stedman Jones, G., *op.cit.*, p. 51; Hilton, B., *A Mad, Bad and Dangerous People?* (OUP, Oxford, 2007), p. 619.

63 See Moss, D., *Thomas Attwood* (McGill, Canada, 1990), pp. 297-305; Cole, G.D.H. *Chartist Portraits* (Macmillan, London, 1941), pp. 327-335; Tholfsen, T., *op.cit.*, p. 479.

Chapter 3: Bright and Birmingham

64 Quinault, R., 'John Bright and Joseph Chamberlain', *Historical Journal* 28, vol. 3, p. 623.

65 Fraser, D., 'John Bright', *Urban History* vol. 8, May 1988, p. 188.

66 Robbins, K., *John Bright* (Routledge, London, 1979), pp. 130-131.

67 Leighton, D., 'Municipal Progress, Democracy and Radical Identity in Birmingham 1838-1886', *Midland History* vol.25, June 2000, pp. 116-117.

68 Hennock, E.P., *Fit and Proper Persons* (Edward Arnold, London, 1973), p. 148.

69 Robbins, K., *John Bright*, p. 132.

70 Robertson, W., *The Life and Times of the Right Hon. John Bright* (Cassell, London, 1884), vol. v, p. 57.

71 Holton, S., 'John Bright, Radical Politics and the Ethos of Quakerism', *Albion*, vol. 34, no. 4 (2002), pp. 584-605.

72 Briggs, A., *Victorian People* (Odhams, London, 1954), pp. 205-239.

73 Taylor, M., 'John Bright', entry in *Oxford Dictionary of National Biography* (Oxford, 2014).

74 McCord, N., *The Anti-Corn Law League* (George Allen and Unwin, London, 1958), p. 171.

75 McCord, N., *op.cit.*, p. 123.

76 Taylor, N., *op.cit.*

77 Walling, R.,(ed.) *The Diaries of John Bright* (Hathi Trust Digital Library), 4 Nov. 1854, p. 178.

78 Ausubel, H., *John Bright, Victorian Reformer* (Wiley and Sons, NY, USA, 1966), p. 74.

79 Ausubel, H., *op.cit.*, p. 76 quoting a letter from Cobden to Bright 11 August 1857, Cobden MSS.

80 Briggs, *op.cit.*, p.209.

81 Evans, E., *Parliamentary Reform, c.1770-1918* (Longman, London, 2000), pp. 37-43.

82 Joyce, P., *Democratic Subjects* (CUP, Cambridge, 1994), p. 100.

83 'The Cave of Adullam', 'everyone that was in distress and everyone that was in debt, and everyone that was discontented, *1 Samuel, chapter 22, verse 2.*

84 Ausubel, H., *op.cit.*, p. 74.

85 Trevelyan, G.M., *The Life of John Bright* (London 1913), p. 1.

86 Joyce, P., *op.cit.*, p. 105.

87 Joyce, P., *op.cit.*, p. 94.

88 Walling, R., *op.cit.*, p. 234.

89 *The Times*, 28 October 1858.

90 Cash, B., *John Bright, Statesman and Orator* (I.B.Tauris, London, 2012), pp. 78-79 quoting Trevelyan and Dale.

91 Burn, W.L., *The Age of Equipoise* (George Allen and Unwin, London, 1964), p. 149.

92 Vince, C., *John Bright* (London, Blackie, 1898), p. 103; p. 94.

93 Ausubel, H., *op.cit.*, p. 120.

94 Ausubel, H., *op.cit.*, p. 153.

95 Blake, R., *Disraeli* (Methuen, London 1966), p. 477.

96 Vince, C., *op.cit.*, pp. 121 ff.

97 Quinault, R., *op.cit.*, p. 626.

98 Quinault, R., *op.cit.*, p. 626.

99 Walling, R., *op.cit.*, p. 536.

100 Bounous, P., 'Bright for Birmingham?' (unpublished M.A. dissertation for the University of Birmingham, 2011).

101 Bounous, P., *op.cit.*, p. 40.

102 Joyce, P., *op.cit.*, pp. 138-143.

103 Quinault, R., *op.cit.*, p. 625.

Chapter 4: Dale, Dawson and the Civic Gospel

104 Marsh, P., *Joseph Chamberlain – Entrepreneur in Politics* (Yale, USA, 1994), pp. 78-94.

105 Ward, R., *City-State and Nation* (Phillimore, Chichester, 2005), p. 78.

106 Hennock, E.P., *Fit and Proper Persons* (Arnold, London, 1973), pp. 117, 125, 127-8; Jones, L., 'Public Pursuit of Private Profit?: Liberal Businessmen and Municipal Politics in Birmingham, 1865-1900', *Business History*, 25/3, 1983, pp. 240-259.

107 Hennock, E.P., *op.cit.*, p. 154.

108 Hennock, E.P., *op.cit.*, pp. 80-93.

109 Hennock, E.P., *op.cit.*, p. 157.

110 Wright Wilson, *The Life of George Dawson* (Percival Jones, Birmingham, 1905) p.149.

111 Mole, D., 'Attitudes of Churchmen towards Society in Early Victorian Birmingham' in ed. Bryman, A., *Religion in the Birmingham Area – Essays in the Sociology of Religion* (University of Birmingham, Birmingham, 1977).

112 Hennock, E.P., op.cit., p. 67; Dale, A.W.W., *Life of R.W. Dale of Birmingham* (Hodder and Stoughton, London, 1898), p. 249.

113 Wright Wilson, *The Life of George Dawson* (Percival Jones, Birmingham, 1905), p. 94.

114 Jones, L., *op.cit.*, p. 244.

115 Dale, A.W.W., 'George Dawson' in ed. Muirhead, J.H., *Nine Famous Birmingham Men – Lectures Delivered in the University of Birmingham* (Cornish Bros., Birmingham, 1909), p. 75.

116 Dale, R., 'George Dawson', *Nineteenth Century* II p. 49.

117 Wright Wilson, *op.cit.*, pp. 107-108.

118 Dale, A.W.W., 'George Dawson', *op.cit.*, p. 95.

119 Wright Wilson, *op.cit.*, p. 149.

120 Wright Wilson, *op.cit.*, pp. 149-150.

121 *Inaugural Address by George Dawson*, MA, Borough of Birmingham, Opening of the Free Reference Library, 26 October 1866 (Birmingham, E.C.Osborne, 1866).

122 Dale, A.W.W., 'George Dawson', *op.cit.*, p. 101.

123 Dale, A.W.W.,'George Dawson', *op.cit.*, p. 100.

124 Wright Wilson, *op.cit.*, p. 94.

125 Wright Wilson, *op.cit.*, p. 150.

126 Dale, A.W.W., 'George Dawson', *op.cit.*, p. 106.

127 Wright Wilson, *op.cit.*, p. 148.

128 Dale, A.W.W., *Life of R.W. Dale* (London, Hodder and Stoughton, 1898) p.249.

129 Horne, C.S., 'R.W.Dale', in ed. Muirhead, J.H., *Nine Famous Birmingham Men – Lectures Delivered in the University of*

Birmingham (Cornish Bros., Birmingham, 1909), p. 273.

[130] Dale, A.W.W., *Life of R.W. Dale, op.cit.*, p. 254.

[131] Dale, A.W.W., *op.cit.*, pp. 278-279.

[132] The Radicals did take advantage of the Forster Act from 1873, when they dominated the Birmingham School Board elections; they then set about building many new schools.

[133] *Op.cit.*, pp. 280-281.

[134] Thomson, D., 'R.W.Dale and the Civic Gospel', in ed. Sell, A., *Protestant Nonconformists and the West Midlands of England: papers presented at the First Conference of the Association of Denominational History Societies and Cognate Libraries* (Keele University Press, Keele, 1996).

[135] Quoted by Dale, A.W.W., *op.cit.*, p. 414.

[136] Quoted by Dale, A.W.W., *op.cit.*, p. 398.

[137] Hennock, E.P., *op.cit.*, p. 162.

[138] Hennock, E.P. *op.cit.*, p. 158, quoting 'The Perils and Uses of Rich Men', R.W.Dale, *Week-Day Sermons*, pp. 175-6.

[139] Dale, A.A.W., *op.cit.*, p. 417.

[140] Dale, A.W.W. *op.cit.*, pp. 403-404.

[141] Boyd, C.W., *Mr. Chamberlain's Speeches* (London, Constable, 1914), vol. 1, p. 55.

[142] Hennock, E.P., *op.cit.*, p. 172.

[143] Jones, L., *op.cit.*, p. 254.

[144] Auspos, P., 'Radicalism, Pressure Groups and Party Politics', *Journal of British Studies*, 20 (1980), pp. 184-204.

[145] Dale, A.W.W., *op.cit.*, pp. 411-412.

Chapter 5: Joseph Chamberlain and Political Survival

[146] Ward, R., *The Chamberlains – Joseph, Austen and Neville, 1836-1940* (Fonthill Media, 2015), p. 9.

[147] See Marsh, P., *Joseph Chamberlain, Entrepreneur in Politics* (Yale, USA, 1994), pp. 10-131; Crosby. T., *Joseph Chamberlain, A Most Radical Imperialist* (I.B.Tauris, London 2011), pp. 7-38.

[148] See Matthew, H., *Gladstone 1809-1874* (OUP, Oxford, 1988), pp. 168-230; Matthew, H., *Gladstone 1875-1898* (Clarendon Press, Oxford, 1995), pp. 99-210; Shannon, R., *Gladstone, Heroic Minister 1865-1898* (Allen Lane, London, 1999), pp. 62-156; pp. 258-364.

[149] Howard, C.H.D., 'Joseph Chamberlain and the Unauthorised Programme', *English Historical Review* 1950 vol. LXV, p. 477.

[150] *The Times*, 6 January 1885.

[151] Quoted by Shannon, R., *op.cit.*, p. 429.

[152] Marsh. P., *op.cit.*, p. 223.

[153] Magnus, P., *Gladstone* (John Murray, London, 1954), p. 193.

[154] Gladstone on 22 October 1868 in a speech at Wigan compared the Protestant Ascendancy in Ireland to 'some tall tree of noxious growth, lifting its head to Heaven and poisoning the atmosphere of the land so far as its shadow can extend'. (Magnus, P., *Gladstone*, John Murray, London, 1954), p. 193.

[155] Smith, J., *Britain and Ireland – From Home Rule to Independence* (Longman, Harlow, 2000), p. 28.

[156] Matthew, H., *Gladstone 1875-1898*, p. 235-254.

[157] Marsh, P., *op.cit.*, p. 233.

[158] Letter from Powell Williams, J. to Joseph Chamberlain, 11 May 1886, JC 5/72/4, Special Collections, University of Birmingham.

[159] Letter Schnadhorst, F. to Joseph Chamberlain, 15 April 1886, JC 5/63/15, Special Collections, University of Birmingham.

[160] Hurst, M.C. 'Joseph Chamberlain and West Midlands Politics, 1886-1895', *Dugdale Occasional Papers* No.15 1962, pp. 15-18.

[161] Ward, R., *The Chamberlains; Joseph, Austen and Neville, 1836-1940* (Fonthill Media, 2015), p.14, and quoting Garvin, J.L., *The Life of Joseph Chamberlain Vol 1* (London, Macmillan, 1932), p. 58.

[162] Lucy, H.W., *A Diary of the Salisbury Parliament, 1886-1892*, quoted in Garvin, J.L., *The Life of Joseph Chamberlain, vol. ii* (Macmillan, London, 1933), p. 358.

[163] *The Times*, Thursday 22 April 1886; Garvin, J.L., *The Life of Joseph Chamberlain, vol. ii 1885-1895* (Macmillan, London 1933), pp. 212-216.

[164] Ward, R., *City State and Nation* (Phillimore, Chichester, 2005), p. 95.

[165] Garvin, J.L., *op.cit.*, p. 215.

[166] Correspondence between Chamberlain, J. and Labouchere, H.,Special Collections, University of Birmingham, JC 5/50/69-88.

[167] Letter from Chamberlain, J. to Dilke, C., quoted by Cawood, I., The Liberal Unionist Party – A History (I.B.Tauris, London, 2012), p. 28.

168 Hurst, M.C., *op.cit.*, p. 26.

169 *Gridiron*, 22 January 1881 quoted by Ward, R., in an unpublished paper 'The Strange Death of Liberal Birmingham'.

170 Tuckwell, W., *Reminiscences of a Radical Parson* pp.59-60, quoted in Garvin, *op.cit.*, p. 255.

171 Marsh, P., *op.cit.*, p. 253.

172 Hurst, M.C., 'Joseph Chamberlain, the Conservatives and the Succession to John Bright, 1886-1889', *The Historical Journal* volume 7, issue 1 p. 70.

173 Hurst, M.C. *op.cit.*, p. 78.

174 Garvin, *op.cit.*, p. 278.

175 Marsh, *op.cit.*, p. 285.

176 Marsh, P., *op.cit.*, p. 274.

177 Garvin, *op.cit.*, p. 427.

178 Quoted in Hurst, M.C. *Dugdale Occasional Papers* No. 15, *op.cit.*, p. 50.

179 Hurst, *The Historical Journal*, volume 7, *op.cit.*, p. 90.

180 JC6/2/1/18, 11 April 1889 Letter Powell Williams to Chamberlain.

181 Hurst, M.C., *Dugdale Occasional Papers*, No. 15 *op.cit.*, p. 50.

182 Cawood, I, *The Liberal Unionist Party – A History* (I.B.Tauris, London, 2012), p. 125.

183 Cawood, I., *op.cit.*, p. 199.

184 Garvin, *op.cit.*, p. 442.

185 Cawood, I., *op.cit.*, pp. 125-145.

Chapter 6: Joseph Chamberlain and Tariff Reform

186 Amery, J., *Joseph Chamberlain and the Tariff Reform Campaign – The Life of Joseph Chamberlain Volume Five 1901-1903* (Macmillan, London, 1969), pp. 192, 195.

187 The publication of *The Ninety-Five Theses* in Wittenberg, Saxony, by Martin Luther in October 1517, an assault on the practices associated with Indulgences, and more generally on the abuses of Papal power, is generally thought to have triggered the Protestant Reformation in Germany.

188 Zebel, S.H., 'Joseph Chamberlain and the Genesis of Tariff Reform', *Journal of British Studies*, vol.7, no.1, p.133.

189 Those debates particularly concerned the extension of British rule into Uganda, East Africa.

190 Jay, R., *Joseph Chamberlain* (Clarendon Press, Oxford, 1981), p. 194.

191 Cain,P., 'The Conservative Party and Radical Conservatism, 1880-1914, Incubus or Necessity?', *Twentieth Century British History*, 1996, vol.7, issue 3, p. 476.

192 Boyd, .C.W. ed. *Mr. Chamberlain's Speeches* (Constable, London, 1914), volume ii, p. 294; Marsh,P., *Joseph Chamberlain, Entrepreneur in Politics* (Yale, New Haven and London 1994), p. 613.

193 Thompson, A., 'Joseph Chamberlain and Tariff Reform', *Historical Journal*, 40, vol.4 (1997), p. 1035.

194 Cain, P., 'The Political Economy in Edwardian England', in O'Day, ed., *The Edwardian Age* (Macmillan, London, 1979), p. 40.

195 Letter, Joseph Chamberlain (JC) to Devonshire, 21 September 1903. Special Collections, University of Birmingham, JC 18/18/47.

196 Sykes, A., *Tariff Reform in British Politics 1903-1913* (OUP, Oxford, 1979), p. 62.

197 Cain, P. 'The Political Economy,' *op.cit.*, pp. 36-37.

198 Sykes, A., *op.cit.*, p. 62.

199 Alfred von Tirpitz was German Secretary of State in the Imperial Navy Office from 1897-1916, effectively the architect of the vast expansion of the German navy designed to challenge British naval hegemony at the start of the 20th century.

200 Sykes, A., *op.cit.*, p. 19.

201 *Monthly Tariff Reform Notes* ed. Vince, C.A., vol. III, 21 November 1905, p. 360.

202 Zebel, S., *op.cit.*, p. 149.

203 Letter, Joseph Chamberlain to Duke of Devonshire, 26 October 1903, Special Collections, University of Birmingham, JC 18/18/48.

204 Letter from Mary Endicott to her mother, 7 October 1902, cited by Amery, J., *op.cit.*, p. 100.

205 Green, E.H.H., *The Crisis of Conservatism* (Routledge, London, 1995), p. 145.

206 Sykes, A., *op.cit.*, p. 288.

207 Webb, B., *Beatrice Webb Diaries* entry for 3 November 1903, quoted by Marsh. P., *Joseph Chamberlain, Entrepreneur in Politics* (Yale, New Haven and London, 1994), p. 581.

208 Crosby, T., *Joseph Chamberlain – A Most Radical Imperialist* (I.B.Tauris, London, 2011), p. 164.

209 Ward, R., *City-State and Nation* (Phillimore, Chichester, 2005), pp. 150-153; Marsh, P., *op.cit.*, pp. 562 ff.

210 Webb, B., *Beatrice Webb Diaries*, http://digital.library.lse.ac.uk/objects/lse:cd528buz pp. 124; 141/2 entries for 29 January 1884.

[211] Boyd, C.W., ed. *Mr. Chamberlain's Speeches*. Vol ii (London, Constable, 1914), pp. 131-139.

[212] *Hansard*, 28 May 1903.

[213] Amery, J., *op.cit.*, p. 311.

[214] Extract from a speech by Joseph Chamberlain to the Constitutional Club, 26 June 1903, quoted in Amery, J., *op.cit.*, p. 268.

[215] Marsh, P., *op.cit.*, p. 589.

[216] 'The Hungry Forties' referred to the 1840s, a bleak decade when widespread unemployment and near starvation in industrial towns fuelled Chartism, and impelled many men of property to espouse an Anti Corn Law campaign designed to cheapen bread and make life more supportable for a distressed workforce. When brandished by defenders of Free Trade, the epithet prompted a Pavlovian response, conjuring dark images of unemployment and deprivation.

[217] Boyd, C.W., *op.cit,.* p. 233-236.

[218] *Birmingham Daily Post*, 8 January 1906.

[219] See Boyd, C.W., *op.cit.*, p. 262, for Chamberlain's hard-hitting Limehouse speech on immigration, 15 December 1904.

[220] *The Times*, 3 January 1906; *Birmingham Daily Mail* 10 January 1906.

[221] Jay, R., *op.cit.*, p. 285.

[222] Ward, R., *op.cit.*, p. 161.

[223] Trentmann, F., *Free Trade Nation* (Oxford, OUP, 2008), pp. 91-97.

[224] Ward, R., *op.cit.*, p. 161; Thompson, J., 'Pictorial Lies – Posters and Politics in Britain, 188-1914, *Past and Present* (2007) pp. 199-202; Marsh, P., *op.cit.*, p. 568/9.

[225] *The Economist*, 2 December 1843.

[226] Trentmann, F., *op.cit.*, pp. 35-64.

[227] Marsh,P., *op.cit.*, pp. 563-580; it is a nice historical irony that C.T. Ritchie had been an articulate Fair Trade supporter in the 1880s, at a time when Chamberlain was a rigorously orthodox opponent of any form of Protection.

[228] *The Times*, 13 July 1904, quoted in Cawood, I., *The Liberal Unionist Party – A History* (I.B.Tauris, London, 2012), p. 234.

[229] Sykes, A., *op.cit.*, p. 91.

[230] Arnstein, W., 'Turbulent Spring or Indian Summer?' in *The Edwardian Age – Conflict and Stability 1900-1914*, ed. O'Day, A., (London, Macmillan, 1979), pp. 60-78. The Taff Vale Judgement in 1901 found in favour of the Taff Vale Railway Company which had sued the Amalgamated Society of Railway Servants for damages incurred by the trade union's strike. The judgement held that a trade union could be sued for damages caused by the actions of officials in conducting an industrial dispute. This effectively eliminated the strike from a trade union's armoury, until the trade Disputes Act of 1906 overturned the judgement.

[231] *Manchester Guardian*, 15 January 1906.

[232] The 'whole hoggers' were supporters of the full extent of protectionism unqualified by ideas of applying protection only as limited retaliation.

[233] *The Times*, 15 January 1906.

[234] Reekes, A.E., 'Birmingham Exceptionalism, Joseph Chamberlain and the 1906 General Election' (Unpublished M.Res. thesis, University of Birmingham, 2014).

[235] Roberts, S., 'Politics and the Birmingham working-class: the General Elections of 1900 and 1906 in East Birmingham', *West Midlands Studies*, 1982; *The Times*, 8 January 1906.

[236] Pelling, H., *Social Geography of British Elections* (London, Macmillan, 1967), p. 202.

Chapter 7: Oswald Mosley – a Socialist in Birmingham

[237] MacKenzie and MacKenzie, *The Diary of Beatrice Webb*, 8 June 1923.

[238] Mosley, O., *My Life*, p. 184.

[239] Taylor, A.J.P., *English History 1914 – 1945*, p. 285.

[240] Skidelsky, R., *Oswald Mosley* (London, Macmillan, 1975), pp. 23-43; p. 134.

[241] Pugh,M., *Speak for Britain – A New History of the Labour Party* (London, The Bodley Head, 2010), pp. 159-163.

[242] Skidelsky, R., *op.cit.*, p. 134; pp. 67-68.

[243] Mosley, O., *op.cit.*, p. 240.

[244] Skidelsky, R., *op.cit.*, p. 69.

[245] Mosley, O., *op.cit.*, p. 182.

[246] The 'Black and Tans' were auxiliary forces to augment the Royal Irish Constabulary in 1920 when forces of law and order faced pressure from the activities of Irish republicans. They gained their name from their clothing of army khaki mixed with official police uniform; and they earned a fearsome reputation for bloody reprisals.

Chanak on the Dardanelles in 1922 was where Lloyd George, the British Prime Minister, briefly threatened the Turkish general Kemal Ataturk with war because the latter was overturning the Treaty of Sèvres (1920), which had given this land to Greece. Lloyd George's belligerence was deeply unpopular in Britain and led to his political downfall in October 1922.

[247] Mosley, O., *op.cit.*, p. 181.

[248] Howell, D., 'The Sheik…. A Valentino in Real Life: Sir Oswald Mosley and the Labour Party, 1924-1931,' *Contemporary British History*, 23:4, pp. 425-443; Skildelsky, R., *op.cit.*, p. 176; Pugh, M., *op.cit.*, p. 197.

[249] *Birmingham Daily Post*, 24 October 1924; Pugh, M., *op.cit.*, p. 160.

[250] Wertheimer, Edon, *Portrait of the Labour Party* (1929), cited by Pugh, M., *Hurrah for the Blackshirts*, (Cape, London, 2005), p. 114.

[251] *Town Crier*, 24 December, 1926.

[252] Wertheimer, E., *Portrait of the Labour Party* (Constable, London, 1929), pp. 187-8.

[253] Cited in Pugh, M., *Hurrah for the Blackshirts* (Cape, London, 2005), p. 112.

[254] Mosley, O., *op.cit.*, p. 159.

[255] *Town Crier*, 7 November 1924.

[256] Quoted by Skidelsky, R., *op.cit.*, p. 232.

[257] Skidelsky, R., *op.cit.*, p. 231-2.

[258] Mosley. O., *op.cit.*, p. 183.

[259] Mosley, O., *op.cit.*, p. 185.

[260] *Town Crier*, 7 November 1924.

[261] Skidelsky, R., pp. 158-159.

[262] *Town Crier*, 17 December 1926; 24 December 1926.

[263] *Birmingham Daily Post*, 22 December 1926.

[264] Pugh, M., *Hurrah for the Blackshirts, op.cit.*, p. 118.

[265] Howell, D., *op.cit.*, p. 428.

[266] Skidelsky, R., *op.cit.*, p. 173.

[267] *The Times*, 20 December 1926.

[268] Pugh, M., *Speak for Britain, op.cit.*, p. 198.

[269] *Town Crier*, 7 June 1929.

[270] Keynes, J.M., *The Economic Consequences of Mr. Churchill* (London, 1925).

[271] *Birmingham Daily Post*, 4 May 1925.

[272] Skidelsky, R., 'Oswald Mosley' entry in the *Oxford Dictionary of National Biography*.

[273] Keynes, J.M., *Tract for Monetary Reform* (London, 1923).

[274] Department of Employment and Productivity, *British Labour Statistics: Historical Abstract 1886-1968* (1971), pp. 306-311.

[275] Churchill, W.S., *Great Contemporaries* (Thornton Butterworth, London, 1937).

[276] Mosley, O., *op.cit.*, p. 241.

[277] Quoted by Marquand, D., *Ramsay Macdonald* (Jonathan Cape, London, 1977), p. 537.

[278] Mosley, O., *op.cit.*, p. 248.

[279] Marquand, D., *op.cit.*, p. 538.

[280] Mosley, O., *op.cit.*, p. 259.

[281] Skidelsky, R., *op.cit.*, pp. 240-245.

[282] *Smethwick Telephone*, 17 January 1931, quoted in Howell, D., *op.cit.*, p. 436.

[283] Skidelsky, R., *op.cit.*, p. 244.

[284] Mosley, O., *op.cit.*, p. 273.

[285] *Birmingham Daily Post*, 19 October 1931.

[286] Roderick Spode, the leader of the Black Shorts, is a character based on Sir Oswald Mosley who appears most prominently in *The Code of the Woosters* (Herbert Jenkins, London, 1938).

Chapter 8: Neville Chamberlain and Appeasement

[287] 'Cato', (Michael Foot, Peter Howard, Frank Owen), *Guilty Men* (London, Gollancz, 1940).

[288] Churchill, W.S., *The Gathering Storm* (London, Cassell, 1948).

[289] Finney, P., 'The Romance of Decline: The Historiography of Appeasement and National Identity' in *Electronic Journal of International History* –Article 1 (2008); Aster, S., 'Appeasement: Before and After revisionism' in *Diplomacy and Statecraft* vol.19 (3), (2008).

[290] Letter, Chamberlain, N., to sister Ida, 19 September 1938, NC/18/1/1069, Special Collections, University of Birmingham.

[291] Crozier, A.J., entry on Neville Chamberlain, *Oxford Dictionary of National Biography* (OUP, Oxford, 2004-14); Self,

R., *Neville Chamberlain* (Ashgate, Aldershot, 2006), pp. 39-137.

[292] Watt, D.C., *How War Came* (Heinemann, London, 1989), p. 78.

[293] Feiling, K., *The Life of Neville Chamberlain* (London, Macmillan, 1946), p. 303.

[294] Self, R., *op.cit.*, p. 12.

[295] Watt, D.C., *op.cit.*, p. 78.

[296] Parker, R., *Chamberlain and Appeasement* (St. Martin's Press, New York, 1993), pp. 12-33.

[297] Self, R., *op.cit.*, pp. 1-12; p. 288.

[298] Parker, R.A.C., 'British Rearmament 1936-1939; Treasury, TUs and Skilled Labour', EHR, 1981, p. 306.

[299] Self, R., *op.cit.*, p. 253.

[300] Crozier, A., *op.cit.*

[301] Gilbert, M., *The Roots of Appeasement* (London, 1966), p. xii.

[302] Finney, P., *op.cit.*

[303] The East Fulham by-election saw a heavy defeat for the Conservative/National Government candidate who advocated significant rearmament, at the hands of a Labour pacifist candidate; the 'King and Country' debate in the Oxford Union in 1933 resulted in a substantial victory for the motion that 'This House will in no circumstances fight for its King and Country'.

[304] McDonagh, F., *Neville Chamberlain, Appeasement and the British Road to War* (MUP, Manchester, 1998).

[305] Charmley, J., *Chamberlain and the Lost Peace* (Ivan R. Dee, Chicago, 1989), pp. 72, 97, 120, 186.

[306] Self, R., *op.cit.*,

[307] Dilks, D., 'Flashes of Intelligence' in ed. Andrew, C., and Dilks, D., *The Missing Dimension* (Macmillan, London, 1984), pp. 101-125.

[308] Parker, R.A.C., *op.cit.*, p. 74.

[309] Parker, R.A.C., *op.cit.*, pp. 124-155; Watt, D.C., 'British Intelligence and the Coming of the Second World War in Europe' in ed. May, E., *Knowing One's Enemies* (Princeton, New Jersey, 1984), pp. 237-271; Wark, W., 'British Military Economic Intelligence: Assessments of Nazi Germany before the Second World War' in *The Missing Dimension*, *op.cit.*, pp. 78-100.

[310] Letter, Chamberlain to Ida, 11 September 1938, NC/18/1/1068. George Canning was one of Britian's most successful Foreign Secretaries, holding the post in 1807-9 then from 1822-1827, when he briefly became Prime Minister.

[311] Letter, Chamberlain to Ida, 19 September 1938, NC/18/1/1069.

[312] Faber, D., *Munich* (Simon and Shuster, London, 2008), p. 430 points out 'that within a fortnight every major Czech border fortification was in German hands; Prague was less than 40 miles from the new frontier, 11,000 sq.miles of territory had been handed over... and the country's communication infrastructure had been disrupted beyond recognition'.

[313] Self, R., *op.cit.*, p. 316; p. 369.

[314] Parker, R.A.C., *op.cit.*, p. 364.

[315] Cockett, R., *Twilight of Truth* (London, 1989); Crowson, N., *Facing Fascism* (Routledge, London 1997) .*op.cit.*, pp. 359-360; 373-4.

[316] Letters to Ida and Hilda, 19 September, 9 October, 13 November 1938, NC/18/1/1069-74.

[317] Self, R., *op.cit.*, p. 344.

[318] Charmley, J., *op.cit.*, p. 120.

[319] Home, A., *The Way the Wind Blows* (Collins, London, 1976), p. 65.

[320] Letter, Chamberlain to Mary, 5 November 1938, NC i/20/1/186.

[321] Watt, D.C., *op.cit.*, p. 164.

[322] Watt, D.C., *op.cit.*, p. 167.

[323] Quoted by Stewart, G., *Burying Caesar* (Weidenfeld and Nicolson, London, 1999), p. 355.

[324] *Hansard*, record of House of Commons Debates, 5s, 345, col 435-50, 15 March 1939.

[325] Nicolson, H., *Diaries and Letters 1930-1939* (Collins, London, 1966), entry for 17 March 1939, p. 393.

[326] Letter, Chamberlain to Hilda, 19 March 1939, NC/18/1.1090.

[327] Self, R., *op.cit.*, p. 352.

[328] Birkenhead, Lord, *Halifax* (Hamish Hamilton, London, 1965), p. 433.

[329] *The Times*, 18 March 1939.

[330] Letters, Chamberlain to Hilda, 19 March 1939 and to Ida 26 March 1939, NC/18/1/1091/1092.

[331] Charmley, J., *op.cit.*, p. 172.

[332] Watt, D.C., *op.cit.*, p. 186.

[333] Chamberlain, A., to Lord Crewe, 16 February 1925, Chamberlain papers, AC 52/189.

[334] Letter, Chamberlain to Hilda, 1/2 April 1939, NC/18/1/1092.

[335] Nicolson, H., Parker, R.A.C., *op.cit.*, p. 11, entry for 20 April 1939, p. 399.

336 Self, R., Parker, R.A.C., *op.cit.*, p. 11, p. 361.
337 Letter, Chamberlain to Hilda, 29 April 1939, NC/18/1/1096.
338 Letter, Chamberlain to Ida, 26 March 1939, NC/18/1/1091.
339 Parker, R.A.C., *op.cit.*, p. 11.

Chapter 9: Enoch Powell and Immigration
340 Powell, E., *Joseph Chamberlain* (London, Thames and Hudson, 1977).
341 Heffer, S., *Like the Roman – The Life of Enoch Powell* (London, Weidenfeld and Nicolson, 1998), p. 342.
342 Rhodes James, R., *Ambitions and Realities: British Politics 1964-1970* (London, Weidenfeld and Nicolson, 1972), p. 164.
343 Sandbrook, D., *White Heat 1964-1970* (London, Little, Brown, 2006), p. 647.
344 Boyd, C.W., ed., *Mr. Chamberlain's Speeches* (London, Constable, 1914), vol. III, p. 262 – the Limehouse Speech, December 1904.
345 Heffer, S., *op.cit.*, pp. 3-115; *Oxford Dictionary of National Biography*, entry on Enoch Powell by Heffer, S., (Oxford, OUP, 2004-14).
346 Heffer, S., *op.cit.*, p. 204.
347 Heffer, S., *op.cit.*, pp. 300-309.
348 Horne, A., *Macmillan 1957-86 Vol. II* (London, Macmillan, 1989), p. 72. Savonarola was a Dominican friar and preacher at the end of the 15th century in Renaissance Florence, who forecast imminent Divine retribution on the wealthy and the corrupt – he was burnt for his pains.
349 Heffer, S., *op.cit.*, p. 309.
350 Cosgrave, P., *The Lives of Enoch Powell* (London, Pan books 1999), p. 171.
351 Kynaston, D., *Modernity Britain – A Shake of the Dice* (London, Bloomsbury, 2014), p. 101.
352 Foot,P., *The Rise of Enoch Powell* (London, Penguin, 1969), pp. 32-46.
353 The Mau Mau Uprising in Kenya from 1952 to 1960 was the work of Kikuyu tribal groups who had suffered more than most Kenyans from British rule; it was an African nationalist movement, expressed in swift brutal attacks on isolated, lightly defended, loyalist groups. It was eventually put down by the colonial authorities.
354 *Hansard*, 610: 232-250.
355 From a speech made by Enoch Powell at the annual dinner of the City of London branch of the Royal Society of St George, 22 April 1961, quoted extensively in Heffer, S., *op.cit.*, pp. 334-340.
356 Foot, P., *op.cit.*, pp. 81-2; Heffer, S., *op.cit.*, p. 378; Sandbrook, D., *op.cit.*, p. 629.
357 Powell, E., *Speech to London Rotary Club, Eastbourne, 16th November, 1968* from 'Speeches of Enoch Powell,' www.enochpowell.net/fr-83.html.
358 Powell, E., *Eastbourne* speech, *op.cit.*
359 Sandbrook, D., *op.cit.*, p. 631.
360 Pimlott, B., *Harold Wilson* (Harper Collins, London, 1992), p. 355.
361 Foot, P., *op.cit.*, p. 55.
362 Powell, E., *Eastbourne* speech, *op.cit.*
363 Cosgrave.,P., *op.cit.*, p. 237.
364 Foot, P., *op.cit.*; the leading articles of many Sunday papers in the aftermath to his 22 April 1968 speech mused on his ambitions.
365 Cosgrave, P., *op.cit.*, p. 242 quoting the Walsall speech of 9 February 1968.
366 Foot, P., *op.cit.*, pp. 109-110.
367 Quoted by Foot, P., *op.cit.*, p. 128.
368 The Midland Hotel is now the Burlington Hotel fronting onto the Burlington Arcade.
369 *The Guardian,* 13 June 1969.
370 Sandbrook, D., *op.cit.*, p. 639.
371 Pabulum means 'food', or 'food for thought'.
372 Powell, E., *Speech at Birmingham 20th April 1968* from 'Speeches of Enoch Powell,' www.enochpowell.net/fr-79html.
373 Foot,P., *op.cit.*, pp. 113-118.
374 *The Times,* 22 April 1968.
375 *The Times,* 22 April 1968.
376 Cosgrave, P., *op.cit.*, p. 254.
377 *The Observer,* 21 January 1973, quoted in the *ODNB* entry on Enoch Powell, *op.cit.*
378 Heffer, S., *op.cit.*, p. 462.
379 This idea makes play of Colombey-les-Deux-Eglises, the home of General Charles de Gaulle; he returned there when out of power in the post-war years, and 'Colombey' or 'Les Deux Eglises' is often used to refer to a

statesman's temporary withdrawal from political life.

[380] Sandbrook, D., *op.cit.*, p. 647.

[381] Crossman, R., *The Diaries of a Cabinet Minister, vol.III* (London, Hamish Hamilton and Jonathan Cape, 1977), p.29.

[382] Quoted in Cosgrave, P., *op.cit.*, p. 9.

[383] *Birmingham Daily Post*, 4 May 1968.

[384] Cosgrave, P., *op.cit.*, p. 281.

[385] Cosgrave, P., *op.cit.*, p. 282.

[386] UK 2001 population census – www.ons.gov.uk/census-2001

[387] There were unsavoury instances of 'Paki-bashing' as it became known in 1969.

[388] Sandbrook, D., *op.cit.*, pp. 644-646.

[389] Heffer, S., *op.cit.*, pp. 462-3.

[390] Evans, S., 'Consigning its Past to History? David Cameron and the Conservative Party,' *Parliamentary Affairs*, 61 (2), 2008, pp. 291-314.

[391] *Daily Telegraph*, 13 December 2014.

Chapter 10: The Twenty-First Century

[392] Yousafzai, Malala and Lamb, C., *I Am Malala*, (this edition, Phoenix paperback, London, 2014), pp. 74 to 255).

[393] *Speech at the Inauguration of the Library of Birmingham*, 3 September 2013, www.libraryofbirmingham.com/article/malala's-speech; also in many versions on YouTube, e.g. www.youtube.com/watch?v=LGg8G35jwuo

[394] Speech made at Ninestiles Academy, Acocks Green, Birmingham, 20 July 2015, https://www.gov.uk/government/speeches/extremism-pm-speech

[395] Wintour, Patrick, *The Guardian*, 17 July 2014.

[396] Ayaan Hirsi Ali, *The Times* 22 July 2015.

[397] Murray, D., 'David Cameron has given his best speech yet on tackling Islamic extremism', *The Spectator*, 20 July 2015.

[398] Leading articles in *The Times; The Telegraph; The Guardian* and *The Independent* on 20 July 2015 all gave the speech a welcome, while recognising that progress would be slow and that much yet needed to be done, especially to realise the goal of greater desegregation. Maria Norris in the *New Statesman* on 20 July 2015 took a contrary view, seeing the Cameron speech as a retread of Blair and Brown government policies, and arguing that extremism was as much to do with the alienation caused by long-standing problems of unemployment, housing and prejudice in deprived communities. Interviews with Birmingham Muslims printed in *The Guardian* by Aisha Garni on 20 July 2015 illustrated the acute sensitivity of the issues raised in the speech for Muslim communities. There was robust criticism online: 'An Open Letter to Britain's Leading Violent Extremist: David Cameron', *INSURGE Intelligence*, by Nafeez Ahmed https://medium.com/insurge-intelligence, for example.

INDEX

Notes: references in bold indicate speech excerpts; italics indicate images; notes with additional information are indicated by page number, then reference number and 'n' (e.g. '149:389n').